THE NEW
BLUE MEDIA

How Michael Moore, MoveOn.org, Jon Stewart and Company Are Transforming Progressive Politics

Theodore Hamm

THE NEW PRESS

NEW YORK
LONDON

Published in the United States by The New Press, New York, 2008
Distributed by W. W. Norton & Company, Inc., New York

LIBRARY OF CONGRESS CATALOGING-IN-PUBLICATION DATA

Hamm, Theodore, 1966–
    The new blue media : how Michael Moore, MoveOn.org, Jon Stewart and company
are transforming progressive politics / Theodore Hamm.
        p.   cm.
    Includes bibliographical references and index.
    ISBN 978-1-59558-040-5 (hc.)
    1. Mass media—Political aspects—United States.   2. United States—Politics and
government—2001–   I. Title.
P95.82.U6H36   2008
302.230973—dc22   2007040353

The New Press was established in 1990 as a not-for-profit alternative to the large,
commercial publishing houses currently dominating the book publishing industry.
The New Press operates in the public interest rather than for private gain, and is
committed to publishing, in innovative ways, works of educational, cultural, and
community value that are often deemed insufficiently profitable.

www.thenewpress.com

Composition by dix!
This book was set in Bembo

Printed in the United States of America

10   9   8   7   6   5   4   3   2   1

For Dad and my stepmom, Yoga

CONTENTS

ACKNOWLEDGMENTS

This book originated at The New Press in collaboration with Colin Robinson, who helped immeasurably in getting the project off the ground. When Colin moved on from The New Press, I felt anything but orphaned, as I benefited greatly from the razor-sharp insights of Andy Hsiao, Marc Favreau, and Furaha Norton. I also send special thanks to my extremely capable research assistants, Caitlin Esch and Vincent Rossmeier, both of whom are well on their way to becoming first-rate journalists.

Through their intellectual encouragement and engagement, not to mention their friendship, my comrades at the *Brooklyn Rail* have contributed mightily to this book. I must first thank Williams Cole, a talented media critic and creator in his own right, for our ongoing dialogue about the news. I also bounced around many ideas with the trenchant minds of Christian Parenti, Donald Breckenridge, Heather Rogers, Meghan McDermott, Doug Cordell, Jason Flores-Williams, and Brian Carreira. In addition to the work of our many other editors, writers, and staff, the *Rail* owes its continued existence to the incomparable Phong Bui, our publisher and tireless champion. It is my good fortune to collaborate with all of these folks. The same can be said of my students and colleagues at Metropolitan College, where I have particularly benefited from the support of Ruth Lugo, Clyde Griffin, and Heide Hlawaty.

As fellow followers of the New Blue Media, my many friends in Brooklyn, San Francisco, and elsewhere have also helped sustain this project. The list includes: Diego Baraona, J. Scott Burgeson, Wayne De Jager, Peter Doolittle, Bob Dowling, Albert Gutierrez, Howard Harrington, Jason Duvalle Jones, Thomas Master, Gary Merowsky, Ray Nedzel, Eulas Pizarro, Leslie Quint, Alan Reeder,

Jonas Salganik, Maddie Soglin, Rebecca Titcomb, and Andrew Wood. Last but not least, I would like to thank Emily DeVoti. Despite some uncertainties in the direction of our relationship over the last few years, we have remained best friends. And for that, most of all, I am truly grateful.

T. Hamm
Brooklyn, New York
January 2008

INTRODUCTION

THE RISE OF THE NEW BLUE MEDIA

The administration of George W. Bush will be remembered for many cataclysmic actions—a disastrous war in Iraq, a criminally inept response to Hurricane Katrina, and a massive upward redistribution of the nation's wealth. Another recurring, but less analyzed, feature of the Bush years is the ongoing attempt by the White House to sabotage the American political news media. In order to advance its agenda, both foreign and domestic, Bush insiders have planted explosive information with sympathetic reporters (Robert Novak and Judith Miller); hired a former male prostitute (Jeff Gannon) to pose as a White House reporter and ask sympathetic questions to the president; and paid an actual syndicated columnist (Armstrong Williams) to write friendly pieces about its education policies. The administration also produced its own "news" segments/propaganda on issues like Social Security for distribution on local TV stations across the country. Meanwhile, nearly all of the nation's leading broadcast and print outlets promulgated the White House's specious rationale for invading Iraq, the alleged presence of WMD. When that charge was shown to be false, the network most sympathetic to the administration, Fox News, never mentioned this essential fact. During Bush's second term, that same network also saw one of its lead reporters, Tony Snow, become White House press secretary; and when Dick Cheney sought to explain exactly how he managed to shoot a hunting partner in the face, he sat down with Fox News's lead anchor, Brit Hume. Ascendant during the Clinton era, right-wing media figures have become omnipresent throughout the Bush years, especially as cable news talk shows have gained a more prominent place on the political landscape. It is yet another depressing sign of the times that Bill O'Reilly, Sean Hannity, Ann Coulter, and many other right-wing zealots have flourished in the Bush era.

This book is not about the growth of the right-wing political media, however. Nor is it another entry into the debate over whether the mainstream media have a "liberal bias," which, as Eric Alterman, Jeff Cohen and others have demonstrated, is a false charge that the right strategically puts forth.[1] Instead, this study examines the growth and—for the most part—commercial success of self-consciously left and liberal political media creators during the Bush years. I have chosen to call this constellation of new outlets the New Blue Media. Both explicitly—as seen in the examples of MoveOn, the *Daily Kos*–led liberal blogosphere, Michael Moore, and Air America—and implicitly—as illustrated by the *Onion*, *The Daily Show*, and *The Colbert Report*—all of these new media creators are seeking to move the Democratic Party to the left. All of these players have been frustrated by the conservative campaigns launched by Al Gore in 2000 and John Kerry in 2004; and, with the exception of Air America's original figurehead, Al Franken, all have repeatedly attacked both the Republicans and the Democrats for the Iraq debacle. At the same time, these new outlets have mounted a counterattack against the right-wing political media. Either via direct confrontation or satirical send-up, the New Blue Media have effectively "taken off the gloves" and fought back, against both the right and the Foxification of mainstream television news coverage. To be certain, more established left-leaning media outlets such as the *Nation*, *Harper's*, and the Pacifica Network have also been at the forefront of the battle against the Bush regime. But the focus here is on the ways in which the new forms of liberal media have helped change the presentation and direction of contemporary progressive politics.

The main stylistic approaches of the New Blue Media—satirical, didactic, and activist—all fit into long-standing traditions in American political life. The roster of successful political satirists includes many of the great figures in American letters, a list headed by Benjamin Franklin, Mark Twain, Ambrose Bierce, H.L. Mencken, and Dorothy Parker. Founded in 1876, *Puck*, a weekly magazine of political cartoons, showed that there was a steady audience for humorous but pointed critiques of current affairs. Twain and Bierce both deflated the pretensions of the Gilded Age, while, from opposite ends of the spectrum, Mencken and Parker tore apart the Harding-Coolidge-Hoover era. Both black minstrel songs and the blues often contained powerful send-ups of slavery and Jim Crow, while the early years of Hollywood produced such classic political spoofs as the Marx Brothers' *Duck Soup* (1933) and Chaplin's *Modern Times* (1936) and *The Great Dictator* (1940). A precedent of sorts was also set during the early years of the New Deal, when Will Rogers, the folksy, enormously popular radio and print satirist, refrained from criticizing FDR, whom he admired. The next generation of leading political satirists often crossed various lines between humor and partisanship, often at their own peril. As historian Stephen Kercher shows, in his 1960 campaign JFK embraced the leading liberal comedian Mort Sahl. But after JFK's victory, Sahl turned his humor back toward the president, who responded by blackballing Sahl. The early 1960s nevertheless became the golden age of American left-wing political satire, the hour of comedians Lenny Bruce and Dick Gregory, cartoonist Jules Feiffer, and Stanley Kubrick's *Dr. Strangelove* (1964), among many other examples. (The Yippies, meanwhile, soon combined comedy with activism, bringing satire onto the floor of the New York Stock Exchange and the streets of Chicago.) The early 1970s were the heyday of *National Lampoon*, although the magazine's often brilliant iconoclastic send-ups originated more from the right than the left. Many creative talents associated with *National Lampoon* influenced the early direction of *Saturday Night Live*, which debuted in 1975. *SNL* renewed elements of the liberal comedic tradition, particularly in its regular "Weekend Update" segment. But it was not until the late Clinton–early Bush years, with the ascendancy of the *Onion* and *The Daily Show*, that humor again formed part of the currency of progressive politics.[2]

The didactic wing of the New Blue Media, led by Air America and Michael Moore, can lay claim to a similarly noble lineage. Because of its success in helping spark the American Revolution, Thomas Paine's *Common Sense* continues to serve as a model for all those seeking to play the role of the righteous tribune. From the great abolitionist William Lloyd Garrison's weekly newspaper, the *Liberator* (1831–66), through the 1960s, expressions of left-wing politics in America typically adopted a strident, crusading style. Liberals, by contrast, have long prided themselves on the civil, sober-minded, cautious nature of their political discussion. In the 1980s and 1990s, the ascent of the right-wing "noise machine," heard first on talk radio, then seen throughout the cable TV era, compelled a response from the left. In the early Bush years, a number of Democratic Party players formed the Air America radio network in an attempt to counteract Rush Limbaugh and the radio right, and to help the Dems win the 2004 election. Swinging further to the left, Michael Moore launched his own effort to become the new Thomas Paine, making his own didactic statement (*Fahrenheit 9/11*) designed to topple a modern King George. Commercially, Moore obviously succeeded, while Air America to date has not; politically, neither accomplished the stated goal of defeating George W. Bush. What this latter fact reveals about the place of didacticism in current political culture remains to be seen.

Led by MoveOn, and by *Daily Kos* and the rest of the liberal blogosphere, the activist flank of the New Blue Media is a somewhat more unique development. From the Populists of the late nineteenth century forward, there have been various insurgent movements aimed at transforming party politics. All such efforts have sought to make use of various advances in media—first printing, followed by film, radio, and television—but the Internet has proved to be an exceptionally conducive tool for grassroots organizing. As a result, both MoveOn and the liberal blogosphere have made a significant impact on contemporary progressive politics:

they have helped keep various issues (e.g., the Iraq War) on the front burner and served as a watchdog of the mainstream media's complicity in pushing the Bush agenda. The netroots have also put pressure on Democratic Party politicians, via petition drives, and most important, by raising significant sums of campaign cash. Unlike the New Left of the 1960s, which was skeptical of LBJ and the Democrats, the leading netroots activists strongly believe that they are, as Jerome Armstrong and Markos Moulitsas (aka Kos) put it in the title of their 2005 book, "crashing the gate," or transforming the Democratic Party. In varying degrees, MoveOn and the Kos-led blogosphere have indeed shaken up the party, and helped lead a counterattack against the right's noise machine.

The basic argument of this book is simple: The New Blue Media have succeeded in transforming the style and, to a lesser extent, the substance of progressive politics. Rather than echo the cautious mush of the 2000 edition of Al Gore or John Kerry in 2004, most leading Democrats have now adopted the combative tone of Howard Dean. Moreover, every liberal politician now makes ample use of all of the Internet tools, from e-mail, Web sites, and Internet fund-raising to blogs and YouTube. In the early stages of the 2008 campaign, for example, Barack Obama announced his candidacy via YouTube; meanwhile, Hillary Clinton's campaign launched a contest in which the public chose her campaign theme song, which was announced via a highly publicized YouTube spoof of the final scene of *The Sopranos* (the would-be first couple thus emulated "known criminals," noted Jon Stewart). Any politician now seeking to curry favor with younger audiences makes the rounds on *The Daily Show* and—if that figure is up for the challenge—*The Colbert Report*. In the 2004 campaign, eventual vice-presidential nominee John Edwards announced his candidacy on *The Daily Show*, and John Kerry chose to give his first post–Swift Boat controversy interview to Jon Stewart; in the pivotal Connecticut Democratic primary in 2006, netroots hero Ned Lamont appeared on *The Colbert Report* a week before he defeated Joe Lieberman. To be sure, Republicans have tried to make use of the new media, launching their own campaigns and appearing on *The Daily Show* (John McCain would officially declare his candidacy for 2008 there). But until the rise of the iconoclastic, antiwar Ron Paul and the Christian populist–fundamentalist Mike Huckabee as 2008 presidential candidates, the Republicans failed to score much success. For reasons of demographics, their positions on social issues, and, most of all, their attachment to the Bush administration, the mainstream Republicans did not make notable inroads into New Blue Media terrain.

The degree to which the New Blue Media have succeeded in moving the Democratic Party away from the centrism and triangulation of the Bill Clinton years, or the caution of the Gore and Kerry campaigns, is an open question. This much is certain, however: the party's leadership no longer can ignore the sentiments of its activist, antiwar base. Harry Reid, Nancy Pelosi, and other party leaders have not been willing to cut off funding for the Iraq War and occupation, but at the very least their feet are being held to the fire over the issue. While the *Onion* and *The Daily Show–Colbert Report* are cagey about their actual positions, Michael Moore, Air America, MoveOn, and the liberal blogs have openly vowed to shake up the party. In practice, that has not always meant a unified strategy. In the early years of Air America, Al Franken often pushed the centrist positions of the party, notably regarding Iraq, while Randi Rhodes, Laura Flanders, Janeane Garofalo, and Sam Seder argued from the left. In the wake of the 2004 election, MoveOn championed the insurgent Howard Dean, whose campaign had helped make the netroots a force to be reckoned with, in his successful bid to become head of the Democratic National Committee. Kos, meanwhile, openly declared war on the Democratic Leadership Council, the influential Clintonite group of pro-corporate, pro-war insiders who continually argued that the party should move to the right. Despite his eventual loss in the general election, Ned Lamont's 2006 campaign provided the Democrats with a blueprint for success in the midterm elections. Backed by the netroots, numerous candidates ran on antiwar platforms, causing even pro-war party strategists like Chuck Schumer and Rahm Emanuel to side with the insurgents. Yet as the 2008 race took shape, the Democratic Congress had mustered only tepid opposition to Bush's Iraq plans. With the exception of John Edwards and long shots Dennis Kucinich, Bill Richardson, and Mike Gravel, the party's presidential candidates seemed determine to strike cautious "out of Iraq" positions. Particularly for the activist wing, the danger confronted by the New Blue Media was that their antiwar stance would again be ignored by the Democratic Party brass.

Each of the following six chapters traces the growth of one of the New Blue Media outlets. In so doing, my aim is to tell two stories at once: the main one concerns how each outlet or figure grew to importance during the Bush years, while the second chronicles the Bush era itself, as seen through the eyes of some of its sharpest observers. For the sake of simplicity, I will use the term "progressive" to describe all those seeking to move the Democratic Party to the left; but I will take note when various commentators define what they mean by a progressive perspective, as opposed to a liberal or leftist one. Although one will hear plenty of observations from all of the key creators of the New Blue Media, those comments are based on what they said at the time of various controversies, not on their subsequent reflections. These figures are nothing if not media savvy, and my preference has been to let their efforts speak for themselves, not to let them spin their reflections. As the Bush years mercifully come to an end, it is well worth remembering the hard work of all the new media creators who not only have helped fight the good fight, but have often also provided a healthy dose of laughter along the way.

1

READING THE *ONION* SERIOUSLY

Many of the liberal media outlets flourishing in recent years did not of course originate in the Bush era. Unless backed by large-scale investors—as in the case of Air America, or countless new magazine titles that start with a whole lot of fanfare but end up having a very short shelf life—it generally takes several years for a new media source to become both a stable business entity and a recognizable brand name that people consume regularly. In media, as in gardening, roots must be planted, and growth cultivated, before the flowers bloom.

While its popular association may be as a product of the Internet boom of the 1990s, the *Onion* actually began in the late 1980s. The paper (a term here used broadly, as the bulk of the *Onion's* readership comes from its Web site edition) most certainly grew to prominence during the Clinton years, and in the reign of Bush II it has become a fixture on the liberal media landscape. But rather than being a nineties start-up, the paper has instead followed a more traditional model of business growth. While obviously abetted by the rise of the Internet, the *Onion's* trajectory—starting in a very small market, then slowly growing to national prominence—has an almost nineteenth-century quality to it.

The *Onion's* signature style of political satire, however, is manifestly a product of the Age of Irony otherwise known as the 1990s. In response to the late-eighties era of political correctness, when language was often treated overzealously, the mid-nineties wave of writers and artistic creators became more playful. As *Guardian* columnist Zoe Williams observed, like postmodernism, the irony that arose beginning in the 1990s "is exclusively self-referential—

its core implication is that art is used up, so it constantly recycles and quotes itself. Its entirely self-conscious stance precludes sincerity, sentiment, emoting of any kind, and thus has to rule out the existence of ultimate truth or moral certainty."[1] As Williams's critique suggests, in the Age of Irony, dogmatism and didacticism were explicitly frowned upon. Relying heavily on pop culture references, this cheeky, self-knowing position pervaded the era's popular music and television shows as well as its high literary production, as illustrated by the journal *McSweeney's* or the work of writer David Foster Wallace. The *Onion*, meanwhile, added a razor-sharp political edge, and even as the nineties fade into the past, irony carries on, and the paper's distinct style continues to feel far from dated.

It's precisely that political edge that is of interest here, and one can argue that even the paper's in-house party line about its politics contains an ironic element. "We're not anti-Left, we're not anti-Right, we're anti-dumb" is the mantra voiced by the paper's business team and editorial staff alike. Upon even a casual reading of the paper, that statement sounds like a marketing ploy—one reminiscent of Michael Jordan's and John Elway's refusals in the 1990s to explicitly name their political parties, because both Republicans and Democrats buy shoes and cars. Though obviously satirical, the *Onion*'s coverage of the key events of the Bush II years shows that the paper's party line doesn't correspond to its actual political content. In tracing the paper's growth, this chapter will show how the *Onion*'s politics should be read as progressive verging on left. And when future historians look back in horror at the current decade, the *Onion*'s satire will be seen as one of the most accurate contemporary portrayals of what the Bush regime was truly all about.

In 1988, as Reagan was passing the torch to Bush I, the *Onion* originated in the long-standing left stronghold of Madison, Wisconsin. Its initial founders, Tim Keck and Christopher Johnson, have since gone on to launch successful, cheeky alt-weeklies—respectively,

Seattle's the *Stranger* and Albuquerque's *Weekly Alibi*. But in the spring of 1988, the *Onion* began as just an eleven-by-seventeen black-and-white sheet, offering a calendar of events and cartoons. That fall, the broadsheet became a full paper, dependent on local advertising. The following year, Keck and Johnson sold the *Onion* to Scott Dikkers and Peter Haise, the former taking over as editor in chief and the latter starting as business manager and then becoming publisher. The pair would help steer the paper over the next fifteen years and beyond. Haise eventually sold his share of the *Onion* in late 2003, while as of late 2007, Dikkers was once again sitting at the editor's desk.[2]

By all accounts, there was never a clear reason for the *Onion's* name. Nor did the paper begin with high literary aspirations. As Haise recalled, the paper was started by a "bunch of dropout History majors. No one was in English or Journalism." (Since the early sixties, of course, the history department at Madison has been a seedbed of radicalism). As Liesl Schillinger wrote in a 1999 *Wired* profile, "some say *onion* is old-time slang for a juicy, multilayered news story." After about six years of publishing a small yet "successful college humor rag," Dikkers wanted the paper "to grow up." In order to do so, the *Onion* forged its signature "multilayered" style. In 1995, Dikkers's plan, according to Schillinger, "was to cut the heavy-handed humor and attempt a more subtle goal: to lampoon *USA Today* with a color-enhanced version that used deadpan journalese to assault the banality of everyday life and to spoof major news events." Robert Siegel, who joined the staff as a writer in 1995 and soon became the editor (from 1996–2003), was responsible for applying the AP style to the paper's news stories. This new version of the *Onion*, which combined the superficiality of *USA Today* with the folksiness of a small-town paper, proved to be an enduring formula for success.[3]

The paper's rise to prominence coincided with the growth of the Internet during the Clinton era. Prior to 1996, the paper was not online, but its stories had begun to circulate via e-mail, often without attribution. One notable story, "Clinton Deploys Vowels to Bosnia: Cities of Sjlbvdnzv, Grzny to be First Recipients," was picked up everywhere from NPR's *Car Talk* to Pat Buchanan's presidential campaign Web site. Nobody credited the *Onion*, however, so Siegel reportedly used this example to persuade Dikkers to take the paper online; clearly they had a good thing going, and at the same time needed to protect their copyright. The site launched in May 1996 and quickly took off—within three years, it reached 1.2 million visitors per month. A short time after the debut of www.theonion.com, the Bosnian vowel story came full circle. The comedian Chevy Chase downloaded it from the Web site and read it at a DNC fund-raising dinner attended by President Clinton, who called it "the funniest thing he'd ever heard." As the *Onion* became a spirited product of the Web generation, readers well beyond Madison gobbled up the paper's instant-classic headlines such as "Clinton Denies Lewinsky Allegations: 'We Did Not Have Sex, We Made Love,' Says President."[4]

In the fateful 2000 election, the *Onion* revealed its left-leaning sympathies. The paper's lead for its first issue that September, "Nation Trying to Fix Up Ralph Nader with a Date," was one of its many memorable campaign stories that fall. "Poor Ralph just looks so sad out there on the campaign trail, giving his little speeches about the excessive concentration of power and wealth in a few hands," a reporter on the campaign trail noted in explaining that some female companionship might lift Nader's spirits. The story suggested that many eligible women would be sympathetic to Nader's positions on free trade, corporate pollution, and campaign finance reform, and quoted an AFL-CIO spokeswoman saying that Nader's support for a large increase in the minimum wage made him "perfect for my Aunt Stella." Nader for his part welcomed the support but found it a distraction, saying that the focus should "not be on me, but on the things I have to say." Neither the real-life candidate nor the *Onion* staff could have predicted how much more the focus would remain on Nader's personal motives, rather than on his issues, well beyond the 2000 election.[5]

In contrast to its dour, but principled and therefore likable

Nader, the *Onion* portrayed the 2000 edition of Al Gore as a stiff. Beside an actual *Washington Post* photo of a robotlike Gore grimacing while holding the Sunday comics, a late-September lead story was headlined "Gore Wondering If Latest *Doonesbury* Is About Him." The latest Trudeau strip was, of course, about him, but in the story the humorless Gore asked, "They don't think I'm some kind of big dork, do they?" The *Onion*, meanwhile, harbored no illusions about George W. Bush. Early in the campaign, its story "Bush Reaches Out to Hispanic Community with Generous Tip" called Bush out as a vapid silver spooner. Its mid-October lead, "Bush Horrified to Learn Presidential Salary," then fully captured how Bush, contrary to his image, could in no way identify with the average American. In the piece, Bush said that instead of a salary of $200,000, he was thinking more in terms of "You know, something like $120 million. That's what my friend Vance Coffman makes as CEO of Lockheed Martin, and that's just an aerospace firm, not a whole country." Bush also saw the president's salary as so low that he told Karl Rove, "And they wonder why they can't get anyone decent for that job. For Christ's sake, a McDonald's manager probably makes that much a year." [6]

"Bush or Gore: 'A New Era Dawns,'" the paper's 2000 elections-week story, would often be cited for its eerily accurate "report" that neither presidential candidate had emerged victorious on election day. Future editor Carol Kolb (2003–5) would later explain simply that the paper's deadline had forced it to run an *Onion*-style variation on the "too-close-to-call" story for the election. But the actual piece treated Bush and Gore as birds of a feather. The story's comedic genius lay in its repetitious use of the dual subject: e.g., "Bush or Gore attributed his victory to his commitment to the issues that matter to ordinary, hardworking Americans." The conceit lent itself to equating the two candidates' positions on the issues. For example, "Throughout the campaign, the Republican or Democrat spoke out in favor of improving educational standards, protecting the environment, reducing crime, strengthening the military, cutting taxes, and reforming Social Security." Here as elsewhere, it was plainly evident that the paper's humor contained a strong critique of the two-party American political system: "Waving to acknowledge his supporters, the Ivy League graduate and scion of a political dynasty called for 'a time of renewal and rebirth in America.'"[7]

After the Supreme Court chose the winner of the 2000 election, the *Onion* served up an extraordinarily prescient, only slightly satirical, critique of the incoming administration. On the eve of Bush II's inauguration in January 2001, the paper's top headline read, "Bush: 'Our Long National Nightmare of Peace and Prosperity Is Finally Over.'" Here again, the story sustained itself beyond a good headline and strong lead (which would not always be the case in *Onion* pieces). "We have reached the end of the dark period in American history that will come to be known as the Clinton Era," Bush rejoiced, referring to "eight long years characterized by unprecedented economic expansion, a sharp decrease in crime, and sustained peace overseas." While the upbeat assessment showed the paper itself to be a product of the Clinton era, the story continued with Bush's remarkably accurate forecasts about his plans, which included "selling off" national parks and "going into massive national debt." Even more prophetically, Bush "promised to bring an end to the severe war drought that plagued the nation under Clinton, assuring citizens that the U.S. will engage in at least one Gulf War–level armed conflict in the next four years." Bush, of course, had run as an isolationist against Gore, but the *Onion* team was on the cutting edge in reading right through W's deceptions.[8]

The inauguration story further revealed that the editors held no illusions about various key players who accompanied the rise of Bush. Then–attorney general nominee John Ashcroft would, in Bush's view, be a "tireless champion in the battle to protect a woman's right to give birth." Responding to the speech, House Speaker Dennis Hastert giddily said, "Under Bush, we can all look forward to military aggression, deregulation of dangerous, greedy industries, and the defunding of vital domestic social-service programs." Rush Limbaugh, meanwhile, was finally satisfied. "[I]n

1996," he noted, "the American public failed to heed my urgent warnings" about Clinton, "but now, thank God, that's all done with. Once again, we will enjoy mounting debt, jingoism, . . . and a massive military build-up." The blistering assault from the left continued with a black woman from Florida stating that Bush "understands the pain of enfranchisement." And the new president then vowed that he would "widen" the gap between rich and poor, while "on the foreign front," he said, "we must find an enemy and defeat it."[9]

Disarmingly realistic, the spot-on predictions about Bush's agenda sounded like they came from the pages of the *Nation*. Ironically, that redoubtably realist magazine's most memorable—and similarly accurate—forecast about the danger of the Bush regime actually came in the form of a satirical cover on the eve of the 2000 election featuring Bush as Alfred E. Neuman from *Mad* magazine, wearing a delirious smile while sporting a button that read "WORRY."[10] As the Bush era actually commenced, though, the world of progressive publishing quickly returned to normal, with the *Onion* providing witty insights and the *Nation* keeping a serious eye on things.

As mentioned in the introduction, the *Onion* fits into a distinguished lineage of political satire in American history. Though obviously not literature per se, many *Onion* pieces read like miniature versions of Mark Twain's brilliant send-ups of slavery (*Pudd'nhead Wilson*) and Gilded Age ideology (*A Connecticut Yankee in King Arthur's Court*); like Twain's classic works, the best *Onion* satires are so true to life that the news stories actually seem genuine. In terms of satirical publications, the *Onion*'s most notable recent predecessors flourished in the 1950s and 1960s, with the rise of *Mad* magazine and the *Realist*, and in the 1970s and 1980s, with *National Lampoon* and *Spy*. All of the publications were by definition iconoclastic, but each adopted its own signature brand in delivering its humor.

Mad was best known for its wide range of cartoon-based stories, which mostly ridiculed the pop culture formulas found on TV and in Hollywood films. Paul Krassner's *Realist*, meanwhile, encapsulated the rebellious spirit of the 1960s in its pages, publishing everything from satirical features (e.g., "I Was an Abortionist for the F.B.I.") to nonfictional radical manifestoes and speeches, to interviews with a wide range of countercultural and political figures. Swinging from the right, *National Lampoon* poked fun at liberal orthodoxy through a grab-bag commercial magazine approach, with various long features written in different styles, as well as short takes and cartoons. Like the editors of the *Onion*, those of *National Lampoon* expressed their opinions only in jest, never in earnest. *Spy*, meanwhile, took aim at media and celebrity culture, but at the same time included long pieces of actual investigative journalism about the entertainment industry; it set the precedent of mocking various tricks of the trade in commercial magazines, like the use of nonsense charts and graphs.

What distinguishes the *Onion* from all of these predecessors is that after it adopted its successful *USA Today*–style formula in 1995, it has never wavered. All of its satire is compressed into fake news stories, mock op-ed columns, and the rest of its standard newspaper format. In the age of branding, audiences need to know what to expect, and the *Onion's* signature style has enabled it to meet that demand. Much of the *Onion's* satire requires a good grasp of current events, so it is not surprising that the paper has a highly educated readership. In fact, more than 90 percent of the publication's readers have at least been to college, with over 30 percent holding undergraduate degrees and a similar number possessing graduate degrees. That same readership is overwhelmingly young (nearly two-thirds between ages eighteen and forty-four),[11] fairly affluent, and nearly two-to-one male, and the vast majority is almost certainly white. While such demographics may explain some of the lesser jokes in the publication about beer and partying, the political satire that most often leads the paper is usually lifted straight from the national headlines. The *Onion's* parodies respond to what's in the news, and are not a form of advocacy journalism. But the paper nonetheless regularly manages to get its point across, loud and clear.

During the first year of the Bush administration the *Onion* expanded both its Web readership and its print presence. By August 2001, its Web site could claim four million visitors per month, and its print circulation of over 250,000 found distribution in four cities—Madison, Milwaukee, Chicago, and Denver. That summer, the paper moved its headquarters from Madison to New York City. In so doing, the *Onion* was making a statement that it was ready for the big leagues. The crew from Madison had only recently set up shop when the towers came down.

After 9/11, the *Onion* stopped its presses for one week. The hiatus allowed the paper to show its respect for the gravity of what had happened in lower Manhattan. But it also enabled its staff to come up with the paper's quite poignant reaction to the terrorist strikes. It was announced by a large banner headline that read, "Holy Fucking Shit—Attack on America." The statement perfectly captured the confusion and fear of the moment. And the paper's lead story, "U.S. Vows to Defeat Whoever It Is We're at War With," accurately recorded the Bush administration's immediate and enduring response to 9/11. To "America's enemy, be it Osama bin Laden, Saddam Hussein, the Taliban, a multinational coalition of terrorist organizations, any of a rogue's gallery of violent Islamic fringe groups, or an entirely different, non-Islamic aggressor we've never even heard of," Bush vowed, "be warned." A pair of newsbriefs in that same issue reported, "American Life Turns into Bad Jerry Bruckheimer Movie" and "Hijackers Find Themselves in Hell" instead of the "Paradise" they had expected. As its new home city and the nation tried to make sense of the attacks, the *Onion*'s 9/11 issue uniquely encompassed a wide range of popular sentiments. "We really were just trying to capture the sadness and anger everyone was feeling, and somehow it came out as humor," Robert Siegel, then the *Onion*'s editor in chief, recalled a year later.[12]

Ironically, perhaps, the most powerful statement the *Onion* made in that landmark issue was not about terrorism or the likelihood of the Bush administration's overreaction to it, but instead about the future of irony itself. That week in *Time*, Roger Rosenblatt's column carried the ominous title "The Age of Irony Comes to an End," with an equally foreboding subheading of "No Longer Will We Fail to Take Things Seriously." As Ground Zero smoldered, Rosenblatt searched for both blame and a sign of hope. He wrote, "For some 30 years—roughly as long as the Twin Towers were upright—the good folks in charge of America's intellectual life have insisted that nothing was to be believed in or taken seriously." It was irony, Rosenblatt suggested, that somehow had blinded us to the rising threat of Islamic fundamentalism. Such an overwrought notion was blown apart by a range of critics, comic and otherwise. For its part, an *Onion* newsbrief announced, "Report: Gen X Irony, Cynicism May Be Permanently Obsolete." In the item, a Gen Xer states, "Remember the day after the attack, when all the senators were singing 'God Bless America,' arm-in-arm?' asked Dave Holt, 29. 'Normally, I'd make some sarcastic wisecrack about something like that. But this time, I was deeply moved.' Added Holt: 'This earnestness can't last forever. Can it?'" Both the newsbrief and the entire 9/11 issue vividly illustrated the *Onion*'s answer to Holt's question, as did its lead story in the next issue, "Shattered Nation Longs to Care About Stupid Bullshit Again." Looking back one year later, Siegel explained to *Alternet*'s Daniel Kurtzman that irony would survive well into the twenty-first century. "Many things about America changed, but you can't kill humor. . . . Obviously people are going to laugh and people will still be sarcastic and snide and ironic and winking and insincere. That's a good thing. That's a sign of the return to normalcy."[13]

Unfortunately, for the Bush administration "normalcy" soon meant outright deception, scare tactics, and bullying in the service of its primary goal of invading Iraq. The *Onion*, as usual, saw right through the jingo. In March 2002, when talk of taking down Saddam was in the air but nearly six months away from becoming an official plan, one of the paper's headlines read, "Military Promises 'Huge Numbers' for *Gulf War II: The Vengeance*." The lead photo for the article showed Donald Rumsfeld giving a typical chesty gesture at a press conference in front of a Photoshopped movie poster of *Gulf War II: The Vengeance*, starring W. and Saddam. The other photo in the piece was even more prophetic, as it featured W. in full military gear, carrying an automatic weapon and hunting down rebel forces. The image smacked more of *Rambo* than the *Top Gun*–style "Mission Accomplished" scene that W. eventually chose, but the prediction was accurate enough. According to the article, the PR blitz for Gulf War II also included a pact with Topps for a series of trading cards; "a first-look deal with CNN, guaranteeing the network full access to the front lines, as well as first crack at interviewing the men and women behind the scenes"; and a "two-cry deal" with Dan Rather.[14] Late that summer, then–White House chief of staff Andrew Card famously stated that the administration was waiting until after Labor Day to unveil its full plan for Iraq because "you don't introduce a new product in August."[15] Six months prior, the *Onion* had already sketched out the marketing plan for that dangerous "new product."

As the White House made its sales pitch for war, the lead article in the *Onion*'s issue in the second week after Labor Day— dated September 11, 2002—declared, "Bush Won't Stop Asking Cheney If We Can Invade Yet." In this case, the story worked a father-versus-impatient-son story line, and so focused less on details of the Iraq question than on Cheney's control over W. At one point, however, the piece did report that "Cheney sat Bush down and explained at length the political ramifications of proceeding with a first strike without creating the appearance of approval from Congress and the American people." It continued by quoting Cheney's advice to Bush: "If we just wait a little longer, Saddam is bound to commit some act of aggression or we'll find some juicy al Qaeda ties or something, and then we can make it look like the whole country's behind it."[16] Here again the satire was right on target. Over the next month, in order to help force Congress into granting the administration the authority to go to war—a vote that would haunt many leading Democrats through both 2004 and 2008—both Cheney and Bush stressed Saddam's alleged ties to al Qaeda. Such outright distortions helped propel the Republicans' success in the upcoming midterms as well as in 2004, and their game plan almost seemed lifted directly from the pages of a satirical publication. While serious liberal news organizations such as the *New York Times* helped disseminate the White House's specious rationale for war,[17] the *Onion*'s lampoons turned out to be far more accurate. The Bush gang, the paper said, was hell-bent on invading Iraq, and it would deploy any means necessary in order to do so.

Throughout the fall campaign, the *Onion* continued to see right through Bush's bluster. For example, the paper's lead story in early October announced that "Bush Seeks U.N. Support for 'U.S. Does Whatever It Wants Plan.'" "As a shining beacon of freedom and democracy, America has inspired the world," Bush told the UN General Assembly. "In this spirit, I call upon the world's nations to support my proposal to give America unrestricted carte blanche to remove whatever leaders, plunder whatever resources, and impose whatever policies it deems necessary or expedient." Such aggressive unilateralism underpinned the rationale W. here gave the UN for overthrowing Saddam: "The time has come for this man to step down, because we want him to."[18] Meanwhile, the question "What should we do about Saddam's WMD?" dominated mainstream media discussion. Based on a false premise, the question itself dictated the answer. It was a sophisticated level of deception, and given Saddam's reputation, it was easy fodder for cable news chatter. But for its part, the *Onion* generally steered clear of that question, and instead frequently pointed out how the war enabled Bush to shift the nation's attention from other problems. In "Bush on Economy: 'Saddam Must Be Overthrown,'" for

example, the war solved problems ranging from a weak manu-
facturing sector to the ongoing corporate scandals, which at the
time involved WorldCom and Enron.[19] Similarly, W.'s answer to
the problem of North Korea was, of course, to invade Iraq; later, he
tried to help sell his tax cuts by offering another $300 on top of his
initial tax rebate, provided that the United States went to war.[20]
Brushing aside the WMD issue, the *Onion* consistently put forth a
satirical but convincing case that the United States was going to
war simply because the Bush administration wanted it.

When the war finally began in March 2003, the paper continued to mock both the Bush administration's theatrics and its claims
to an easy victory. One memorable lead story again foretold Bush's
"Mission Accomplished" moment with remarkable accuracy. Beside a photo of W. leading an invading squad of soldiers through
desert combat, the paper's top story explained how "Bush Bravely
Leads 3rd Infantry into Battle." In that same issue, a newsbrief reported, "Dead Iraqi Would Have Loved Democracy," which in just
six words refuted most arguments for the war.[21] With notable foresight, the lead in the following week's top story then stated, "Following a 12th consecutive day of fighting, a puzzled and frustrated
President Bush confided to military advisors Monday that he
'really figured the war would be over by now.'" In that story, and in
many others, Bush came across as juvenile and incompetent, a
frontman for Cheney, Rumsfeld, Wolfowitz, and the other neocons.[22] In the fall of 2002, Beltway media mainstay Bob Woodward
had, in *Bush at War*, legitimized the notion that W. really was in
charge of his administration's war plans; four years and two books
later, Woodward's analysis mirrored that found in the *Onion*.

As the overthrow of Saddam became the occupation of Iraq,
the paper stayed on the attack. It fired back at Bush shortly after he
gave his spurious speech aboard the USS *Abraham Lincoln* declaring victory; here was the Hollywood moment that the paper had
sagely predicted, with Bush effectively combining two Tom
Cruise films (*Top Gun* and *Mission: Impossible*). But in the *Onion*'s
account, instead of stating that the mission was over, the sign be-

hind Bush read "screw you, vets," and the story detailed a ribbon-cutting ceremony at which Bush cut veterans benefits. The piece also featured what was by *Onion* standards an unusually earnest photo, of a homeless African American vet dejectedly panhandling.[23] Such sentimentality was short-lived, however, as the next week's lead story returned to form: "Gen. Tommy Franks Quits Army to Pursue Solo Bombing Projects." "The years I've spent with the Army have been amazing, and we did some fantastic bombing," Franks stated. "But at this point, I feel like I've taken it as far as I can. It's time for me to move on and see what I can destroy on my own."[24] Amid the chaotic aftermath of the invasion, many media observers, as well as Democratic Party officials, began to turn against the Bush administration, attacking its incompetent handling of the occupation. The *Onion*, however, continued its relentless assault on *both* the design and the execution of the war.

By mid-2004, the paper had become a recognized brand, and it now had localized editions in six markets: New York City, Chicago, Madison, Milwaukee, Boulder/Denver, and its newest addition, Minneapolis. (Four more cities—San Francisco, Los Angeles, Austin, and Washington, D.C.—lay ahead in the company's near future.) Each edition carried the same initial sections, providing fake news reports and columns, mock lifestyle features, and send-ups of other *USA Today*–type ephemera such as pointless opinion polls and person-on-the-street responses (always with the same people). The national pages would then be followed by actual (i.e., nonsatirical) entertainment previews and reviews, geared toward local markets. The satire was still the selling point, but each local edition also carried its own elements of sincere arts coverage, thereby attracting more local advertising. The *Onion*'s Web site, meanwhile, now claimed over three million "unique" visitors per month. As it had done for established liberal media outlets like the *Nation* and others, the lunacy of the first Bush term spurred the business growth of the *Onion*.

Yet, despite its relentless trashing of the Bush regime, the paper still clung to its avowed nonpartisanship. As the *Chicago Tribune's* Leon Lazaroff noted in August 2004, the company's president, Sean Mills, "likes to trumpet" the aforementioned claim that " 'we're not anti-Left, we're not anti-Right, we're anti-dumb.' " Lazaroff also quoted a prominent New York media executive as saying that part of the paper's success with advertisers was that it remained "political without being stridently partial." [25] Its nonpartisan marketing claims aside, the *Onion* continued to be partisan and often downright radical.

In the opening salvo of its campaign coverage, the paper appeared to move toward the "Anybody but Bush" camp. In "Bush 2004 Campaign Pledges to Restore Honor and Dignity to the White House," Vice President Cheney, "addressing a crowd of 2,500 supporters from the tobacco and soft-drink industries," explained that "[a]fter these past three years, we need to rebuild a government based on old-fashioned American values: duty, dignity, and responsibility." [26] But the following week's lead zinger also suggested that Bush would face rather weak competition. "Democrats Somehow Lose Primaries" showed that the Democratic Party, "struggling to find a strong voice," was in disarray. "We're going to keep fighting," said a puzzled but determined John Kerry. "I'm not going to throw in the towel just because I have no idea how it is even remotely possible for all of us to lose our own primary." [27] In the paper's estimation, the hapless Democrats nonetheless had many causes to fight for. Throughout the spring of 2004, the *Onion* periodically slammed Bush with top stories such as "Bush to Cut Deficit from Federal Budget" and "Bush Addresses 8.2 Million Unemployed: 'Get a Job.' " [28]

The paper's portrayal of Kerry, meanwhile, bespoke both a popular hope that Kerry would reignite his former left-leaning passions as well as a begrudging acceptance that the Democratic challenger was in fact simply anybody but Bush. In early June, as the mainstream media started to speculate on who Kerry's running mate would be, an *Onion* top story offered its own rather ingenious suggestion: "Kerry Names 1969 Version of Himself as Running

Mate." "My running mate is smart, hard-working, and, above all, unsullied by compromise," Kerry said of his younger self, adding, "To tell you the truth, sometimes I wish I were more like him." Regarding Vietnam, the war hero turned war opponent now running as a pro-war senator observed, "Yes, my running mate has made remarks that have been critical of certain decisions made in Washington. . . . He and I do not agree on every point. But may I remind you that this man *voluntarily* enlisted to serve in Vietnam?"[29] The paper's hope that the younger, more principled John Kerry could inspire the current one stood in sharp contrast to Kerry's presentation of himself, which well beyond the Democratic National Convention emphasized only his "war hero" past. More in sync with Kerry's campaign was a lead article in early August, "Kerry Unveils One-Point Plan for Better America."[30] The story's one point—that Bush must go—would unfortunately become Kerry's only consistent message throughout the rest of the campaign.

From the end of August through the November election, the *Onion* regularly pilloried the Bush regime, and notably, it did so without ever fully embracing or attacking Kerry's muddled campaign. During the week of the Republican National Convention, the paper's mock heroic top story told how a "Small Group of Dedicated Rich People Change the World." Beside a photo of celebrating oil magnates, Republican National Committee chair Ed Gillespie explained that "[t]he Republican Party has always been blessed with idealists, but really, it's a handful of discreet men behind the scenes who drive our party. Whether self-made corporate moguls, inheritors of vast familial wealth, or heirs to decades-old political dynasties, these men and the effects of their contributions cannot be underestimated."[31] All of the GOP's attempts to put on a diversified front at the convention thus appeared to be false advertising. And any of its efforts to champion itself as the party of integrity and moral virtue were called out in the *Onion*'s lead story the following week, "Hundreds of Republicans Injured in Rush to Discredit Kerry." Somberly, the final paragraph of the story reported Rush Limbaugh's tragic death, which occurred when a bus full of pro-Bush Vietnam vets smashed into his studio.[32]

In late September, as the mainstream media focused on Bush's war record—a controversy that led to the downfall of Dan Rather at CBS—the *Onion* unearthed a far more pertinent scandal: "Documents Reveal Gaps in Bush's Service as President." On matters both foreign and domestic, from Iraq to public education, the documents revealed that Bush had shirked his duties over the preceding four years. Objecting to such "partisan smear tactics," House Majority Leader Tom DeLay said that he "wouldn't be surprised if all 11 billion of these words turn out to be forgeries." Meanwhile, Bush campaign strategist Matthew Dowd seemed unfazed by the revelations, precisely because in the past, "[w]e've faced down widely reported, fully researched, carefully documented accounts of Bush's alcoholism, drug use, private-sector business failings, ignorance in matters of state, smug arrogance, and general self-serving lackadaisical behavior."[33] In reality, Karl Rove displayed a unique and imposing ability to discredit any and all negative stories about Bush. But while Rove may have been "the Architect" of Bush's reelection, the *Onion* consistently went after the real commander in chief. "Cheney Vows to Attack U.S. If Kerry Is Elected," read the headline of a mid-October lead story.[34]

In both the run-up to the election and its aftermath, the *Onion* cynically, but accurately, lampooned the Republicans' commitment to real democracy. "Countdown to Recount 2004," the paper's painfully hilarious lead feature published a week before the election, addressed such important issues as "How to make *your* vote recount," "When will the next president be appointed?" and "Polls Show Supreme Court Split 5–4: A Closer Look at the Swing Justices." In that same issue, a frighteningly prescient newsbrief said, "Republicans Urge Minorities to Get Out and Vote on Nov. 3," the day *after* election day.[35] Several actual reports later confirmed that Republicans in various swing states, particularly Ohio, had indeed issued such phony advice about when to vote—a true testament to both the *Onion's* savvy and the Republicans' sleaze.

The paper's election-week edition then carried a story detailing how the "U.S. Inspires the World with Attempt at Democratic Election."[36] The piece didn't quite pack the same wallop as the paper's "Bush or Gore" story from four years earlier. But given the subsequent revelations of the Conyers Report about the extensive voting irregularities in Ohio, the story's basic premise—that there was merely a superficial attempt at a fair election in 2004—proved to be largely on the mark.[37]

Regardless of what happened in Ohio, Bush had indeed won the popular vote, causing many observers to search for blame. For its part, the *Onion*'s postelection analysis seemed to be a variation on P.T. Barnum's dictum, "Nobody ever went broke underestimating the intelligence of the American people." In "Nation's Poor Win Election for Nation's Rich," the paper combined class analysis with class ridicule. "The Republican party—the party of industrial mega-capitalists, corporate financiers, power brokers, and the moneyed elite—would like to thank the undereducated rural poor, the struggling blue-collar workers in Middle America, and the God-fearing underprivileged minorities who voted George W. Bush back into office," said an appreciative Karl Rove. The story line, however, wasn't exactly a riff on Tom Frank's *What's the Matter with Kansas?*, as it made a case that Kerry had actually promised something for working-class America. "The Republicans," the article reported, "found strong support in non-urban areas populated by the people who would have benefited most from the lower-income tax cuts and social-service programs championed by Kerry." The paper's anger at the election's outcome then produced an overview of American democracy that owed more to Mencken than to Whitman. On behalf of the "tiny fraction at the top of the pyramid," Bush thanked the "teeming mass of mouth-breathers . . . who help us stay rich," and said "God bless America's backwards hicks, lunchpail-toting blockheads, doddering elderly, and bumpity-car-driving Spanish-speakers." Whatever else it was—classist, borderline racist—such a critique was anything but a call for healing with Red State America.[38]

The *Onion*'s righteous indignation at the reelection of Bush led it to continue spewing venom toward the Republicans in the month after the election. As one of the paper's prominent news-briefs explained, "Citing the 'extreme inefficiency' of this month's U.S. presidential election, key Republicans called for future elections to be conducted by the private sector."[39] And a lead story in late November reported, "Swift Boat Vets Still Hounding Kerry." According to Swift Boat founder and longtime Kerry nemesis John O'Neill, "We've made great progress in spreading the truth about John Kerry's treasonous past, but our job isn't over just because he lost the presidency."[40] Rather explicitly, the *Onion* thus presented the outcome of the 2004 election as resulting from a combination of Republican smear tactics and an ignorant voting public. The paper's mild criticisms of Kerry as a candidate never turned into a full takedown of the Democrats' exceedingly weak campaign. While it was not encouraging a Hillary Clinton–style reconciliation with the Red States, the paper did seem to accept the view of many mainstream liberals that the problem of Kansas had nothing to do with the Democrats' lack of a real agenda.

In mid-October 2005, as the war in Iraq showed no signs of progress and the Bush administration's response to Hurricane Katrina was—naturally—disastrous, the *Onion* came up with another classic headline: "Bush to Appoint Someone to Be in Charge of Country." The president, who in reality had shown up in New Orleans and reminisced about his days partying on Bourbon Street, here declared, "I've been talking to folks from across this country, from Louisiana to Los Angeles, and people tell me the same thing: This nation needs a strong, compassionate leader." His short list for the new "secretary of the nation" included "fellow Yale graduates, Midland, TX business associates, and various GOP fundraisers with connections to the Bush family." Just like the disgraced FEMA director Michael Brown, "[d]espite their inexperience in government, [all on the list] clearly passed the Bush character test."[41] Here again the *Onion*'s satire had foresight. Over the next month, as the Valerie Plame affair heated up and the Harriet Miers confirmation process melted down, political pundits would constantly discuss how the American ship of state lacked a captain.

Word soon spread that the White House had been fighting back against the *Onion*'s jabs. On its regular Web site parody of Bush's weekly radio address, the *Onion* had been using the official administration photo and insignia for the program. As Katharine Q. Seelye reported in the *New York Times* in late October 2005, Grant M. Dixton, associate counsel to Bush, had written a letter to the *Onion* the previous month, stating that the seal "is not to be used in connection with commercial ventures or products in any way that suggests presidential support or endorsement." Editor Scott Dikkers responded with a letter expressing surprise that Bush would "spend taxpayer money for his lawyer to write letters to *The Onion*" and suggesting that the administration should instead support tax breaks for satirists. Seelye reported that Rochelle H. Klaskin, the paper's lawyer, drove home her point about the "inconceivable" notion that anyone would see the seal as an endorsement by referring back to the paper's headline about Bush "appointing someone to run the country." The fast-circulating story about the spat between the White House and the *Onion* again illustrated that the Bush gang's own antics themselves often verged on satire.[42]

The absurdity of the White House threats against the paper only served to deepen the *Onion*'s slams against the administration and its cronies throughout Bush's second term. After the notorious Cheney hunting accident, in which the vice president sprayed his hunting partner Harry Whittington with shotgun pellets from head to chest, the paper accomplished a remarkable feat: it gave an already darkly humorous situation even more comedic bite. "White House Had Prior Knowledge of Cheney Threat," declared the lead headline the week after the incident; the subhead furthered the 9/11 reference, claiming that "Aug. 2005 Briefing Warned, 'Cheney Determined to Shoot Old Man in Face.'" The story then poured it on, stating, "The brief, which urged the White House to take 'the most thorough possible precautions to disable this threat to the faces, necks, and chests of the nation's elderly,' was issued a full six months before the events of Feb. 11."[43] A few months later, the paper's lead story reported, "Oil Executives March on D.C." Attended by "more than 1,000 majority shareholders and executive officers from the nation's largest petrochemical companies," the march on Washington for "petrochemical corporations' rights" enabled an oppressed minority to make their "voices be heard at last."[44] An ongoing conflict of interest never fully exposed by either the Democrats or the mainstream political media, the coziness between the Bush-Cheney White House and the oil lobby could not have been lampooned any more forcefully.

In the late summer of 2006, as the fall midterms began to take shape, the *Onion* kept hammering away at the administration, with lead stories including "Bush Grants Self Permission to Grant More Power to Self" and "Bush Urges Nation to Be Quiet for a Minute While He Tries to Think."[45] Yet while the hapless president and his party received the brunt of the attack, the paper also ridiculed the Democrats for their feeble resistance. After his "decisive 1–0 decision" granting himself the constitutional power to grant the executive branch more power, the president, who earlier that year had notoriously referred to himself as the "Decider," faced only mild criticism from Senate minority leader Harry Reid. "The only thing we can do now is withhold our ability to grant him more authority to grant himself more power—unless he authorizes himself to strip us of that power," explained the ineffectual Reid. Similar to the paper's 2004 portrayal of Kerry, the *Onion*'s implicit message was that the Democrats needed to fight back much harder against the Bush regime; if they continued to sound as ridiculous as Reid did here, the Dems stood no chance that fall. That the paper pulled for a Democratic victory in the fall was further illustrated by a lead story it ran during the week prior to the election, in which Bush asked registered Democrats to accompany him on an "Extremely Important Mission" (i.e., so they wouldn't vote).[46] The *Onion*, however, also harbored a healthy skepticism that a Democratic victory would produce real change, as evidenced by the paper's election-week headline, "Politicians Sweep Midterm Elections."[47]

Even more stinging than its jabs at Bush or the weak-kneed Democrats were the paper's volleys against the Iraq disaster that both parties had continued to support. As the war turned three years old in March 2006, Rumsfeld proudly declared, "Iraqis Now Capable of Conducting War Without U.S. Assistance." While politicians on both sides of the aisle vainly hoped that U.S.-trained Iraqi security forces would restore order, the reality on the ground was that the U.S. invasion had only unleashed spiraling chaos. Hence, Rumsfeld now felt comfortable in withdrawing, because "[t]he scope and intensity of the combat in Iraq is such that I believe the presence of American forces in the country will no longer be required to help the Iraqi people plummet into meaningless violence." Instead of a bold attempt to implement democracy in the region, the U.S. invasion was really an act of neocolonial plunder. According to Rumsfeld, while the United States had accomplished "a lot, . . . there's still so much to take from the people of this rich country. . . . We look forward to working very, very closely with Iraq, once there's a friendly government in place that we can do business with." The piece drove home its message about the true nature of the U.S. occupation in its closing sentence, as Rummy noted, "We plan to be around for a long, long time."[48] The war, now three, was only reaching early childhood. And, in the *Onion*'s view, even if American troops were to leave Iraq, that wouldn't mean an end to U.S.-initiated conflict in the region. As debuted on the war's second anniversary and reprinted on its fourth, a classic headline thus declared: "Bush Announces Iraq Exit Strategy: 'We'll Go Through Iran.' "[49]

Consistently entertaining and—as illustrated here—often quite prescient, the *Onion*'s political satire has reached audiences well be-

yond its twenty- to thirty-something demographic. Throughout
the Bush years, the paper's headlines cropped up frequently
throughout the mainstream political media—particularly in the
columns of two of the *New York Times*'s leading liberal voices, Paul
Krugman and Frank Rich. Krugman began a 2003 column, "*The
Onion* describes itself as 'America's finest news source,' and it's not
an idle boast." As he would in another column two years later,
Krugman referred back to the paper's mock inauguration for Bush
in 2001 (about how "Our long national nightmare of peace and
prosperity is finally over"). In particular, the economist Krugman
saw this statement from Bush as particularly prescient: "We must
squander our nation's hard-won budget surplus on tax breaks for
the wealthiest 15 percent. And, on the foreign front, we must find
an enemy and defeat it."[50] For the media critic Rich, the *Onion*
flourished precisely because the pro-Bush political media played so
fast and loose with the truth. Citing one of many examples, Rich
noted that a *New York Post* account of a CIA report about WMD
did not mention that "no stockpiles . . . were found in Iraq" until
the story's sixteenth paragraph. "This would be an *Onion* parody
were it not deadly serious," Rich wrote.[51]

The *Onion* in many ways exposed the subservience of the
mainstream media to the Bush White House, but it also consistently went after deeper targets, including the complicity of liberals in Congress and the political media in accepting the terms of
debate put forth by the White House on Iraq and other issues. Its
comedic brilliance owed much to the necessary skepticism the
paper held regarding the statements made by those in power. By
injecting that element of doubt into contemporary political debate, the *Onion* helped popularize media self-criticism; it is no surprise that one of the paper's early editors back in Madison, Ben
Karlin (1993–96), would become a key player in the rise of *The
Daily Show* and *The Colbert Report*. In the fall of 2007, the *Onion*—
its Web readership still over three million per month, and with ten
local print editions—appeared to be in solid shape. The same

could not be said of either the Bush-led Republican Party or the war in Iraq. Of course, the *Onion* bore only a small sliver of responsibility for turning the tide of public opinion, but in many respects it had been at the cutting edge in its criticisms of the Bush regime. And, despite the paper's own party line, its scalpel had consistently sliced decidedly in support of the left.

2

A LIBERAL FRANKEN-STEIN: THE RISE AND FALL OF AIR AMERICA

Somewhat belatedly, talk radio became an important front of the New Blue Media during the Bush years. The right had discovered talk radio's ability to rally the base in the late 1980s, and by the early 2000s, nationally syndicated figures such as Rush Limbaugh and Sean Hannity drove home the Republican line to twelve million to fifteen million listeners per week. By the second Bush era, liberals had finally had enough. With direct support from key Democratic Party players, Air America made its much-ballyhooed debut in the spring of 2004—with the avowed intent of defeating George W. Bush. The network's intellectual origins, however, lay in the 1990s, and, like the Democratic Party itself, Air America struggled with the legacy of Clintonism. Throughout his two terms, Clinton had triangulated the party to the right on many key issues. On matters of war and the economy, the mainstream Democrats differed little from the Republicans. It was now primarily the so-called culture wars that separated the two parties. Throughout the culture wars of the 1980s and 1990s, talk radio had been a key element in disseminating the Republicans' message, and by the early 2000s the Democrats desperately sought to steal some of their opponents' thunder.

In seeking to combat the right head-on, Air America led the didactic wing of the New Blue Media. Neither nuance nor subtlety was present in the vocabularies of Limbaugh, Hannity, and company, and Al Franken and the rest of Air America's flagship team promised a similar barrage of heavy fire. Of course, Franken and fellow original host Janeane Garofalo were both known for their political comedy, and one of the network's initial main players was Lizz Winstead, co-creator of *The Daily Show*. But humor was a decidedly secondary feature in Air America's original programming. From the outset, the network's lead hosts, Franken and Randi Rhodes, positioned themselves as the liberals' answer to Limbaugh, Bill O'Reilly, and the rest of the right's attack machine. Air America's creation was thus an experiment of sorts—namely, to see whether liberal politics could flourish in a commercial talk-radio format. While a range of other factors have stunted its growth—including its own management problems, the inherent difficulty of starting as a national network, and the persistent scrutiny and attacks it has faced from the right—Air America's ongoing struggles to survive also cast doubt on whether contemporary progressive politics lend themselves to didactic styles of delivery.

Al Franken may not have been the driving monetary force behind the creation of Air America, but he clearly was the marquee figure, the name that would build the new brand. He brought to it his star power, his connections in the media, entertainment, and political worlds, and, most important, his reputation for wanting to confront the right head-on. Franken, Air America's founders predicted, would be a good "lead dog" for the network, or the star to build the team around. And in the network's first year and half of operation, Franken's signature blend of satire and advocacy would define Air America's house style.

A former *Saturday Night Live* skit writer and performer, Franken had earned his stripes as a liberal political commentator with his wildly successful 1996 book, *Rush Limbaugh Is a Big Fat Idiot and Other Observations*. By the mid-1990s, Limbaugh had made himself a household name by Clinton bashing, and in the book Franken went after Limbaugh, hard. Franken mixed together jokes, ad hominem assaults, and pointed criticisms of Limbaugh's attacks on Clinton's policy record. Franken further showed that he actually had a bigger target in mind than just Rush by slamming

Newt Gingrich, Phil Gramm, and that year's Republican presidential candidate, Bob Dole. By taking on the right in the name of Clintonism, Franken established himself as a key Democratic player. That the book spent twenty-three weeks on the *Publishers Weekly* bestseller list during Clinton's reelection year solidified Franken's status with liberals both inside and outside the Beltway.

The right tried in vain to squash Franken's rise. Reagan-era henchwoman Jeane Kirkpatrick began her memorable hatchet job in the *New York Times Book Review* by stating, "It remains a mystery why the *New York Times* would ask me to review this dreadfully foul little book. I am an expert on geopolitical strategic paradigms, not on the cheap, mindless mockery that seems to be Mr. Franken's forte." In Kirkpatrick's estimation, Franken's book was "not just unfunny. It is confused." And it was filled with "invective and scurrilous accusations that remain totally unproven." However, Kirkpatrick's main example of Franken's "scurrilous accusations" was itself unintentionally funny: "Nowhere in the 288-page screed does Franken actually show any real evidence that Limbaugh is indeed fat." The self-described "expert" cold warrior concluded her "review" of Franken's book by saying, "If this is the kind of mindless political tripe that passes for political satire these days, I fear for this nation!"[1]

The battle lines had been drawn. The right would reflexively attack the liberals' ad hominem attacks on the Republicans' ad hominem attack machine. In this case, Kirkpatrick brazenly dismissed Franken's "mindless tripe" in defense of a belligerent—and yes, hefty—right-wing attack dog. But in Franken, the right was now facing someone who proved that he was willing to take off the gloves and fight—with low blows, if he saw fit to do so. The commercial success of Franken's book further established that there was indeed a market (at least in publishing) for a new style of liberal politics. Amid the Clinton-era reign of the technocratic policy wonks, Franken helped inaugurate the rise of hard-edged liberal political satire. And, in Franken's case, the two perspectives have continued to inspire each other.

Beyond Bill and Hillary themselves, it is indeed difficult to find anyone with a rosier assessment of the Clinton era than Franken. In his two major books, *Rush Limbaugh . . .* and *Lies and the Lying Liars Who Tell Them* (2003), Franken reveals himself to be a dyed-in-the-wool Clintonite. His support goes beyond defending Bill Clinton from the right-wing attack machine that Limbaugh ignited, Fox News stoked, and Kenneth Starr turned into a fiery inferno. In his books and elsewhere, Franken has indeed defended what he views as the resounding success of nearly every Clinton policy—on matters both foreign and domestic, from Kosovo to the expansion of Medicaid coverage for children. In general, Franken supports his points with mildly humorous barbs backed by an array of statistics and policy indicators. As one of just many examples, Franken contradicts what he calls an "imbecilic," "shit-for-brains 2003 editorial" in the *Wall Street Journal* about crime rates in the Clinton era by using graphs and statistics drawn from FBI Uniform Crime Reports.[2] At the same time, Franken's glowing endorsement of Clinton's crime policies manages to overlook two rather significant facts about the 1990s: the decade saw the largest prison boom in American history, and the death penalty was carried out far more frequently than it has been during the Bush years.

Franken's readiness to go to bat for the Clinton legacy placed him in stark opposition to Rush Limbaugh and Fox News, but also to the more intellectual voices of the right. Of the latter camp, Franken's most notable skirmishes came with Rich Lowry, editor of the *National Review*. In March 2004, the two engaged in a protracted battle in the pages of the *New York Post*, the *National Review*, and *Spinsanity*, a now-defunct Web magazine. It started when Franken took on Lowry after the latter insisted that the Clinton-era Democrats had "feminized," "sissified," and created an "Oprah-fication" of American politics. In *Lies*, Franken, a former wrestler, challenged Lowry to a fight; and after Lowry trashed his book in the *Post*, Franken repeated the challenge.[3]

The two then converted their conflict into lengthy written critiques of each other's work. Franken slammed Lowry for arguing—in his book *Legacy*, about the Clinton years—that for anything "good that happened during [the Clinton era], the credit belongs elsewhere—mainly to Ronald Reagan." Lowry fought back by calling Clinton "merely a placeholder" presiding over Reagan-era policies. In the end, Lowry won the pissing match. It wasn't simply because he demonstrated that Franken—contradicting his own argument against the right—could also distort the factual record (namely by stating that upon leaving office, Clinton had a specific plan to go after al Qaeda that Bush ignored) in order to make a point. It was also because he showed that Franken's willingness to dish out ad hominem attacks could backfire. In their exchange, Franken singled out one of Lowry's dedications in *Legacy*—"To Robert / Who laughs more than anyone I know"—and wondered, "Doesn't an author so obsessed with masculinity owe it to his readers to explain who Robert is?" In return, Lowry clarified that Robert is not, as Franken implied, his lover, but instead his brother, and rightly faulted Franken for his "sexual McCarthyism."[4]

Franken fills *Lies and the Lying Liars Who Tell Them* with similarly blustery invective, mostly aimed at the fanatical right. Ann Coulter, Sean Hannity, and, of course, Bill O'Reilly are his main targets. Coulter is up first, and Franken's takedown establishes what will become a recurring pattern of critique in the book: outright name-calling, as shown by the chapter title, "Ann Coulter: Nutcase"; harsh but witty analysis, as seen in passages such as "Ann Coulter, for those of you lucky enough to not have been exposed to her, is the reigning diva of the hysterical right. Or rather, the hysterical diva of the reigning right"; and highly specific, borderline nitpicking examples of each figure's willful "lies," which here stem from Coulter's 2002 book *Slander* (its subtitle, *Liberal Lies About the American Right*, inspired the title of Franken's book). In *Slander*, Coulter wrongly refers to her list of sources as "footnotes" instead of "endnotes," and she incorrectly calls *Newsweek* Washington bureau chief Evan Thomas the "son" of Socialist Norman

Thomas, instead of the grandson. No one opposed to the right would disagree with Franken's goal of fighting back against the truly repugnant Coulter; but whether Franken's critique in *Lies* irrevocably damns her work remains an open question.[5]

Against the equally repugnant O'Reilly and Hannity, Franken deploys a similar method, and again achieves mixed results. O'Reilly, says Franken's chapter subtitle, is a "Lying, Splotchy Bully." With mock nobility, Franken "dare[s] to hope that O'Reilly can be saved. From himself." The bulk of the chapter recounts Franken's showdown with O'Reilly at the June 2003 BookExpo America in Los Angeles; there Franken memorably went after O'Reilly, working the latter into a lathery rage. The main issue? O'Reilly's "lies" about *Inside Edition*, his former TV show, having received two prestigious Peabody Awards, when it actually received one not-as-prestigious Polk Award. Later in the chapter, Franken documents O'Reilly's intentional, grossly distorted statements about real policies such as welfare and meaningful issues such as black enrollment in colleges. In the end, however, Franken seems to think that the reader will share his hostility to O'Reilly over the Peabody incident—but compared to the bigger lies of the Bush administration that O'Reilly (among many others) helped promote regarding Iraq, this one seems minor.[6] Regarding Hannity, Franken calls him an "Irish ape-man" and says he is a leader of the "lying right," for which it is a "sacred tenet . . . that Ronald Reagan did not cause the massive budget deficits of the eighties."[7] The no-holds-barred approach Franken adopted in *Lies* made for lively reading, but here as elsewhere, his criticisms often centered on specific policy issues such as deficit spending.

While Fox News came onto the scene disseminating a far-right agenda, Franken thus launched his critique in the name of Clintonian neoliberalism. In a lengthy feature profile in the *New York Times Magazine* on the eve of Air America's debut, journalist Russell Shorto indeed characterized Franken as "a devout party man, one who says, for example, that the Democratic Leadership Council is a moral force for good." Shorto further noted that

"Franken's political views are more eclectic than you might imagine. He's a big booster of the military and counts John McCain as one of his heroes. 'On trade, I would have voted for Nafta,' [Franken] said, 'but now I'd be working to fix it and get more environmental and labor standards into it.'" Against the far right, Franken promoted DLC-style centrism, albeit with a different tone. Former Clinton adviser (and CNN analyst) Paul Begala told Shorto that by early 2004, Franken now ranked beside the Clintons as a "rallying point" for Democrats. And, Begala said, "The thing about this year is, 'liberal' and 'wimp' have become decoupled. Al has been one of the real sparks of that. Liberals are ready to fight."[8]

The contrast between Franken's preferred political style and his actual centrist politics became quite clear in his choice of Democratic candidates for the 2004 campaign. By the summer of 2003, Howard Dean had moved to the front of the pack. What sparked the former Vermont governor's campaign was both his message—against the war—and his use of medium, the Internet, as an organizing and fund-raising tool. But Dean's fighting style also initially separated him from the other contenders. Echoing Paul Wellstone, Dean told CNN's Larry King in the summer of 2003, "What the American people are going to see, should I get the nomination, is a Democrat who is not afraid to be a Democrat again."[9] Meanwhile, the architect of Dean's rise, his initial campaign manager, Joe Trippi, declared, "We have to be the most aggressive campaign [and] the most unpredictable" in order to stay ahead in the race.[10] Dean's readiness to go to battle against the Republicans sounded Frankenesque, and his freewheeling rants against Bush at times made him seem to be a talk radio–type figure. But the centrist Franken backed a different horse.

Franken was indeed instrumental in helping Kerry move to the forefront of the liberal fight. In early December 2003, Franken invited Kerry to his Upper West Side apartment for a meeting with various leading political reporters, including the *New Yorker's* Hendrik Hertzberg, *Time's* Jim Kelly, and the *Nation's* Eric Alterman, among many others. As Shorto reported, "Alterman grilled Kerry on his vote on Iraq, and he gave a long, tortured answer. Then he was asked about it a second time. 'By the third goround, the answer was getting shorter and more relevant,' Kelly said." Kerry's unique inability to provide convincing sound bites was thus already evident, but Franken helped lay the groundwork for Kerry's rise as the "electable" candidate. Franken told Shorto that his rationale for hosting the gathering was that "I liked Dean, but I also think Kerry is just a really smart, capable man."[11] Stylistically, he shared more in common with the combative Dean than with the more elusive Kerry. But politically, he was more in sync with Kerry, a supporter of NAFTA, the Iraq War, and the DLC. Franken's only real strong show of support for Dean came in late January 2004, when the former wrestler literally took a Dean heckler down to the ground at a New Hampshire rally. Even then, Franken was quick to note that he "would have done it if [the heckler] was a Dean supporter at a Kerry rally."[12]

By the time of Air America's debut, in late March 2004, Dean was out of contention and John Kerry was well on his way to becoming the Democratic nominee. Franken was by no means solely responsible for these developments, but he was plainly a leading player in the process. Neither was Franken chiefly responsible for creating the new liberal radio network, although he obviously had a hand in that as well. For both the 2004 Democrats and fledgling Air America, getting Bush out of office was the rallying cry. And with John Kerry and Al Franken at the respective forefronts, the fight would be spearheaded by Clintonian centrists.

A great deal of media fanfare accompanied the launch of Air America at the end of March 2004. A fair amount of controversy over the business dealings and practices of the early founders has continued to swirl since then, a pot stirred by right-wing bloggers and promulgated by far-right media outlets such as Fox News and the *New York Post*. Until the network's bankruptcy in 2006, the issue of Air America's funding was debated as much as its political positioning, with the right trying to use the former in order to damn the latter.

The original concept behind Air America was created by Sheldon and Anita Drobny, a husband-and-wife team of investors based in Chicago. Both had been active in Democratic Party fundraising, and their idea received initial public support from Bill Clinton. In December 2003, Clinton told *Chicago Magazine* that the Drobnys' goal in creating the liberal radio network was "to do something good for our country by working to restore a sense of balance."[13] In mainstream political parlance, such balance is between "right" and "left," but for the Clintonians, it more accurately could be termed as the "center" versus the "far right."

As Russell Shorto reported in his *Times Magazine* profile of Franken, Clinton's influence was indeed present throughout Air America's initial rise. The network's first CEO, former AOL executive Mark Walsh—a friend of close Clinton ally and then–DNC chair Terry McAuliffe—was brought into the project by David Goodfriend, a former Clinton White House staff member. Former Clinton White House chief of staff John Podesta also pledged his "advice" as well as an "information pool," the source of both originating from his think tank, the Center for American Progress. "We'll be a resource for them, much the same way that the Heritage Foundation provides stuff that right-wing talkers use," said Podesta.[14] Other than serving as an early guest on *The O'Franken Factor*, in order to promote both his book and the Democrats' vision, Clinton was not connected personally to the network. But via his acolytes, his political presence was nonetheless abundantly clear.

Where the far-right media had gained traction by bashing Clinton, the new liberal radio network would do much of its Bush bashing in the name of Clintonism. But, according to Walsh, it would do so by adopting its own distinctly liberal style. Air America's product promised to be "comedic rather than didactic," he told *USA Today*. "You'll be entertained, maybe have a chuckle and when you arrive at work you'll have the well-thought-out sort of argument that you can give to the right-wing guy at the coffee urn talking about how Bill Clinton ruined this nation."[15] Walsh no doubt had Franken in mind when he said that the network should both be comedic and mount a persuasive argument. And, as Shorto reported, when Franken initially found out about the effort to create Air America, he was "immediately interested."[16]

But Franken was not the only creative inspiration for the network. Comedienne Lizz Winstead, co-creator of *The Daily Show*, initially served as a key player as well. Beyond co-hosting a late-morning show with rapper Chuck D, Winstead's actual role in steering the early creative direction of the network was the subject of dispute. But in early media coverage, she appeared to be a central figure. Shorto referred to her as one of two lead members of the network's "creative team," the other being veteran broadcast news producer Shelley Lewis. In the introduction to a *Mother Jones* interview between Winstead and media fixture Kurt Andersen, Winstead was dubbed the "comedy czar" of the network.[17] Regardless of her official title, Winstead clearly brought to the network a vision different than that of the Clinton insiders.

In her interview with Andersen, Winstead spoke of her desire to incorporate a variation on the *Daily Show* model of blending real news with satire. "There will be information," she said, "but the hosts will feel free to be witty, and there will be a few 90-second comedy pieces each hour. So you come for the news and stay to hear the satirical response to it." She agreed with Andersen's response, which was that this would be "sort of the opposite of *The Daily Show*, where you come for the entertainment but you get, shockingly enough, your information." What Winstead described indeed sounded more oriented around comedy and news than Franken's model of policy discussion with some comedy mixed in. Winstead also revealed her politics to be further to the left than Franken's. Asked by Andersen whether a John Kerry victory would be "bad for Air America," Winstead said no, explaining that Kerry "gave away the farm on so many issues that there's a lot to fix." Later she observed, "I don't know why Joe Lieberman is a Democrat."[18] Winstead's views showed that like the Democratic Party itself, Air America faced internal divisions between leftists and centrists—and, echoing the Dean versus Kerry debate, conflicts over both style and content would be present at the network's launch.

The media blitz over Air America's launch included an appearance on NBC's *Today* show by Walsh and Franken on the morning of the network's debut. The booking itself showed two things: Air America was considered a serious media player from the get-go; and Franken was not only the network's marquee name, but also the spokesman for its creative vision. Asking the question that was ostensibly on her audience's mind, then–*Today* show host Katie Couric pressed Franken on whether Air America should, in fact, be "rename[d] the 'John Kerry for President' network." "Oh, no," Franken replied. "It would be more the 'Get Rid of Bush Network.' . . . [W]e're going to be around for a long time. So after Kerry becomes president, then we'll be going after the Congress." Franken further clarified that conservatives would be welcome on the show, mentioning John McCain, Gary Bauer, and G. Gordon Liddy as upcoming guests. Before a large national TV audience, Franken announced his goal for Air America to become a key contributor to the national debate, from that day forward and well into the "Kerry presidency."[19]

In launching a national radio network with the explicit aim of influencing a presidential election, Air America set a rather lofty goal for itself. Other attempts at building left-leaning networks had started with more grassroots ambitions. Founded in 1949, Pacifica originated to spread the ideals of pacifism. As the historian Matthew Lasar demonstrates, Pacifica's founders had been conscientious objectors in World War II, and during the McCarthy era, they were painted as Communists. In truth, few of the original members supported the Communists or held allegiance to any political party. Instead, they were adherents to Gandhian idealism, which during the cold war gained little traction in national politics.[20] Since its founding, Pacifica has stayed on the left, but it has never become a thriving national network; its strongholds have instead remained on the coasts—KPFA in Berkeley, KPFK in Los Angeles, and WBAI in New York. The radical leanings of Pacifica's programming have generally precluded it from becoming a major presence in mainstream national politics. But at times, leading liberals have sought out the support of the network's audience, with mixed results. On election day 2000, for example, in order to dampen left enthusiasm for Ralph Nader, Bill Clinton phoned in to *Democracy Now!*, the network's most popular program, trying to drum up support for both Al Gore and Hillary Clinton. After Amy Goodman, Pacifica's leading figure, peppered him with questions about NAFTA, the death penalty, and sanctions against Iraq, the president complained that "every question you've asked has been hostile and combative."[21] Clinton obviously would be a much more welcome presence at Air America.

There was a right-wing precedent for creating a national radio network aimed at influencing national politics. It had been done in the 1930s by the Detroit-based Father Coughlin, whose attacks on the New Deal reached a staggering forty million listeners. Coughlin's drift to the far right eventually led him to support Hitler and Mussolini, and FDR's administration finally shut him down. Conservative talk radio experienced a resurgence in large local markets in the 1960s and 1970s, with staunch anti-Communist Joe Pyne dominating the Los Angeles area and Bob Grant filling the New York City airwaves with right-wing invective.[22] The recent reemergence of national right-wing radio began in the mid-eighties with the rise of Rush Limbaugh, who would eventually contribute such insipid phrases to political debate as "feminazi." After being syndicated by the ABC Radio Network in 1988, Limbaugh became a major player in the Republican Party. In 1994, after he helped Newt Gingrich and the far right sweep Congress, Limbaugh was even given an "honorary member of Congress" award by incoming Republicans. Limbaugh's success paved the way for the more recent rise of the radio programs of right-wing TV hosts Bill O'Reilly (syndicated by Westwood One) and particularly Sean Hannity, who by 2006 reached over 12 million listeners per day (also on ABC), second only to Limbaugh's 13.5 million. Those numbers would dwarf the audience share that Air America received during the Bush years.

In 2007, the Center for American Progress issued a report that grimly assessed the dominance of the right in talk radio. The average adult American, the study found, listened to nineteen hours of radio per week. More than fifty million listeners specifically tuned in to talk radio each week, a number second only to country-and-western music. What they heard was overwhelmingly voices from the right. In the top 257 stations, owned by five major companies, more than 90 percent of the talk show hosts were conservative; in terms of the number of hours aired, the ratio stood at ten-to-one conservative to progressive. These trends, the report maintained, were a consequence of the deregulation of national media, which eliminated local station ownership as well as programming, replacing the latter with syndication.[23] The Center for American Progress study documented a trend that was already common knowledge by the time Air America got off the ground. The need to counterbalance the right's dominance of talk radio was clear to many liberals, but it was indeed a daunting challenge. Supported by large media companies, the right had control of the airwaves, and its politics of resentment played out well in the talk radio format.

Air America came on the air at noon eastern standard time on Wednesday, March 31, 2004, with *The O'Franken Factor* reaching a handful of major markets (including New York, L.A., and Chicago). "We're angry!" Franken assured his listeners. "This show is about taking back our country. It's about relentlessly hammering away at the Bush administration until they crack and crumble this November, because, don't get me wrong, friends, they are going down." Such fighting words pointedly distinguished Air America from National Public Radio (NPR), which is officially required to be nonpartisan in order to maintain public funding; but NPR, as Winstead observed, is also characterized by "aw-shucksy folksiness," where there's always that "nine-minute story about the goat-cheese farm that you tune out." [24] The connections to NPR nonetheless remained present, at least in terms of Air America's original staffers. Franken's co-host (until October 2005) was Katherine Lanpher, who came from Minnesota Public Radio, and Jo Ann Allen, a familiar voice from WNYC, served as Air America's original news anchor. Yet from its first minutes on the air, the "angry" new network showed that it would be charting a course quite distinct from NPR's.

Franken's early roster of guests showed that the anger on the network's flagship show would be voiced by Democratic Party insiders and supporters. Al Gore, Hillary Clinton, Bob Kerrey, Robert Reich, Richard Clarke, and Paul Krugman all came on the show in its first two days. Joe Biden would be a frequent guest as well—like Franken, he was really worked up about the Bush administration's "bad management" of the occupation of Iraq, not the decision to go to war in the first place. "We can't lose Iraq," Franken adamantly concurred with Biden. The show's guests were not all Clintonites, however. Michael Moore also weighed in, voicing the contempt for the Bush administration that would soon hit the theaters. From day one, Franken's show was openly going after Bush, O'Reilly, and Limbaugh, and he was doing in it in his own style. As Rachel Straus noted on *Alternet*, Franken mixed "satiric skits with political commentary culled from an impressive guest lineup." [25] Yet more often than not, Franken echoed the same centrist views of his notable guests.

The same could not necessarily be said for the hosts of Air America's other main inaugural shows. Winstead, Chuck D, Randi Rhodes, Laura Flanders, Janeane Garofalo, and Sam Seder all came out swinging against Bush, often assuming positions much further to the left than Franken. But the "Anybody but Bush" line dominated Air America throughout the 2004 campaign. Rhodes, of course, in her first show notoriously squared off with Ralph

Nader. She demanded that he drop his third-party candidacy, telling him, "We can't afford you this year, Ralph!" After Rhodes cut him off several times, Nader hung up. The bluster deprived Air America listeners of a serious discussion of how Nader's candidacy actually might benefit the Democrats by forcing them to take a tougher stand on corporate corruption and the Iraq War.[26] In May 2004, Garofalo and Seder made their view of Kerry more explicit: "We need to get him in office, then move him to the left." By moving to the left during the campaign, at least on some of the issues Nader and others raised, Kerry might have articulated a clear alternative to the Bush regime. Many of Air America's various programs' guests—especially on the *Laura Flanders Show* and on Garofalo and Seder's *Majority Report*—in fact advocated such a move. But amidst the "ABB" fervor of the 2004 campaign, the new network was hardly alone in encouraging liberals and the left to close ranks behind Kerry.

As soon as Air America debuted, the far-right media began their assault, lambasting the network's politics and chances for success. Franken's previous battles with Limbaugh and O'Reilly had laid the groundwork for the counterattack. Now, by naming his show *The O'Franken Factor* and running it in the same time slot as Limbaugh's, Franken openly invited it. His call to arms may have further heightened the media buzz around Air America's launch, but for the right, it provided an easy measuring stick—namely, a comparison of the ratings between the Franken and Limbaugh shows. On TV as well as radio, and in print, various right-wing commentators continually seized any opportunity to slam Air America.

The Fox News entourage greeted the network's debut with a variety of responses. "All forms of free speech are welcomed in this country. We wish them well," Fox News said in an official, conspicuously neutral statement.[27] O'Reilly, of course, was more combative, forecasting failure on the eve of the network's debut. "These pinheads backing the venture will lose millions of dollars because the propaganda network is simply tedious, and tedious doesn't

sell," O'Reilly told his television audience.[28] Hannity, as one reporter noted, was "uncharacteristically silent" on his radio show
about his liberal competitor's debut. But his silence naturally didn't
last long, as Hannity, according to one observer, soon "mockingly
suggested that the only way liberals and left-wingers could secure a
place on the airwaves was if they were subsidized by the government."[29] Meanwhile, Limbaugh—not a Fox News employee, but
its spiritual figurehead—scoffed at Air America's small size, com-
paring Air America's outlets to "1,000-watt blowtorches."[30] And
the *Drudge Report*, a fellow traveler on the right, gleefully distributed word of the network's early contractual troubles, which
forced it off the air in Chicago and L.A.[31] The right's main bullies
clearly wanted to give the new punk kid on the block a beatdown.

In print, the right-wing critics often raised more interesting
questions than those simply pertaining to market share. To find
those questions, however, a reader needed to first wade through a
thicket of standard right-wing distortions. The most enduring of
these, of course, has been the myth of the "liberal media." "[T]he
left already dominates the networks, NPR, CNN, Hollywood, and
so on," David Skinner wrote in a preview of Air America's launch
in the *Daily Standard*, the online companion to Rupert Murdoch's
Weekly Standard. Such a dubious statement, presented here as elsewhere as a "fact," soon gave way to Skinner's real question. "What
made Rush Limbaugh successful?" Skinner asked, rhetorically.
He later answered by observing, "When you look at the conservative personalities of the twentieth century who fundamentally
changed the art and sport of political debate in the mainstream,
you find a history of outsiders." As predecessors to Rush, he offered the "socially awkward, spiritually tormented, overweight"
anti-Communist zealot Whittaker Chambers; and William F.
Buckley, whose elitism placed him outside the mainstream. Skinner also should have added Father Coughlin to the list, but
Coughlin's fascist sympathies have made him persona non grata on
the right. Regardless, as Skinner suggested, Franken's "insider" status potentially limited his ability to create a new mass audience.[32]

In the *National Review*, editor Rich Lowry generally let writers other than himself keep up the battle with Franken. Jonah Goldberg, the magazine's lead columnist and here a pop psychologist, early on decided that the network's main role would be to boost liberals' "self-esteem." He then took pointed swipes at Franken's style: "He's schizophrenic; unwilling to decide whether he's a comedian or political commentator. This is different from being a funny commentator or a political comedian. Franken wants to be both, which often makes him fail at both because he's too serious to be one and not funny enough to be the other."[33] Where O'Reilly, Hannity, and Limbaugh went after the network's chances for success, Goldberg now slammed its leading figure's style. The network's political substance has rarely proven the basis for right-wing critique.

A leader in the right's mission to damn the left, the *National Review*'s Byron York has kept a watchful, cynical eye trained on the exact size of the network's audience. York, author of the revealingly titled *The Vast Left-Wing Conspiracy: The Untold Story of How Democratic Operatives, Eccentric Billionaires, Liberal Activists, and Assorted Celebrities Tried to Bring Down a President—and Why They'll Try Even Harder Next Time* (2005), has assailed Air America from its inception. In the first week of the network's existence, when no real numbers had yet been compiled, York cited one unnamed "radio expert" who called the size of Air America's audience "microscopic." "After the intense media attention that surrounded Air America's debut fades away," York predicted, "the network will likely spend the rest of this year trying to build a tiny listenership into a small one, and then to go from there."[34] In the summer of 2004, when Franken scored growing success competing against Limbaugh in the New York City market, York promptly wrote two articles aimed at rebutting the numbers. Later, in an April 2005 column titled "Air America's Year of Decline," York was pleased to report the network's low ratings for the winter of 2005.[35] And the following August, York wrote a lengthy article—ominously titled "Radiogate"—about a dubious loan the network had received.[36] Although his writing appeared in a magazine ostensibly devoted to championing free-market conservatism, York consistently tried to dash the hopes of the start-up radio network.

Yet York's criticisms of Air America were indeed tepid when compared to those of Michelle Malkin, an ultraright blogger, columnist for the *New York Post*, regular on *Hannity and Colmes*, and both regular guest and occasional fill-in host on *The O'Reilly Factor*. Malkin, who gained notoriety by writing a book defending World War II internment camps for Japanese Americans, truly despised Air America. In her syndicated columns and especially on her blog, Malkin tried to stir up any and all possible allegations of corruption, infighting, and controversy within the network. Along with research partner Brian Maloney, Malkin spearheaded the effort to turn the Air America loan scandal—a complicated tale involving a deal made between Evan Cohen, Air America's initial CEO, and a Bronx charity—into a major story. From late July through September 2005, Malkin's blog published all sorts of legal documents about the "scandal," and in her nationally syndicated column she questioned why figures she called "race hustlers" such as Al Sharpton and Jesse Jackson remained silent about it.[37]

Not satisfied with Air America's efforts to repay the loans, in late September 2005, Malkin and Maloney went on *The O'Reilly Factor* to further trash Air America. Maloney said that Air America's alleged financial woes were "the result of Soros and some of the big wigs not contributing what Air America would like." (For the right, Rupert Murdoch's largesse is rarely mentioned, whereas anything George Soros funds is immediately demonized.) Malkin for her part saw two main problems with the network: a "bad business model" and "the content of the programming on the air." Regarding the latter, she said, "[Y]ou've got any number of these Air America hosts saying outrageous things that I think even rational liberals have to agree is just beyond the pale." As an example, Malkin said that Randi Rhodes had "advocat[ed] . . . the assassination of President Bush and jok[ed] about it." When O'Reilly interjected that Rhodes had "apologized,"

Malkin responded that Rhodes had called for Bush's head "twice." What's more, Malkin said, Rhodes had recently been "caught on-air cheering the looters in New Orleans." O'Reilly responded skeptically, saying "Really?" Malkin then explained that Rhodes had "basically rationalized their criminal behavior," before quickly going back to slamming Air America's business model and current financial condition. Malkin's sensationalized attacks on Air America proved to be so fanatical that they made O'Reilly look like the voice of reason—a monumental feat indeed.[38]

The obsessive effort to crush the new liberal network illustrates a number of key points about the far-right media. One is that despite their proclaimed "differences," the major outlets—the "respectable" opinion journal *National Review*; Murdoch's Fox News Channel, *New York Post*, and *Weekly Standard*; and the right-wing talk show hosts on ABC Radio—invariably end up spouting the same line. In this case, Air America's "scandalous" business dealings provided the fodder for most stories, while on occasion its "outrageous" politics came under attack. Such coordinated assaults were always destined to show up nearly everywhere in the right-wing media, on both the airwaves and in print via syndication, at virtually the same time. The right's effort also shows its "kitchen sink" style of argument—Air America was a bad business model, run by operators who were either shady or desperate, and full of "unfunny" personalities who are either "tedious propagandists" or "beyond the pale." Indeed, the only consistent point the right-wing critics made is that they didn't like Air America. Nonetheless, aimed at scaring away both listeners, and, more important, investors for Air America, the right's persistent assault would partially succeed.

By October 2005, Air America could count seventy stations in its network, covering most major markets and a range of tiny ones such as Ely-Hibbing, Minnesota, and Lihue, Hawaii. It also now had a combative, media-savvy CEO in Danny Goldberg, who was ready to defend the network against the various right-wing charges. In late September 2005, for example, Goldberg swung back at what he called "the same cast of right wing media characters who have attacked the network for ideological reasons from day one." Both the *New York Post* and O'Reilly had recently reported that the network was in financial trouble. But while O'Reilly was telling his TV audience that Air America "could be on its last legs," Goldberg, writing in the *Huffington Post*, maintained that the network in reality was "in strong financial shape." He then spelled out details regarding Air America's response to the loan scandal, its expanding number of stations, and its growing ratings. And he defended the "spirited progressive opinions" voiced on the network from the "litany of attacks, lies, half-truths and smears from various members of the right-wing media." [39]

Named the network's new CEO in late February 2005, Goldberg brought to Air America a successful track record in the music industry. Among other efforts, he had managed the Beastie Boys and Nirvana as well as founded Artemis Records. In his 2003 book, *Dispatches from the Culture Wars: How the Left Lost Teen Spirit*, Goldberg discussed his work on behalf of Ralph Nader's controversial 2000 campaign; in the updated, 2005 edition of the book, Goldberg then explained why he had broken with Nader in 2004 and supported Kerry. In the earlier campaign, Nader had provided an alternative to Gore and especially Lieberman, whom Goldberg rejected largely because of their efforts to censor the entertainment industry. In 2004, Nader now appeared to be a "prisoner of his own bitterness," and, like his friend Michael Moore, Goldberg was not sufficiently impressed with Nader's efforts to force corporate corruption or withdrawal from Iraq onto the Democrats' agenda. Goldberg, however, was against the war, and initially sympathetic to Dean; but he soon joined the groundswell of support for Kerry, for whom he had a "soft spot," only to be disappointed by Kerry's lack of clear positions on the issues. Leaning leftward, Goldberg also blasted a darling of the DLC: "I would never under any circumstances support or vote for a ticket with Joe Lieberman on it," he said. [40]

Other than his distaste for Lieberman, Goldberg was generous in his appraisal of most major Democrats. "Bill Clinton's victories were inspiring," he wrote, although "Clintonism without Clinton failed miserably." He hosted a fund-raiser for Hillary Clinton, only to become upset by her subsequent support of Lieberman's crackdown on the entertainment industry. And of the Kerry campaign, he found the result "deeply disappointing," but saw a "silver lining": "[U]nlike any election in my lifetime, the campaign left many progressive footprints, an infrastructure of activists, media, and organizations that have at long last begun the work of creating a true progressive electorate." Air America is the first example of the new infrastructure that Goldberg offered, and his goal for the network was indeed to perpetuate the growth of the "progressive campaign catalyzed by MoveOn.org, Michael Moore, and Howard Dean." [41]

The Nation would seem a likely ally for Air America, as it too seeks to contribute to the conversation over the Democratic Party's direction; its editor, Katrina vanden Heuvel, has been a regular guest on *The Majority Report*, and one of that show's original co-hosts, Janeane Garofalo, appears in *Nation* ads. But shortly after Goldberg's arrival, the magazine published a lengthy diatribe against the network written by the pugnacious critic Nicholas von Hoffman. In it, von Hoffman took swipes at the network's business plan, arguing that the syndicated model of Air America competitor Democracy Radio made more sense—as illustrated by the growing audience for heartland populist Ed Schultz. Von Hoffman also ripped what he saw as Air America's "hipper-than-thou," "noise-making," "overwrought" hosts, particularly singling out Garofalo, who struck him as either a "confused avenging liberal angel or venomous pixie." As for the new CEO, von Hoffman maintained that "Goldberg himself is part businessman and part red-hot. He is not one of your modern mumbling liberals who isn't sure he wants people to know what his opinions are. He shouts them with a self-assured truculence." Von Hoffman ended on a more sober note, arguing that the problems he heard on Air

America were not exclusive to the network. "Progressive talk-radio has to be *for* something," he said, adding "When liberalism and liberals do find their platform, their new, progressive talkers will surely broadcast it."[42]

Both Air America co-founder Sheldon Drobny and Goldberg—along with several Air America devotees—took von Hoffman's bait and fired back angry letters. Goldberg in particular confronted the charge regarding the lack of a progressive vision. "[A]ny fair assessment of Air America's programming would acknowledge that its hosts and dozens of authors, elected officials and public interest leaders have numerous positive ideas," he said, without citing specifics.[43] Nonetheless, one of Goldberg's first moves was to bring in TV host Jerry Springer, an established left-liberal, yet one more known as a trash-talking fight promoter than a positive thinker. What the Goldberg era promised for Air America was thus an eclectic mix of new progressive ideas—not beholden to DLC-style centrism, but not isolated from it by any means. As in the 2004 campaign, virtually any position that Republicans didn't agree with could be termed "progressive." The Democrats could be home to Clintonians, Deaniacs, New Dealers, and many others. Yet the unity found in their contempt for the Bush regime concealed their division over the not-insignificant matter of Iraq.

Along with Goldberg, by the fall of 2005 the vast majority of Air America's on-air hosts had clearly and repeatedly stated their opposition to the war in Iraq, with most raising at least the need for discussion of the withdrawal of U.S. forces. All of the hosts, including Al Franken, continually attacked the Bush regime for lying about WMD. Randi Rhodes even went so far as to state that Bush and company started the war in order to benefit their defense-contractor friends. "War is a racket; it's always been a racket," Rhodes stated.[44] Such attacks on the war increasingly corresponded with public opinion, which by the fall of 2005 had turned against the war. But the rising tide of support for withdrawal was not echoed by the Democratic leadership, whether Clintonian centrists or Democratic National Committee chair Howard Dean. And Franken, whom Goldberg called the network's "franchise player," continued to be in sync with the party leadership's response to the most pressing issue of the Bush era.[45]

In mid-October 2005, in the week leading up to an important vote in Iraq on a new constitution, Franken devoted significant time on his show to the war. That Monday, he spoke to Iraqi feminist Zainab Salabi about her book *Between Two Worlds: Escape from Tyranny; Growing Up in the Shadow of Saddam*, which among other things reminded audiences about the horrors of the Hussein regime. Also coming on the show that day was Coleen Rowley, the ex–FBI agent and 9/11 whistle-blower, who discussed her upcoming run for Congress. When Franken asked what her main issue would be, Rowley readily replied, "The war in Iraq, and how spending on it is taking away funding from education, and causing the Bush administration to spend down the Social Security surplus." Uncomfortable, Franken then said that the "million-dollar question" was "What can we do about it?" Rowley then cited the argument made by former Reagan National Security Agency director Lieutenant General William Odom for withdrawal, as well as various legislation—proposed by Senator Russ Feingold and others—calling for the same. Franken didn't express support for such a position, and it was the last time that the idea of a U.S. pullout was mentioned that week.[46]

Instead, Franken discussed the Bush administration's disastrous handling of the occupation. That Tuesday, he spoke to Noah Feldman, a New York University law professor and adviser to the occupation government, about the mismanagement of the occupation: "We're all looking toward Saturday and the results of the election," Franken assured him. The next day he led off the show with a discussion of how the Bush gang willfully ignored several official, detailed, and ultimately accurate warnings about what would happen after the regime fell. And that Thursday, the *New Yorker*'s George Packer came on to discuss his book, *The Assassins' Gate*, in which he expresses his dismay over the bungled occupation. Manifestly shaken, Franken at one point told Packer that the Bush team was not made up of "adults," and that the administration's antics in Iraq "make me so angry I want to cry." Packer for his part wondered whether Americans possessed "the will, the patience and the stamina" to continue the occupation until it succeeded. Why anyone was surprised at the chaos created by an administration openly disdainful of "nation building," and why the cost of the war was not a pressing issue, went unasked.[47]

Franken, who made little secret of his desire to challenge Paul Wellstone's Republican successor, Norm Coleman, for a Senate seat from Minnesota in 2008, thus seemed trapped in the same quagmire of Iraq that plagued the Democratic Party's leadership. At the same time, his status as Air America's "franchise player" was only increasing, as his radio show was now telecast on the Sundance Channel. Through early 2007, when Franken officially left the network and announced his run for the Senate, he would continue to use Air America as his bully pulpit; meanwhile, the Clinton-inspired Center for American Progress would provide regular guests on his show. Most important, Franken's hawkish foreign policy views kept him close to the DLC and Democratic Party insiders, but distanced him from both the party's base and his fellow hosts at Air America.

By mid-2007, the next presidential campaign season was already well under way, but Air America was fighting simply to stay alive. Goldberg had left in the spring of 2006, as the problems he had largely inherited from his predecessors—in particular the mounting debts—became insurmountable. That summer, Air America moved from its flagship channel in New York, WLIB, to a weaker station further down the AM dial, and it had begun losing its affiliates across the country (although it still had over ninety). The network claimed to have just under 2.5 million weekly listeners nationwide, which paled in comparison to Limbaugh and Hannity's numbers. In mid-October 2006, after losing more than $40 million since its launch, the company filed for bankruptcy. True to form, two of Air America's most prominent foes expressed their delight. "They're haters and no one listens," Bill O'Reilly told his radio listeners. "They got what they deserved."[48] For his part, Rush Limbaugh insisted that the problem was not that Air America's hosts were "not funny enough." Instead, in his view, "They just aren't any good. You can't just put idiots on the radio and expect twenty million listeners."[49] Venomous and arrogant, the right's talk radio hosts would continue to dominate the airwaves in the foreseeable future.

But the question remained, why had Air America failed to get off the ground? As von Hoffman suggested, its founders' business model of starting as a twenty-four-hour national network was a leading factor; that overly ambitious plan coincided with the equally lofty goal of unseating a president. The alternative would have been to start slowly, with syndication of a few programs that, if successful, could form the basis of a national network. This long-haul approach has worked for Democracy Radio, which launched both the Ed Schultz and Stephanie Miller shows that became syndicated as part of Jones Media. By the fall of 2007, the trade publication *Talkers Magazine* (the self-described "Bible of Talk Radio") reported that Schultz had now tied O'Reilly in the number of daily listeners (3.25 million); Miller, meanwhile, ranked even with Air America's two leading hosts, Randi Rhodes and Thom Hartmann (Franken's successor), with 1.5 million.[50] Yet as Air America's experience also demonstrated, even when successful in gaining a foothold in the marketplace, liberal commercial talk radio faces another problem: large advertisers steer clear of it. In late October 2006, the ABC Radio Network circulated a memo instructing its affiliates to black out ads from several leading corporations on any Air America programming the affiliates carried. Bay Area veteran progressive broadcaster Peter B. Collins first leaked the memo, which was then posted on the Web site of Fairness and Accuracy in Reporting (FAIR), the left-leaning media watchdog outfit. ABC Radio listed Hewlett-Packard, Microsoft, Wal-Mart, Visa, and McDonald's as among the many companies unwilling to air their ads on Air America.[51] In following up on the story, the

New York Times noted that those same five companies were all listed as sponsors of the Fox News TV programs of Bill O'Reilly and Sean Hannity.[52] Many of America's leading corporations clearly feel comfortable sponsoring programs on the right, not the left—which will likely prevent progressive media from ever becoming as large as right-wing media, at least in the broadcast domain.

Even after bankruptcy, however, leading liberals were not ready to give up the fight for Air America. As noted in *PR Week*, the network's many business troubles actually served as "liberal talk radio's saving grace, because it is easy to pin the problem on bad management rather than on an inherent lack of a market."[53] But the growing success of Schultz continued to suggest otherwise, and in early 2007, new ownership took over Air America, again with strong liberal credentials. Real estate mogul Stephen Green bought the company for the bargain basement price of $4.25 million, and his brother, Mark Green, a longtime fixture in New York City liberal politics, now presided over it. In May 2007, Green relaunched the network as Air America 2.0. Leading Democrats including Hillary Clinton and Barack Obama came on for interviews, while a pep talk about the new network by Bill Clinton was soon featured on Air America's Web site. In a format that rewarded hard-edged arguments and straight shooting, Air America under Green promised to be even more tied in to the Clintons and the mainstream Democrats. One of the problems with the original version of Air America, as FAIR's Steve Rendall observed, was that its hosts "tend[ed] to cleave to a Democratic Party line that has itself often been hard to decipher in recent years." By contrast, Rendall continued, there is "a spirit of independence in conservative talk that leads hosts to sometimes criticize the Republicans for not taking a principled right-wing stand."[54] In addition to its business troubles, from a content standpoint, Air America has also encountered a larger problem: by trying to didactically deliver the same mush that has characterized mainstream Democratic Party politics from the Clinton years through the Gore and Kerry campaigns, the network has continued to serve up less than appetizing fare.

3

THE PASSION OF MICHAEL MOORE

Ascendant through the 1990s, Michael Moore's star burned ever more brightly during the Bush years. Moore first rose to prominence with his 1989 documentary *Roger & Me*, in which he memorably chased down CEO Roger B. Smith of General Motors, blaming the automaker for the demise of the filmmaker's hometown of Flint, Michigan. In 1996, Moore became a best-selling author, penning *Downsize This!*, a similarly scathing appraisal of corporate America. Relying on his signature blend of in-your-face satire mixed with blunt-edged left critique, Moore amplified his populist views in two TV series during the decade, *TV Nation* and *The Awful Truth*. Given his anticorporate stance, it was not surprising that in 2000, Moore, along with Tim Robbins, Susan Sarandon, and other left-leaning entertainment figures, vigorously campaigned for Ralph Nader, for whom Moore had once worked at *Mother Jones*.

In 2000, the man from Flint showed the strength of his Naderite convictions all the way through the first Tuesday of November, when he posted a "Final Election Day Letter" on his highly trafficked Web site. In it, he attacked the Clinton-era Democrats for their retreat on welfare as well as their allegiance to large corporations. Nader's campaign, in Moore's view, tapped into growing support for economic change, and the best way that the nascent movement could show its strength, he said, was "to go into the voting booth today and vote for Ralph. If he scores big tonight, it will send a shock wave through the system." The shock waves, of course, did ripple, but the result was not what Moore hoped for. Over the next several years, while liberals pilloried

Nader—blaming him for staying in the race rather than Gore for losing his home state—the Democrats continued to pledge allegiance to corporate America. Though he held fast to his populism, throughout the next presidential campaign, Moore would consistently urge Nader not to run again. In fact, just after the Democratic National Convention of 2004, the activist filmmaker, along with liberal TV host Bill Maher, even dropped to his knees before Nader on the set of Maher's HBO show, begging the anticorporate candidate to bow out so as not to hurt the Democrats' chances that November. "Come home," Moore pleaded to Nader.[1]

Rather than suddenly becoming a born-again Democrat, Moore's conversion was better explained by his growing contempt for a president he viewed as almost satanic. From 2001 forward, Moore regularly pounded away at George W. Bush on his Web site, paying special attention to the White House's loyalty to its many corporate cronies. In his 2002 documentary *Bowling for Columbine*, his most successful film since *Roger & Me*, Moore showed Bush to be in the hip pocket of the far-right National Rifle Association. In general, the work was more of a critique of America's fanatical progun culture than an indictment of Bush. But after *Bowling for Columbine* took the top prize at Cannes, Moore noted on his Web site that "[m]y favorite quote I read during the festival was, 'This film will single-handedly guarantee that George W. Bush will never see a second term.' Well, one can only dream. After all, it is just a movie." Just two years later, Moore would boldly and loudly claim that his next film indeed promised to accomplish such a Herculean task.[2]

In the interim, Moore became a leading voice of liberal outrage against the Bush regime. When *Bowling for Columbine* won the 2002 Oscar for Best Documentary, the filmmaker took advantage of the Hollywood stage to deliver a bracing indictment of all things Bush. The Academy Awards in 2003 were held on Sunday, March 23, just a few days after the beginning of the U.S. invasion of Iraq—and the war was on everyone's mind. After receiving a standing ovation from many Hollywood celebrities, Moore was joined on stage by the other Best Documentary nominees. He explained that he had invited them up there to make a point: "They're here in solidarity with me because we like nonfiction." Shaking, his anger rising to a crescendo, Moore continued:

> We like nonfiction and we live in fictitious times. We live in the time where we have fictitious election results that elect a fictitious president. We live in a time where we have a man sending us to war for fictitious reasons. Whether it's the fiction of duct tape or the fictitious Orange Alerts, we are against this war, Mr. Bush.

Though his acceptance speech had not yet exceeded one minute, the band started up, which, along with the mixture of cheers and a few loud boos from the audience, drowned out Moore's next statement: "Shame on you, Mr. Bush, shame on you. And any time you got the pope and the Dixie Chicks against you, your time is up."[3] Moore's comments not surprisingly provided plenty of fodder for the right-wing talk radio and cable news airwaves. Yet in Moore, the far-right media now met its match: a figure on the left who also drove home his points with a sledgehammer. And rather than John Kerry versus George Bush, the 2004 presidential campaign would soon play out in the political media as a contest between Michael Moore and Bill O'Reilly.

On the road to *Fahrenheit 9/11*'s release date in late June 2004, Moore continued his assault on Bush. In the fall of 2003, he went on a fifty-three-city tour across the United States and Europe promoting *Dude, Where's My Country?*, his best-selling book and an anti-Bush diatribe. Along with Al Franken, Moby, and many others, Moore was a headliner at MoveOn's star-studded campaign kickoff event in mid-January 2004. Two days later, he stunned many among the MoveOn crowd by announcing his support for Wesley Clark rather than Howard Dean. He did so even though Clark, a former Republican, had been a prominent general in the

Kosovo campaign, which Moore had opposed; Clark, however, was willing to propose an exit strategy for Iraq, thus potentially luring away some of Dean's antiwar voters, including Moore.

Moore's choice stemmed from both strategic considerations and personal preferences. Despite Clark's lack of political experience, Moore felt that he possessed two essential qualities that made him the most electable of the Democratic challengers: Clark was a decorated war hero, and, unlike John Kerry, he was from the South. Moreover, he had once defended Moore's right to voice dissent on the Kosovo conflict (which the latter compared to the Columbine incident), a principled stance for which Moore was deeply grateful. The filmmaker's dislike for Howard Dean also may have had a personal edge. Rumor had it that Moore had reached his decision after he and his wife had dinner with Dean and his wife. While no specific details of the prandial tiff emerged, Clark, Moore wrote in a letter explaining his endorsement, "is clearly not a professional politician. He is clearly not from Park Avenue," which were oft-repeated slams made against Dean. In any case, Moore's embrace of Clark confirmed the former's reputation as a mercurial figure of the left who marched to the beat of his own drum.[4]

Moore's main contribution to Clark's fledgling campaign would be a dubious one. Right after announcing his endorsement, Moore traveled to New Hampshire to help stump for the general. There Moore memorably derided Bush as "a deserter," a charge based on the president's unaccounted-for time in the National Guard during the Vietnam War. The problem with Moore's characterization is that it was inaccurate: a deserter is someone who flees the service for more than thirty days, whereas being gone for under thirty days (as in the case of Bush) constitutes AWOL status. Such a distinction amounted to more than just a technicality—a deserter can be punished by lengthy prison sentences and in some cases even by death. The more temperate Clark, however, did not immediately distance himself from the hyperbolic Moore, instead saying, "I've heard those charges. I don't know whether they're established or not. He was never prosecuted for it."⁵ Like the former general's campaign, the relationship between the two figures did not exactly take off after the deserter controversy. For Dean, Moore's refusal to throw his considerable weight behind the then-front-runner's campaign was quite damaging. But for the film-maker himself, the exaggerated denunciation of Bush did little harm to his reputation as someone ready to deploy any means necessary in the fight to bring down the president.

One clear sign that Moore had become a major player in the national political scene was the attention he received from the *New Yorker*, which during the Bush years also became a leading contributor to the national political debate. In a late-February 2004 double issue, Moore received the type of treatment that the magazine usually reserved for figures like Kofi Annan: a lengthy profile, in this case checking in at over 11,500 words. Titled simply "The Populist," Larissa MacFarquhar's piece turned out to be surprisingly sympathetic to Moore, especially given the magazine's overall cynicism regarding left politics. MacFarquhar assured readers that "Moore is of the left, but it is also important to him that he is mainstream. He wants to change things, and he knows that to do so he must prove to his followers that they are the majority." His methods, she observed, were far from radical: "He tells people to vote. He tells them to take over their local Democratic party. . . . He asks people to spend a weekend next October in one of the congressional districts where the race promises to be close, handing out flyers. Last month, he endorsed Wesley Clark, ignoring howls of protest from pacifist fans." After interspersing Moore's bio with lengthy scenes of him colorfully interacting with audiences in England, MacFarquhar spelled out some more of his positions. While Moore "believes that the government should regulate companies to prevent them from making an excessive profit," she added that "[h]e is not an old-style populist buy-American type, however; he thinks that foreign competition has been used as a bogeyman to distract Americans from corporate bad behavior. In Flint, he drove a Honda." The writer further noted that in *Dude,*

Where's My Country?, Moore had slammed the nineties left's obsession with the Mumia Abu-Jamal case, and she quoted Kathleen Glynn, Moore's wife, explaining her view of the left as "stifling." MacFarquhar, in short, was painting Moore as coming from the left, but not dogmatically so, thus making him more palatable for the *New Yorker's* more mainstream audience.[6]

As with her analysis of the *Onion*, MacFarquhar provided keen insights into the recent rise of political satire. Moore's humor, she maintained, bears some resemblance to the antic spirit of Abbie Hoffman, Jerry Rubin, and the Yippies, who memorably threw dollar bills on the floor of the New York Stock Exchange and ran a pig for president in 1968, among many other provocations. Similarly, in past years, Moore had sponsored the candidacy of a felon for president, and run a ficus for Congress. But Moore, MacFarquhar argued, is far less critical of the institutions of American power than the Yippies. At least until *Sicko* (2007), his attacks have almost always been personal, against Roger Smith (of GM), Philip Knight (of Nike), and George W. Bush, Dick Cheney, and Donald Rumsfeld, as opposed to CEOs in general or the American war machine. (Moore's method could be defended on the grounds that story lines with clear individual villains make for more popular films, except that Mark Achbar and Jennifer Abbott's *The Corporation* (2003), a historical overview, Eugene Jarecki's *Why We Fight* (2005), an analysis of the military industrial complex, and *Sicko* show that institutional critique can be combined with box-office success.) Radical or not, for MacFarquhar, Moore's style had helped the left regain the ground it had lost on the front of political satire during the 1980s. While the left fretted about political correctness, the "right of money and Martinis and Wall Street," as personified by P. J. O'Rourke, steadily monopolized political humor. But by the Bush years, left-leaning humor—as created by Moore, Al Franken, Jon Stewart, and many others—had returned, poking holes in the overzealous rhetoric and actions of the right.[7]

Moore's work, of course, had long combined satire with direct attack on his chosen targets, thus blending comedy with a didactic message. The first of Moore's films with a clear, timely goal—i.e., to influence the outcome of the 2004 presidential race—*Fahrenheit 9/11* would ultimately be much more serious than humorous. As the publicity buildup continued through the spring, the many obstacles Moore faced in getting the film out only contributed to its gravity. The filmmaker's showdown with Disney over distribution of the film previewed the David versus Goliath story line that would take hold upon *Fahrenheit*'s release.

In early May of 2004, a front-page story in the *New York Times* reported that Disney, which owned *Fahrenheit*'s producer, Miramax, would block distribution of the film. When Miramax initially agreed to finance the film one year earlier, Disney had come under fire from conservatives. But as the *Times* story suggested, the conflict involved self-interest as well as ideology. Ari Emanuel, Moore's high-powered agent (and brother of influential Democratic congressman Rahm Emanuel), explained that Disney's then-CEO Michael Eisner had told him that distributing Moore's film potentially threatened the tax breaks that Disney received from Florida, since Jeb Bush controlled that state. In the *Times* story, a Disney executive ducked that allegation, instead declaring, "It's not in the interest of any major corporation to be dragged into a highly charged partisan political battle." However, as *Times* reporter Jim Rutenberg pointed out, the primary interest of corporations is to make money, and both of Moore's most recent projects, *Bowling for Columbine* and *Dude, Where's My Country?*, had reaped handsome dividends.[8]

For his part, Moore quickly spun the conflict into something greater than a dispute between a filmmaker and a distributor. "Should this be happening in a free and open society where the monied interests essentially call the shots regarding the information that the public is allowed to see?" he said to the *Times*.[9] On his Web site that same day, Moore began a note to his fans in similar fashion: "I would have hoped by now that I would be able to put my work out to the public without having to experience the profound censorship obstacles I often seem to encounter." Disney's claims of political neutrality, Moore rightly argued, were contradicted by the presence of Sean Hannity and Rush Limbaugh on the company's ABC radio affiliates.[10] The filmmaker would soon gain a powerful ally in his fight. Arguing that the "Walt Disney Company deserves a gold medal for cowardice," a *New York Times* editorial stated that a "company that ought to be championing free expression has instead chosen to censor a documentary that clearly falls within the bounds of acceptable political commentary."[11] In response, Eisner turned the argument on its head, insisting that Disney was exercising its own free speech right *not* to distribute the film.[12] For a brief moment, it thus appeared that not only *Fahrenheit*'s future was at stake, but so, too, was the meaning of the First Amendment.

While Disney's announcement seemed to threaten *Fahrenheit*'s future, its timing was actually rather fortuitous for the film's publicity buildup, as it came just prior to the opening of the Cannes Film Festival. In April, *Fahrenheit* had been selected as one of the eighteen films in competition at the festival, only the third time that a nonfiction film had been chosen in fifty years. A.O. Scott, lead film critic for the *Times*, now wondered whether the ongoing controversy reflected "Mr. Moore's appetite for publicity or . . . the timidity of Disney management?" In either case, the dispute hardly hurt Moore's cause. As Scott observed, "However it was cooked up, the confrontation between Disney and Mr. Moore looks like a ready-made scenario for one of his films, since it casts him, once again, as a populist Paladin going into battle against a corporate enemy."[13] Amidst the Cannes buildup, Moore reportedly received some input from advisers from the Clinton and Gore camps, although he hardly needed it. He was already extremely popular in Europe, and his film's antiwar message promised to be warmly received there; the filmmaking community just as surely stood to respond favorably to a director's battle on behalf of his art against the censorship of an all too familiar corporate giant. Furthermore, it certainly did not hurt that Quentin Tarantino, one of

Miramax's most successful directors, was the jury president for the festival's top prize. In short, the conditions were ripe for Moore to clean up at Cannes.

And triumph he did. The premiere of *Fahrenheit 9/11* received a twenty-minute standing ovation, and the film soon won the Palme d'Or, the festival's top prize. Caught up in the excitement of the moment of winning the Palme, Moore told a news conference, "I did not set out to make a political film. I want people to leave thinking that was a good way to spend two hours. The art of this, the cinema, comes before the politics." Soon, of course, Moore would be boasting that his film would be a primary reason for George W. Bush's demise. Yet even as he declared his commitment to his art, the filmmaker launched his offensive against his critics. "I fully expect the Fox News Channel and other right-wing media to portray this as an award from the French," said Moore, while also noting that only one member of the jury actually was from France.[14] The battle lines had shaped up in Moore's favor, pitting him in alliance with the international community against the arrogant American empire, as represented by both the Bush administration and Disney. Within two weeks after the end of Cannes, Disney had sold the rights back to Miramax, which in turn cut a deal with Lions Gate Films—a Canadian-owned company, as Moore quickly pointed out—and IFC for distribution. The forces of both international opinion and, correspondingly, international capital had triumphed.

But hurdles still remained prior to *Fahrenheit*'s late-June release date. In mid-June, the Motion Picture Association of America (MPAA) ratings board gave the film an R rating, thus restricting access for people under seventeen. In explaining its decision, the board cited the film's "violent and disturbing images and strong language." In response, Moore issued a statement emphasizing his hope that fifteen- and sixteen-year-olds would be able to see the film, particularly because they could end up in Iraq. "If they're old enough to be recruited . . . they certainly deserve the right to see what's going on," he said.[15] Former New York governor Mario

Cuomo then entered the fray on Moore's behalf, offering to help appeal the ratings board's decision. Meanwhile, an IFC spokesman noted that a less-restrictive PG-13 rating could result in a 20 percent boost in the film's box office. In a Web site missive that week, Moore wryly observed, "I would like to think the MPAA is saying that the actions by the Bush administration are so abhorrent and revolting, we need to protect our children from seeing what they have done. In that case, the film should be rated NC-17!"[16] Neither Moore's appeals nor Cuomo's efforts on his behalf would change the board's mind, however. "This is a classic example of how the voluntary rating system works to benefit parents," said MPAA chief Jack Valenti, a former insider in Lyndon Johnson's administration.[17]

Moore soon faced off with a far more aggressive foe in the form of a group called Move America Forward. The so-called 527 organization (a nonprofit group aimed at influencing elections) was formed initially to combat Moore's film, but it has since continued to serve as a stalking horse for the War on Terror. Its founder, a far-right former California assemblyman named Howard Kaloogian, had recently scored two major right-wing victories: he had launched the Recall Gray Davis Committee, which ultimately succeeded in bringing down the conservative Democratic California governor; and he had orchestrated a screeching PR campaign that cowed CBS into canceling a made-for-TV movie about Ronald Reagan. Move America Forward's goal in this case was to pressure movie theaters into not screening *Fahrenheit*. "Michael Moore has the right to free speech," Kaloogian explained to *Daily Variety*. "But so do millions of Americans who find his anti-military propaganda and attacks on our troops offensive."[18] The organization's Web site listed phone and fax numbers for the heads of various theater chains, and its views helped shape the right's rhetorical counterattack against Moore's media blitzkrieg. MAF's goal stated goal was simple: "To support our troops and the war on terrorism," said Siobhan Guiney, its executive director, who added that the group's actions did not amount to censorship, because "only the government can censor something." Such a view was disingenuous, of course, since market censorship—the organization's real goal—is potentially far more powerful. But such an effort automatically stood to backfire. As John Fithian, the president of the National Association of Theatre Owners, spelled it out, "Any time any organization protests against a movie, they ensure that the movie will do better at the box office than it would have done otherwise. If they have any doubt about this, just ask Mel Gibson."[19]

As with Gibson, albeit from the opposite end of the spectrum, Moore's passion would have to overcome the hostility he faced. And like Mad Max, Moore was equally ready for the task of defending himself. "The right wing usually wins these battles. Their basic belief system is built on censorship, repression, and keeping people ignorant," he stated on his Web site, championing the efforts of his supporters to overcome their many foes.[20] One week prior to the film's release, Moore reported that over five hundred theaters across the country would ignore the pleas of Move America Forward and screen *Fahrenheit*. The film's distributors, meanwhile, announced that they would spend $10 million on publicity for the film (which cost only $6 million to make), far and away the most money ever spent on marketing a documentary. Moore soon began a flurry of network television appearances, starting with the *Late Show with David Letterman* a week before the film's opening. Apparently, George Bush I's characterization of Moore (in the *New York Daily News*) as a "slimeball" responsible for a "vicious personal attack on our son" dampened no one's desire to talk to Moore. In any case, the filmmaker's manifest knack for self-promotion made him more than ready to take on all comers.[21]

Even before the film had opened, the right's main attack on the content of both the film and its creator's character was in play—namely, that Moore "lies." Joe Scarborough, the right-wing former congressman from Florida turned cable talk show host, spearheaded the charge against Moore. The feud between Scarborough and Moore had been building since the fall, when the host accused the filmmaker of lying in *Dude, Where's My Country?*. It escalated considerably after Moore—as reported by MacFarquhar—began circulating a true story about a female aide who died in Scarborough's district office. According to MacFarquhar, Moore told book tour audiences "that he'd done a little research on the medical examiner who ruled out foul play, and discovered that he had been fired from his previous position for mishandling a similar case." While Moore claimed that he "was just kidding around" and that "[h]e didn't really think that Scarborough had killed his aide," the innuendo was obvious.[22] In both the run-up to *Fahrenheit*'s release and its aftermath, Scarborough fervently fought back. After Moore confessed (to the *San Francisco Chronicle*) that he had possessed footage of the Abu Ghraib torture scandal well before it became public but not released it, Scarborough pounced on the "so-called truth seeker," accusing him of "a cover-up." "Americans," he assured his MSNBC viewers, "can't stand hypocrites, and the more people get to know Michael Moore and his work, the more they are going to find out that he's a self-proclaimed working class hero, who attacks corporations while flying around in corporate jets, [and] who claims to seek the truth while spreading his own version of lies."[23] Rest assured that the talk show host had only just begun to fight.

But Moore was ready to answer the charges of the legions of other right-wing pundits who were poised to accuse Moore of "playing fast and loose with the truth," as Scarborough put it. A lengthy and prominent story in the *New York Times* on the Sunday before the film's release highlighted the filmmaker's concern with the veracity of the work's many potentially explosive points. Moore, the *Times* reported, had hired prominent Democratic consultant Chris Lehane, who was well known "as a master of the black art of 'oppo,' or opposition research, used to discredit detractors." More important, he had hired a crackerjack team of fact-checkers, headed by the *New Yorker*'s former general counsel, Dev Chatillon. Even though *Fahrenheit* "is an Op-Ed piece, it's not a news report," Chatillon observed, "the facts have to be right." "We have gone through every single word of this film—literally every word—and verified its accuracy," stated Joanne Doroshow, a public interest lawyer and Oscar-winning documentary filmmaker who was also a member of Moore's team of scrutinizers. For his part, Moore made it abundantly clear to the *Times* that he would sue anyone who accused him of lying. "Any attempts to libel me will be met by force," Moore declared, adding, "The most important thing we have is truth on our side. If they persist in telling lies, knowingly telling a lie with malice, then I'll take them to court." [24] The filmmaker's chesty threat would not stop many on the right from trying to call his bluff.

Amid considerable fanfare, *Fahrenheit* finally opened nationally on Friday, June 25, 2004. It did so in 868 theaters, with only two chains opting not to screen the film. Over 100,000 MoveOn members pledged to see the film over the weekend, and Moore scheduled a town hall–style Internet meeting with the group's members for the following Monday. (In Sacramento that same night, Move America Forward organized an advance screening of the Disney documentary *America's Heart and Soul*, which Kaloogian called "a very patriotic film. It's in the finest tradition of inspiring Disney movies.")[25] The day *Fahrenheit* opened, Moore told *USA Today*—for which Moore would serve as a guest columnist during the Republican National Convention—that he hoped that its influence on the fall election would be similar to that of Ralph Nader's book *Unsafe at Any Speed* on car safety. "This may be the first time a film has this kind of impact," said a buoyant Moore. Over the next few months, such a lofty prediction would seem like more than just hype.[26]

After so much buildup, the views of critics thus mattered less than usual in shaping popular reaction to a film. In general, the notices were favorable—in fact, 81 percent of them praised the film, according to one compilation. Yet even many sympathetic reviewers, like A.O. Scott in the *Times*, raised some important criticisms of the work. *Fahrenheit*, Scott wrote, "is many things: a partisan rallying cry, an angry polemic, a muckraking inquisition into the use and abuse of power . . . [but while it] has been likened to an op-ed column, it might more accurately be said to resemble an editorial cartoon."[27] Similarly, in the *Rocky Mountain News*, reviewer Robert Denerstein likened the film to a "drive-by attack," which he presciently saw as "the cinematic equivalent of talk radio, a melange of accusations and provocations that may dominate the national discussion for weeks."[28] The bombastic quality of the work also troubled *New York Times* columnist Nicholas Kristof. Moore's work, he maintained, "marks the polarization of yet another form of media. One medium after another has found it profitable to turn from information to entertainment, from nuance to table-thumping." Such a didactic style, Kristof lamented, had been "pioneered" by talk radio, but it had then begun to dominate cable news and had steadily taken over political books, Internet debate, and now documentaries.[29] The right, of course, clearly dominated both talk radio and cable news, and the airwaves were soon filled with ceaseless invective against Moore. In general, the assault was led by the usual suspects—Scarborough, O'Reilly, Hannity—but it also featured some notable new combatants.

A former leftist turned raging hawk, Christopher Hitchens stridently tried to provide intellectual cred to the right's attack on Moore. On the Monday before the film's opening, *Slate* ran the provocatively titled "UnFairenheit 9/11: The Lies of Michael Moore." In typical Hitchens fashion, the piece began with a sweeping condemnation of the left, which was nonetheless noteworthy in that it addressed some of the dilemmas of the new liberal media. After calling the left "too solemn, mirthless," and many other variations thereof, Hitchens recalled his days at the *Nation*, when his colleagues used to wonder, "Where was the radical *Firing Line* show?" and "Who will be our Rush Limbaugh?" Citing "Al Franken's unintentionally funny Air America network" as one example that "an answer to this long-felt need is finally beginning to emerge," he then went for the jugular. *Fahrenheit 9/11*, he said, offered a "glimpse [of] a possible fusion between the turgid routines of MoveOn.org and the filmic standards, if not exactly the filmic skills, of Sergei Eisenstein or Leni Riefenstahl."[30] Surely his hero George Orwell would have applauded Hitchens's high-minded rejection of totalitarian filmmaking.

Once past the opening bluster, Hitchens did make some accurate criticisms of the film. Notably, he singled out the way in which the work's discrete points about bin Laden, the Saudis, and the U.S. war in Afghanistan do not amount to a coherent argument. For Moore, Hitchens noted, "[e]ither the Saudis run U.S. policy . . . or they do not. As allies and patrons of the Taliban regime, they either opposed Bush's removal of it, or they did not. . . . Either [the United States] sent too many troops, or we were wrong to send any at all . . . or we sent too few." Moore's rather rosy portrayal of Iraq before the 2003 U.S. invasion also rightly drew the writer's ire—although what Hitchens termed Moore's "peaceable kingdom" would be more memorably shot down, via satire, in *South Park* creators Trey Parker and Matt Stone's *Team America* (2004). Hitchens, however, hurt his own cause by ardently defending the Bush administration's war in Iraq, never criticizing the White House's deceptions or its disastrous handling of the invasion's aftermath. The self-proclaimed heir to Orwell further raised doubts about his own intellectual independence when he defended Bush from the ridicule that Moore's film, *The Daily Show*, and many others had heaped on him for a notable moment on a golf course. After making a stock comment about fighting terrorism, Bush had nonchalantly told reporters, "Now, watch this drive." Rather lamely, Hitchens wrote, "Well, that's what you get if you catch the president on a golf course." The British contrarian then concluded by dealing the "pacifist card," quoting Orwell's caricature of those who hold such a position ("There is a minority of intellectual pacifists, whose real though unacknowledged motive appears to be hatred of western democracy and admiration for totalitarianism").[31] Yet Moore, as MacFarquhar's *New Yorker* profile had clarified, is not a pacifist. And so Hitchens ended his diatribe on a decidedly Bush League note.

A week and a half after the *Slate* article appeared, Hitchens joined in the almost nightly barrage of anti-Moore ranting on *Scarborough Country.* He had told *Slate* readers about the origins of his feud with Moore, which began when they appeared as co-panelists at the Telluride Film Festival in 2002. Now he revived that event by bringing a tape of that panel debate to the Scarborough show. At Telluride, Moore had taken the shockingly "un-American position" that Osama bin Laden was innocent until proven guilty; two years later, his film argued that the Bush administration had been too cozy with the bin Laden family and that the Iraq War was a diversion from the hunt for bin Laden. Egged on by Scarborough, who called these not-incompatible positions "complete hypocrisy," Hitchens labeled Moore a "moral cretin" and a "political idiot." [32] The following Sunday morning, Hitchens continued to hammer Moore on CNN's *Reliable Sources,* hosted by Howard Kurtz. The Fourth of July edition of the show opened with quotes from right-winger Tucker Carlson, at the time co-host of CNN's *Crossfire,* who assured viewers that "there's nothing deeply patriotic about Michael Moore"; and also from Carlson's co-host, the far-right Robert Novak, who argued that Moore "is a demagogue. He's anti-American. He lies." [33] Already responsible for outing Valerie Plame as a CIA agent (in order to retaliate against her husband Joe Wilson's criticisms of Bush's dubious case for the Iraq War), Novak fit nobody's definition of a neutral reporter.

In line with Carlson and Novak, Hitchens soon mixed it up with MSNBC analyst Bill Press, who had just published a book called *Bush Must Go.* Press objected to the "double standard" being applied to Moore: "If we are going to pick, pick, pick at everything Michael Moore says, let's pick, pick, pick at everything Bill O'Reilly says, Rush Limbaugh says, Sean Hannity says, and everybody else on the right." Hitchens responded by referring to the veracity of his own work on documentaries (in particular, Eugene

Jarecki's 2002 work *The Trials of Henry Kissinger* was based on Hitchens's book). Always ready to stress the independence of his judgments, he then said, "I'm not a friend of Limbaugh or Hannity, thanks all the same."[34] Yet as in the War on Terror, in the War on Moore, Hitchens had joined forces with the shock troops of the far right, who sought to defend both Bush and the Iraq War from a left-wing "demagogue."[35]

Nonetheless, the question of whether Moore's use of evidence added up to a coherent argument remains open to debate. In the aforementioned *Reliable Sources* discussion, *Newsweek*'s Michael Isikoff, despite having led that magazine's effort to discredit Moore's facts, actually struck a sensible middle ground between Hitchens—who said "documentary means documentary," meaning that Moore's alleged lies placed the film in another category—and Press, who defended Moore's right to be "a polemicist" and characterized him as the "Rush Limbaugh of the left." *Fahrenheit 9/11*, Isikoff said, "does raise a lot of legitimate questions and is provoking a lot of real debate," but it nonetheless amounts to a "highly selective use of the facts."[36] Moore's argument indeed relied on the kitchen sink–type approach common on the right, in which everything gets thrown in so as to make one large point: in this case, it was that Bush must not be reelected. The facts he used were verifiable, whereas many of his arguments—e.g., that the Bush family relationship to the bin Ladens explains both the Afghanistan and Iraq interventions—were not persuasive. Ultimately, and perhaps surprisingly, the most accurate assessment of the film may have come from none other than Karl Rove: "It's an artful piece of propaganda," Rove told the *National Review*'s Byron York.[37]

One month after *Fahrenheit 9/11* made its opening splash, Moore became a controversial presence at the Democratic National Convention in Boston. It was here where he finally got to climb in the ring with Bill O'Reilly. On the convention's opening day, the show's host had run "into Moore on the street and persuaded him to enter the No Spin Zone," a dubiously named segment where O'Reilly rips into guests whose politics he doesn't like. When Moore insisted that the exchange should take place in a "neutral setting," O'Reilly tried to coax him by offering Moore something unique: "I never give anybody the opportunity to ask me questions," the host said, implying that he would give his guest that rare honor. Instead of highlighting Moore's "lies," O'Reilly proceeded to flip the script by arguing that the filmmaker had unfairly called Bush a "liar" for his claims regarding WMD in Iraq. When Moore said that the president plainly had done so because "he said something that wasn't true," O'Reilly shot back that Bush's statements had been "Based upon bad information given to him by legitimate sources."[38] Pro-war mainstream commentators like ABC's Ted Koppel would soon echo O'Reilly's defense of Bush.

Such tit-for-tat volleying between Moore and O'Reilly continued for some time, before giving way to a wide-ranging, increasingly heated debate over examples of possible parallels for the Iraq conflict including Nazi Germany, apartheid South Africa, and the fall of the Soviet Union. Each figure refused to concede a single point, and each sanctimoniously sought the higher ground. The clash of the titans ended thusly:

> MOORE: You would sacrifice your life to secure Fallujah?
>
> O'REILLY: I would.
>
> MOORE: When can we sign him up? Let's sign him up right now.
>
> O'REILLY: That's right, you'd love to get rid of me.
>
> MOORE: Where's the recruiter? No, I want you to live, I want you to live.
>
> O'REILLY: I appreciate it. Michael Moore, everybody. There he is.[39]

Even as they swung from different sides of the plate, the two cleanup hitters used the same heavyweight bat. And in spite of their mutual contempt, the two media titans appeared to deserve each other.

The battle was by far the biggest viewing attraction of the evening's convention coverage, the bulk of which took place on cable TV, since the major networks allotted only one hour of coverage to the DNC per night. O'Reilly, not surprisingly, felt that he had emerged victorious. As he stressed on the following night's show, the host believed that he had effectively rebutted the charge that Bush had lied the nation into war, and that he "didn't get baited" by Moore's "red-meat questions" about Fallujah. (For *New York Times* television critic Alessandra Stanley, however, Moore's questioning had "badger[ed] O'Reilly into submissive silence.")[40] Notably, one of O'Reilly's guests on the follow-up show, *Boston Globe* political reporter Rick Klein, questioned whether either figure had won the showdown. It was "great theater, great gladiator theater," Klein said. A bit peeved, O'Reilly then asked whether Klein had gained any insights from the interview. Klein responded, "I learned that when two people get in the room and they both strongly believe their arguments[,] you're not going to convince each other of it. I think Mr. Moore made an argument, you made an argument, and it was great to watch." Klein's larger point was that didacticism, no matter whether from the right or the left, results only in preaching to the choir, not winning over new converts.[41]

Yet as soon as it debuted in late June, Moore loudly began to trumpet what he saw as *Fahrenheit*'s resounding success in winning the hearts and minds of Red State voters. On the Monday after it opened, Moore addressed thousands via the Internet at "Turn Up the Heat: A National Town Meeting on *Fahrenheit 9/11*," an event organized by MoveOn. "It was the number-one movie in every single red state in America," announced a gleeful Moore. "Every single state that Bush won in 2000, it was the number-one film in it."[42] Moore's fever pitch continued with a letter dated July 4 that he posted on his Web site. "Where do I begin? This past week has knocked me for a loop," the missive began. It continued, "*Fahrenheit 9/11,* the #1 movie in the country, the largest grossing documentary ever . . . Did Karl Rove really fail to stop this? Is Bush packing?" The filmmaker then cited a slew of box-office records it set—including that *Fahrenheit* "instantly went to #2 on the all-time list for largest per-theater average ever for a film that opened in wide-release," and that it surpassed *Rocky III*'s record for the biggest opening weekend gross for any film that opened in fewer than one thousand theaters. Indeed, over three million viewers saw the film that weekend, for a gross of nearly $24 million, which already made it the most successful documentary of all time.[43]

But beyond the numbers, it was the numerous examples of the work's apparently glowing reception in the heartland that Moore found most encouraging. From the Deep South to Anchorage, the film was opening eyes, he said. NASCAR champion Dale Earnhardt Jr. had taken his crew to see it, thus inspiring the filmmaker to write: "Whoa! NASCAR fans—you can't go deeper into George Bush territory than that! White House moving vans—START YOUR ENGINES!" In places including Greensboro, North Carolina, and Oklahoma City, audiences gave it standing ovations, and theater managers reportedly "were having a hard time clearing the theater afterwards because people were either too stunned or they wanted to sit and talk to their neighbors about what they had just seen." Not far up the road from Oklahoma City, "[l]adies' church groups in Tulsa were going to see it, and weeping afterwards." Similar anecdotes poured in from across the nation, many having been reported in reputable outlets like the *New York Times* and *Los Angeles Times.* "The most heartening response to the film," Moore said, "has come from our soldiers and their families. Theaters in military towns across the country reported packed houses." The local paper in Fort Bragg, North Carolina, reported the reaction of a soldier's wife who declared her strong support for the film, which gave Moore "the resolve to make sure as many Americans as possible see this film in the coming weeks."[44] Moore was certainly no novice in the art of self-promotion, but, based on the box-office numbers and the amount of media attention, his hype about the film did indeed appear to have substance.

Moore was also confident that the film was winning over audiences not associated with the left, whether in Red State or Blue. He told Charlie Rose that he agreed with an unnamed reviewer who had predicted that the film "is going to preach to a second choir, not the choir of the left, but the choir of the left out."[45] The filmmaker had heard many reports of moviegoers coming out of the theater explaining their desire to vote for the first time. Accordingly, Moore's team had made voter registration cards available in many theaters. Moore's many detractors nonetheless found a silver lining in the public reaction to the film. In mid-July, Scarborough happily reported a *Washington Post* poll's finding that "Americans' approval of the president's handling of the war on terror has actually shot up since the release of *Fahrenheit 9/11*. And John Kerry's numbers have gone down during that same time period." For Scarborough, the time was right for John Kerry to launch a "Sister Souljah moment," meaning that Kerry should take a page from Bill Clinton's playbook by very publicly disavowing a controversial left figure—in this case, it would have been Kerry attacking "Michael Moore's brand of hate speech."[46]

That the Democrats needed to distance themselves from Michael Moore quickly became conventional talking-head wisdom. During the DNC, *Nightline* devoted an entire program to the filmmaker's apparently problematic presence in Boston for the convention. "Inside the hall, it's all about projecting a positive message," began Ted Koppel's opening voiceover. Then came a flurry of bromides—"All of us can win," "We are one people," etc.— from Ted Kennedy, Barack Obama, and other party figureheads. This stood in sharp contrast to Moore, who was shown outside the convention declaring that "Bush lied." This facile distinction between the "upbeat" Democrats and Moore's "overheated rhetoric" soon gave way to a substantive discussion between Koppel and Moore regarding the party's position on Iraq. Though Koppel maintained that Bush did not lie about WMD, but had instead relied on bad intelligence, the host did share Moore's criticisms of Kerry's position at the time, which was that the United States needed to "internationalize the job." Koppel for his part observed that "talking about internationalizing the war sounds lovely, but [there are] no armies out there that are going to be coming." Moore was then forced to explain how he could support a candidate whose views of the war were out of sync with his own, as well as those of a majority of the party's delegates. "Because John Kerry will have to respond to the will of the people," Moore said, hopefully.[47] Thus, beneath the superficial story line regarding the "problem" Moore was creating for the party, there actually lay no real conflict at all: Moore was rallying the base behind a candidate and a party that had no line on the war. Along with MoveOn and many other antiwar activists, Moore was letting the Democratic Party leadership off the hook for its nonposition on Iraq.

A month later, at the Republican National Convention in New York City, the filmmaker's highly visible presence inside the convention—which he was covering for *USA Today* as a columnist—nonetheless helped the Republicans in their effort to portray the Democrats as the party of Michael Moore. On the convention's opening evening, GOP "maverick" John McCain went after Moore, in the name of defending the Bush administration's invasion of Iraq. (The day before, Sunday August 29, upwards of one million people protested against both Bush and the war in the streets of New York City, impressing even the *New York Post* and forcing the Republicans into a counteroffensive.) "Our choice wasn't between a benign status quo and the bloodshed of war. It was between war and a graver threat," McCain declared. "Don't let anyone tell you otherwise," the Republicans' own "war hero" continued, "Not our political opponents. And certainly not, certainly not, a disingenuous filmmaker who would have us believe that Saddam's Iraq was an oasis of peace."[48] Sitting in a balcony seat, Moore was then memorably shown flashing an "L" (for loser) sign with his hand to both McCain and the booing delegates. *Fahrenheit 9/11* and its creator had thus become such a hot button for Republicans that McCain could rile up the party faithful by merely mentioning the filmmaker, even though McCain later admitted (to MSNBC's Chris Matthews) that he had not even seen the film.

In one of his *USA Today* columns, Moore lashed back at McCain ("a courageous war hero now reduced to carrying water for the Bush campaign") and rather unconvincingly defended his portrayal of preinvasion Iraq: "Human-rights groups say thousands of civilians were killed because of our bombing. I thought it would be worthwhile to show some of the faces of Iraqi people who might soon meet their death." The column, however, barely concealed the filmmaker's evident glee at being the center of attention on the RNC's opening night. "I know Republicans are mad that my film may have convinced just enough people to tip the balance in this election," the provocateur said. In case anyone questioned the work's influence, Moore noted that twenty million people had now seen it. McCain, he maintained, had lost his audience on the convention floor after making his comment about the film. Instead, the delegates now began to focus on their preferred target: the enemy liberal filmmaker. McCain, the director stated, "must have wondered why a party that promises to protect us from terrorists booed my name more loudly than Saddam's or Osama's."[49] The answer was twofold: Moore had succeeded at inserting himself into the center of political debate during the 2004 campaign, and the Republicans were glad to keep him in the spotlight.

Moore's publicity offensive continued after the RNC, when he began to create a stir about whether he would allow *Fahrenheit* to be nominated in the Oscar category of Best Documentary. A *Rolling Stone* cover story in the first week of September, sympathetically titled "Michael Moore's Patriot Act: How a Blue Collar Screw-up Became the White House's Worst Nightmare," reported that Moore was deciding whether to withhold entering the film, in hopes that it could be broadcast on PBS, cable, or network television before the November election (at the time, the Academy's rules stipulated that a nominated documentary couldn't be shown on television within nine months of its release). In any case, the film's resounding box-office success, observed *Rolling Stone*'s Mark Binelli, had "made Moore a real-life summer action hero for the left. Who needs Bruce Willis running from a fireball when you can watch a fat guy in jeans and a Michigan State Spartans cap taking on an entire Republican administration?"[50] In a letter on his Web site dated that Labor Day, the action hero expounded upon his success. He told of a Republican pollster who, while watching *Fahrenheit*, "got so distraught he twice had to go out in the lobby and pace during the movie," which the pollster apparently referred to as the "atomic bomb of this campaign." That observer's anecdotal report—which was that whereas 80 percent of people going to see the film were already Kerry supporters, 100 percent of those leaving the theater were now against Bush—was somewhat supported by various concrete polling data Moore cited, including that Bush's approval rating among Ohio audiences dipped by 21 percent after seeing the film. Meanwhile, a Gallup poll found that 56 percent of Americans had seen, or had plans to see, the film, either in the theaters or upon its video release, which Moore had managed to move up to October. Moore stated that there were no guarantees of its being shown on TV, mainly because his contract with the DVD distributor prevented that from happening. But he would continue to push for such a screening because "[i]f there is even the remotest of chances that I can get this film seen by a few million more Americans before election day, then that is more important to me than winning another documentary Oscar."[51]

Moore also cast his decision not to seek the Oscar in light of the commercial success that other documentaries were having in the late summer of 2004. "Last week," he said, "1 out of every 5 films playing in movie theaters across America was a documentary! That is simply unheard of. There have been so many great nonfiction films this year, why not step aside and share what we have [i.e., an Oscar] with someone else?" At the end of his letter, he urged readers to go see *Super Size Me*, Morgan Spurlock's scathing critique of McDonald's; *Control Room*, Jehane Noujaim's critically acclaimed portrayal of Al Jazeera; *The Corporation*, Mark Achbar and Jennifer Abbott's historical overview in which Moore serves as a talking head; *Orwell Rolls Over in His Grave*, a critique of the major media's soft coverage of the Bush administration, in which Moore also appears; *Bush's Brain*, an attack on Karl Rove; Robert Greenwald's many films; and *The Yes Men*, about a pair of political pranksters infiltrating WTO meetings, a film Moore not only appears in but also helped inspire.[52] With *Fahrenheit* shattering all box-office records for documentaries (grossing over $115 million by the end of August), and a slew of other successful docs in the theaters, it did indeed seem like the shining hour of nonfiction filmmaking.

While most political documentary filmmakers sought to emulate Moore's model—making an informed but entertaining film that would start out with a theatrical release—Robert Greenwald adopted a notably different approach. Greenwald's method involved much more reliance on the progressive grass roots, in terms of both production and especially distribution. A former B movie and television producer in his late fifties, Greenwald's initial foray into documentaries came in 2002 with *Unprecedented: The 2000 Presidential Election*. He followed that up the next year with *Uncovered*, a harsh critique of Bush's case for the war in Iraq that Greenwald put together in just over four months. He distributed *Uncovered* via DVD, successfully relying on MoveOn.org, the Center for American Progress, the *Nation*, and other liberal outlets to spread the word. While the participation of MoveOn and the *Nation* seemed obvious, given their strong antiwar stances, the financial and publicity help provided by the Center for American Progress was more surprising. But as the *New York Times Magazine*'s Robert Boynton explained, the center's John Podesta saw "this kind of multimedia, multiorganization project [as] an effective way of reaching a younger demographic, which policy groups traditionally have difficulty courting." MoveOn volunteers would actually help provide the source material for Greenwald's next project, *Outfoxed: Rupert Murdoch's War on Journalism*; in addition to drawing on talking heads and leaked information about Fox's various strategies of covering the news, the documentary cited several examples of the network's biases that had been monitored by the MoveOn volunteers. Relying on similar grassroots networks, Greenwald followed up these works with docs critical of Wal-Mart, Tom DeLay and the Republicans, and the use of military contractors in Iraq—as well as a sympathetic series about the efforts of the ACLU. Nearly all of Greenwald's work during the Bush years qualified as quick-hitters, designed to rally the progressive activist base. Produced at such a rapid pace, none of the docs served up new or especially controversial arguments. But as Boynton observed, in "meld[ing] grass-roots politics with the culture of the Internet," Greenwald's efforts augured a future in which "young political filmmakers will be as likely to wield a camera phone as a digital camera." [53]

Moore, by contrast, remained very much an auteur, one who obviously loved to go to battle against the right, which relished the chance to return the fire at him. For a brief moment, the overwhelming commercial success of *Fahrenheit* indeed seemed to be opening the door for other left-wing documentaries to find wide theatrical release. Within a few years, that wave seemed to have subsided, with documentaries again on the margins of commercial filmmaking. In the fall of 2004, however, the filmmaker had a concern greater than the future of his craft on his mind.

In late September, Moore launched a high-profile national tour, which would bring him to twenty states, both Red and Blue (particularly battleground states like Michigan, Ohio, and Pennsylvania), and sixty-three cities in the remaining six weeks of the campaign. His goal? "To try and convince the fed-up, the burned-out, and the Nader-impaired to leave the house for just a half-hour on November 2nd and mark an 'X' in a box (or punch a chad or touch a screen) so that America and the world can be saved." [54] On Tuesday, October 5, Moore posted an excited letter on his Web site announcing that the documentary was now available for purchase and rental; that same day, Simon & Schuster released his *Fahrenheit*

9/11 Reader, which provided the screenplay, various sympathetic reviews, and most important, factual information to counter the right's charges that he had "lied." The film's release meant far more than just increased revenue for Moore, however. This was because, in his words, "All surveys have shown that, the more people who see it—especially those still sitting on the fence—the more likely we will have regime change come November 2nd." Accordingly, Moore suggested that his fans help spread the word, whether by hosting neighborhood premieres, serving as their own local video stores (i.e. by lending out the film), organizing large screenings, or buying it and giving it away. Such mass dissemination would pay off, he assured. "Let's flood the country with this movie. It's the Republicans' worst nightmare."[55] For his part, O'Reilly, who had dubiously claimed to be "undecided" in the race up until that point, in late September made his already-known sympathies abundantly clear. In a no less than three-part interview with President Bush aired on *The O'Reilly Factor*, Murdoch's chief lieutenant lobbed mostly softballs at the president, beginning with "Are you surprised [the Iraqis] don't appreciate the American sacrifice more?" and moving on to statements like "Fallujah: Should we have crushed it when we could have?" On the first night of the interview (Monday, September 27, 2004), O'Reilly posted his highest ratings of the year—4.5 million viewers, about 2 million more than his regular numbers.[56]

Throughout October, Moore valiantly attempted to register as many new voters as he could on what he termed his "Slacker Uprising Tour." As the title suggested, Moore pitched his appeal to young, first-time voters. In order to win over these slackers, he rewarded them for registering with new underwear (to the men) and Ramen noodles (to the women). His effort stirred up the most controversy in, of all places, Michigan, where the state Republican Party filed criminal complaint charges against him on the grounds that he was bribing voter registrants. For Moore, this petty action took the cake. After recalling the Disney affair, the right's harassment of the theater owners, the FEC battles, the R rating, the media assault, and a slew of counter-documentaries (which he termed "attack dog tapes"), Moore observed that "with no tricks left in their bag, [his right-wing foes] just decided, 'Let's toss his sorry ass behind bars—him and his noodles and his gift of clean underwear!' "[57] Like the other flanks in the multifaceted assault on Moore, this one never succeeded in stopping the filmmaker's juggernaut. But the right, sad to say, would soon have the last laugh.

The days in and around the November 2 election saw a flurry of communiqués from Moore to his many fans. With "One Day Left," he reminded "Decent Conservatives and Recovering Republicans" that "Bush refused to go after and capture Osama bin Laden. He fought, every step of the way, the investigation into the 9/11 attacks. Who on earth would oppose such a thing?" And he told his "Friends on the Left" as well as "Nader voters" that Kerry—whom Bush derided but Moore lauded as the "number one liberal in the Senate"—"is not the tweedledee to Bush's tweedledum." Addressing the president directly, he asked, "Why did you and your friends fund SIX 'documentaries' trashing me—but only ONE film against Kerry? C'mon, he was the candidate, not me."[58] On the night before, and the day of, the election, the man from Flint felt confident that Kerry would win, and that *Fahrenheit* was playing an instrumental role in sending Bush back to his ranch in Crawford. Like many liberals, he was ready for a "victory party," only to be jolted by the ultimate outcome. Published two days after the election on his Web site, his initial reaction suggested deep despair. "My first thoughts after the election" simply was a list of all of the names of the American soldiers killed in Iraq up until that date. Yet Moore quickly perked up, and his next two missives found plenty of silver linings. Both "17 Reasons Not to Slit Your Wrists" and "The Kids Are Alright" stressed the fact that young voters (ages eighteen to twenty-nine) turned out in record numbers and voted overwhelmingly (54–44 percent) for Kerry. Moore saw this as a distinctly hopeful sign for the future, and as evidence that his hard work had paid off. On tour, he said, "Each night from the stage I could see it in people's eyes that they were not going to give up—and they, too, would not rest until Bush was removed from the White House." *Fahrenheit's* message would thus live on through the next generation.[59]

Yet barely had the dust begun to settle on the election before conservative factions in the Democratic Party began to kick it up again, aiming it specifically in the direction of Moore. The Democratic Leadership Council, or DLC—a small but highly influential group that had nurtured conservative New Democrats like the Clintons and Joe Lieberman—immediately blamed the Moore crowd for the party's stinging defeat. In an early December op-ed in the *Wall Street Journal*—provocatively titled "Get the Red Out"—DLC figureheads Al From and Bruce Reed argued that the party lost because of its position in the war on terror. Henceforth, they said, the party needed to adopt a "muscular foreign policy." The Democrats, From and Reed maintained, need to "be the party of Harry Truman and John Kennedy, and not of Michael Moore . . . [who] does not represent the Kennedy or Truman tradition in the Democratic party of patriotism and security."[60] Moore eagerly returned the fire. On his Web site, he referred to the "pathetic sight of the DLC (the conservative, pro-corporate group of Democrats) apologizing for being Democrats and promising to 'purge' the party of the likes of, well, all of US!" The DLC, he said, was small in number, with the group's annual dinner attended by only about two hundred people. This he contrasted with MoveOn's membership (over two million), and the total audience for *Fahrenheit* (over fifty million), among other indicators.[61] While Moore expressed confidence that his views in fact represented those of the majority of Democrats, From and other members of the DLC stressed their belief that the country was now dominated by a Republican majority, which is why the Democrats needed to move to the right. That Moore's positions on Iraq or the war on terror had not been in any way adopted by the Kerry campaign seemed not to matter to either side in the debate. The DLC simply wanted to blame Moore in order to suit its own agenda, while the filmmaker rightly stood his ground in the name of his.

Hyperbole notwithstanding, the question of Moore's actual influence on the 2004 election remains in dispute. In his book *The Vast Left-Wing Conspiracy* (2005), the *National Review*'s Byron York offered an analysis more detailed and specific than the book's overheated title would suggest. Seeking to dispel the idea that *Fahrenheit* had won over Red State voters, York broke down the box-office numbers using information provided by Nielsen EDI, a film division of the ratings giant. The Nielsen data, York said, "revealed a picture of *Fahrenheit 9/11*'s performance that bore almost no resemblance to Michael Moore's hype." The Nielsen numbers measure a film's performance in various regional markets. As York summarized the findings, *Fahrenheit*, in fact, did well only "in blue states, and even then only in the most urban parts of those blue states." Its strongest market shares were in cities like New York, Chicago, San Francisco, Seattle, Portland, Boston, Philadelphia, and Washington, D.C. The film's weak showing in Red State cities like Dallas and Houston may not have been surprising, but more problematic was its poor performance in Orlando, Tampa, and other Florida cities, as well as in Raleigh-Durham, Charlotte, and other places in the South. Las Vegas and Phoenix were not located in battleground states, but the film's lackluster returns in those cities suggested that it was not resonating in the Sun Belt, either. Despite Moore's initial boasting about how the film had sold out in its opening weekend in Fayetteville, North Carolina, and Tulsa, the numbers in those places ended up being way below market share. Based on the actual numbers, York maintained that "Moore's claim that his documentary was a 'red-state movie' was simply untrue, and all the articles based on its alleged national appeal were, in the end, just hype."[62]

But even if the film did not swing any of the Red States, *Fahrenheit*'s impact on shoring up the resolve of voters in the Blue States to go to the polls cannot be underestimated. To an extent unmatched in the annals of media history, a documentary film had become a focal point of national debate. That same work now stands as a document of a particular time, capturing as it did the feverish desire of many millions of Americans to get rid of the Bush II regime. The dust has now settled, and what remains is a provocative, but not particularly persuasive, critique, perhaps most valuable as a compilation of archival footage of the Bush gang's first term in office. Its success in becoming a lightning rod during the campaign ultimately owed much to Moore's unmatched appetite for, and ability to generate, media controversy. In a response to a postelection rumor that Hollywood, in retaliation for Bush's victory, might honor *Fahrenheit* at the Academy Awards, O'Reilly vowed, "If Hollywood nominates this propaganda tract as Best Picture, you will see a backlash against the movie industry that you have never seen."[63] That laurel was never bestowed, of course. But when Moore returned with his next film in 2007, O'Reilly was still very much on the warpath.

In *Sicko*, Moore would not exactly depart from his didactic style, but—in highlighting an issue (the need for national health care) without backing a specific policy or politician—the work followed in the tradition of *Bowling for Columbine* far more than *Fahrenheit*. The mostly positive critical reaction saw a recent nemesis return, this time with a nod of the cap. Writing in *Counterpunch*, Ralph Nader, who after the 2004 election wrote a column there asking "Will the *Real* Michael Moore Ever Re-Emerge,"[64] now viewed *Sicko* as Moore's "best move yet." Nader did express hope that Moore would go beyond his general endorsement of national health care to contribute his resources and influence to the widespread grassroots movement behind HR 676, John Conyers's legislation calling for a single-payer system.[65] In a memorable showdown with CNN's Wolf Blitzer, in which the activist filmmaker berated the host and his network for their coverage of the war, Moore would in fact express his support for the bill. (On Blitzer's show, Moore would also speak favorably about the new Al Gore, and not rule out supporting Hillary Clinton.)[66] Meanwhile, the *New Yorker*, a fixture in doctors' offices across the land, ended up running two separate pieces about the film, first a blistering assault by the magazine's lead film critic,

David Denby, who objected to Moore's rosy portrayal of socialized medicine, calling him an "absurdist of outrage."[67] The following issue then carried a critique from Atul Gawande, an author and practicing surgeon. Although far more favorable in his assessment than Denby, Gawande nonetheless concurred with the critic in stating that *Sicko* "doesn't offer solutions" and that it's simply "an outrage machine."[68]

Somewhat surprisingly, in arguing that Moore had not advocated a specific solution, the left and liberal critics missed the larger message of *Sicko*, which at one point included Soviet propaganda footage and ended with an almost socialist realist portrayal of Cuba. Indeed, Moore's film went well beyond making a case for why private health care insurance companies should be put out of business or why national care was so necessary. It was most surprising (or, perhaps, least) that the critic who best captured the real solution that Moore put forth was none other than Bill O'Reilly. In early July 2007, O'Reilly renewed his attack on Moore in one of the host's "Talking Points Memo" segments (which he followed that night with the "Ridiculous Item of the Day," about Hollywood liberals' financial support for the "far-left zealot" Al Franken). Early in the segment, O'Reilly played a clip from a 2002 interview he did with Moore, in which the host asked the filmmaker, "How liberal are you? Are you a socialist, a communist?" Moore responded to the red-baiting by stating that he had "never understood those terms. Because when you grow up in a place like Flint, Michigan, there's no liberal or left community there." But for O'Reilly, *Sicko* clearly demonstrated that "Moore is a socialist. He wants a liberal government to provide cradle-to-the-grave entitlements and to have the right to seize personal assets through draconian taxation." Just in case socialized medicine appealed to any of his viewers, O'Reilly felt compelled to sketch out the greater dangers it portended. If "national health care is passed," Fox's leading man stated, "I can assure you that Michael Moore and his acolytes will tell you that decent food is a human right, and so is decent housing. And a dignified retirement. And child care for working people, and on and on and on." O'Reilly, of course, derided such a pleasant-sounding society as a "nanny state."[69] Thus, while Michael Moore may often seem like an outsized presence on the American political landscape, and the left's version of Bill O'Reilly, in the final analysis, only one of these figures is creating propaganda calling for a more egalitarian world.

4

NETROOTS I: THE RISE OF MOVEON

Although MoveOn grew exponentially during the Bush years, it is clearly a product of the Clinton era. It originated in Berkeley, amid the Bay Area–led Internet boom of the 1990s. Wes Boyd and Joan Blades, the couple who co-founded the group, made a killing when they sold their software company, Berkeley Systems, which had produced the famed "flying toaster" screen saver as well as "You Don't Know Jack," a popular online game show. In 1998, during the high point (or low) of the Lewinsky scandal, the duo decided to apply their resources, skills, and passion to a more meaningful pursuit: trying to stop Bill Clinton from being impeached. Boyd and Blades would do it through the means they knew best, the Internet. They began to circulate a pithy petition asking Congress to "Immediately Censure President Clinton and Move On to Pressing Issues Facing the Nation." Within three weeks, 240,000 people across the country had signed on, thus planting the seeds of a movement; the number of supporters of the Clinton petition eventually reached a half million. "This is groundbreaking," Blades told the *New York Daily News*. "If it's effective, it's going to mean representatives are going to have to be more responsive to their constituents." MoveOn, she said, is "about giving people an opportunity to come together on something that crosses geographic and party lines," which was necessary because "[c]onsensus building is something our politicians are not doing enough of."[1] Yet by the 2000 campaign and through the present, MoveOn would be considered nothing if not a highly partisan organization.

As the dust settled on the Clinton impeachment scandal, the

group possessed the infrastructure but not necessarily the driving issues that could make it grow. In response to the Columbine massacre in 1999, MoveOn issued an online petition calling for gun control. While the number of signers shrank considerably, reaching only seventy thousand, the *New York Times* nevertheless identified MoveOn "as distinguishing itself as a model for online plebiscites."[2] Such a characterization suggested that the group's early role was more as a new source of liberal advocacy than as a media outlet. At the same time, MoveOn had already established itself as an early pioneer in Internet fund-raising. By the 2000 election, it had collected over $2 million in small contributions, which would be spent on trying to defeat any politicians who had supported impeachment; in a five-day span before an FEC filing deadline at the end of June, the group had raised $250,000. Such numbers were impressive, and the organization plainly stood as a force to be reckoned with. After MoveOn helped fund several successful candidates in the fall elections, Steven Weiss of the Center for Responsive Politics predicted that the group "certainly will set an example of how the Internet can be used to finance campaign contributions to candidates."[3] Still, like the Gore-Lieberman-era Democratic Party, MoveOn lacked any compelling cause that it could rally its troops behind. In the first year of Bush II's reign, the group did not generate any notable enthusiasm behind its calls for campaign finance reform, to fight Bush's tax cuts, or to push for energy price controls.

Like the rest of the American political landscape, MoveOn was transformed by 9/11. Yet while the Bush administration went hard right, and the mainstream Democrats capitulated, MoveOn began to swing left. In November 2001, Boyd and Blades hired Eli Pariser, a precocious and energetic twenty-year-old organizer from Maine. In the immediate aftermath of 9/11, Pariser had created 9-11peace.org, which—taking a cue from MoveOn—was an online petition, in this case calling for military restraint and a multilateral response to the World Trade Center attacks. That both MoveOn and Pariser expressed concern about going to war with

Afghanistan would later be used against them. In any case, within three weeks, the petition had 500,000 signatures. Pariser came aboard as MoveOn's campaigns director, and he soon oversaw the group's efforts against the Iraq War. In the fall of 2002, as the Iraq War became the Bush administration's selling point for the midterm elections, the organization helped fund antiwar candidates. Senator Paul Wellstone topped the list of such voices against the invasion of Iraq, and his vote against the preemptive war in early October had helped spur MoveOn's efforts. In a forty-eight-hour span after that vote, MoveOn raised $1 million to help fund antiwar candidates; all told, it raised more than $600,000 for Wellstone alone. After Wellstone's tragic death in late October, the group raised $200,000 for his replacement as candidate—Walter Mondale—in a mere two hours. By November 2002, MoveOn had become more than just the technologically advanced flank of the Democratic Party's base. It was now one clearly identified with a cause—stopping the Bush administration's Iraq War—that the leadership of the Democratic Party did not want to touch.

After rising to prominence in the 2002 midterms, the technoactivist group's next splash came with its foray into traditional media in its effort to stop the Iraq War. Working with Fenton Communications, a leading Democratic PR outfit, MoveOn produced an updated version of LBJ's 1964 "Daisy" commercial, in which a young girl picked petals off a flower while a mushroom cloud hovered behind her. In the original ad, the girl counted to nine, and then a voice-over counted backward to zero, at which point the cloud enveloped her. In MoveOn's version, the setup was the same, but this time the counting was interspersed with shots of burning Iraqi oil fields and vocal antiwar protests. It ended with the statement that "maybe the unthinkable" could happen in the coming war. In mid to late January 2003, two months before the war commenced, the ad aired in eleven cities. It screened in the Washington, D.C., area during the Super Bowl, but—after a firestorm of reaction from conservative pundits—it was turned down in two major markets, Los Angeles and Boston. This dramatic media statement coincided with the group's direct action against the war, which struck a more cautious note in arguing against the invasion. On Tuesday, January 21, more than nine thousand MoveOn members gathered across the country to deliver "Let the Inspections Work" petitions to the home offices of more than four hundred senators and representatives. In describing her organization's efforts to the *San Francisco Chronicle*, Blades characterized MoveOn as "bipartisan and issue-focused." During the war and its immediate aftermath, such terms seemed appropriate. MoveOn indeed led a multifaceted counterattack against the war, flooding in-boxes, filling the airwaves, and putting bodies into politicians' offices and onto the streets.[4]

As it helped lead the antiwar movement, MoveOn increasingly became a major political player on the national and even international stage. In the run-up to the war, the group delivered its petition calling for more inspections, signed by more than one million people worldwide, to the UN Security Council. MoveOn's focus on the war helped expand the group's numbers, such that by early 2003 it boasted over one million members worldwide. More important, MoveOn's rank and file showed that they were willing to do more than click, sign, and contribute. As Pariser observed in early 2003, "We've changed the way that we do organizing in the last eight months. One of the things is to move past e-mailing and phone calls and get people back out on the street and use the Internet as a backbone for catalyzing that." The large contingents that turned out in many U.S. cities for the February 15 worldwide protests against the impending war helped illustrate MoveOn's reach. MoveOn became a leader in the Win Without War coalition that had been established the preceding fall. This coalition of stalwart liberal and left advocacy groups—including the NAACP, Greenpeace, and an array of religious organizations—had been formed in response to ANSWER, the far-left antiwar outfit that spearheaded the initial large protests against the invasion. MoveOn was instrumental in pushing for Win Without War to sign on to the February 15 day of protest, a plan that originated at the European Social Forum in Rome in November 2002. United for Peace and Justice, the largest peace coalition group, came aboard in December, and helped organize the February protest; in New York City, UFPJ also led the fight against the Bloomberg administration's denial of a right to hold an antiwar march. But MoveOn's central role in the national protests was illustrated by Pariser's presence onstage in the huge rally that was held near the UN. "For each person who's here, there are a hundred who weren't able to make it," he told the massive crowd that shivered on an icy cold Saturday. "I know—I get e-mail from them. They're ordinary, patriotic, mainstream Americans." [5]

The meteoric ascent of both MoveOn and Pariser soon captured the attention of the *New York Times Magazine*. In early March, as the U.S. invasion appeared imminent, the pro-war liberal journalist George Packer penned a lengthy feature story about the group. Titled "Smart-Mobbing the War," the piece focused mainly on Pariser, who impressed Packer, in spite of what the writer saw as the antiwar movement's ultimate naïveté. For Packer, comments such as the ones Pariser made at the February protests suggested that MoveOn's new figurehead "seems to exist so that patriotic, mainstream, duct-tape-buying Americans can't dismiss the antiwar movement as a fringe phenomenon of graying pacifists and young nihilists." Indeed, the methods applied by Pariser and MoveOn were nothing if not contemporary: an interactive Web site allowed members to debate ideas, resulting in automated reports ranking those ideas and steering the group's actions. However futuristic their methods, Packer maintained that "Dot-org politics" nonetheless amounted to simply "the latest manifestation of a recurrent American faith that there is something inherently good in the vox populi," and that they "confirm what Tocqueville noticed over a century and a half ago: that Americans, for all our vaunted individualism, tend to dissolve in a tide of mass opinion." Packer's skepticism aside, his comments illustrated that what would be eventually called "netroots" politics had begun to be recognized as a potential molder of mass opinion. Even so, Packer clearly—and most condescendingly—disagreed with the antiwar movement on the conflict, maintaining that it neglected to consider "that the Iraqi people, while not welcoming the threat of bombs, might be realistic enough to accept a war as their only hope of liberation from tyranny." Somewhat more presciently, Packer predicted that once the war began, MoveOn would turn its attention to fund-raising for Democratic contenders in 2004. And a bit more ominously, he suggested that "[w]hile Pariser is too cautious to declare any political ambitions of his own, the party would be foolish not to pursue a young activist with his talents."[6]

In terms of the organization's independence from the Democratic Party, the protests on the eve of the war stood as a high-water mark for MoveOn. Principle, rather than pragmatism or partisan politics, guided the group's actions. While leading Democrats from John Kerry through Hillary Clinton caved in to a Republican Party hell-bent on invading Iraq, MoveOn teamed with peace activist groups across the land in order to show the world that not every American shared the bloodlust of the Bush administration. After a winter of petitions, visits to politicians' offices, and large-scale marches and rallies, MoveOn continued to take a stand even as American and British forces moved toward the Gulf. In mid-March, the group helped coordinate peace vigils across the world, with some three thousand slated to take place on Sunday, March 14. In Minneapolis–St. Paul, for example, activists assembled at seventy scheduled locations. At the largest gathering, of more than one thousand people at Lake Harriet, Gary Chisholm, a technology consultant, told the *Minneapolis Star Tribune* that he saw the protests as "bringing light to the darkness."[7] The same could be said more generally about MoveOn's initial role in the national debate over the war. Yet, over the next year and a half, as the invasion of Iraq became a nightmarish occupation, the group would try—tirelessly, but unsuccessfully—to channel its antiwar zeal into transforming the Democratic Party.

•   •   •

A key political player by early 2003, MoveOn would by no means focus exclusively on the war, however. Its next notable campaign, in fact, challenged the consolidation of major media, a trend personified in the figure of Rupert Murdoch. Joining with the advocacy groups Common Cause and Free Press, MoveOn sought to stir public outcry against the Federal Communications Commission's proposed relaxation of restrictions on corporate media domination of local markets. In late May 2003, a series of TV commercials produced by the trio of liberal groups began to air in a handful of markets, including New York City. In one of the spots, Murdoch's face appeared in front of four TV screens labeled ABC, CBS, Fox, and NBC, the caption in the foreground reading, "This Man Wants to Control the News in America. The FCC Wants to Help Him." The choice of Murdoch as the campaign's target seemed obvious to anyone on the left. As Pariser told the *New York Times*, "News Corporation is a great example of a company that takes a political ideology and merges it with its news-making."[8] Murdoch's primary outlets—Fox News, the *Weekly Standard*, and the *New York Post*—had certainly helped stoke the bonfires of public support for the Iraq War; indeed, according to media critic Eric Alterman, "No one—not even *Times* superhawk William Safire—was more important in the media debate over Iraq than the *Weekly Standard's* William Kristol," a noxiously ubiquitous figure on the cable talk shows.[9] MoveOn's participation in the FCC controversy—in which Murdoch, Viacom, and other media giants emerged victorious, but only after spirited debate—thus could be seen as flowing directly from the group's antiwar work. Yet once again, the timing of the controversy altered MoveOn's direction. Just when it appeared to have settled on a primary issue—stopping the war—the group now charted a new course. Unlike most other advocacy groups, MoveOn's focus has constantly moved all over the map.

In early June 2003, MoveOn joined with other progressives in an attempt to wake up the Democratic Party. Boyd served as a featured speaker at the Take Back America conference, a three-day summit among liberals held in Washington, D.C. As the *Washington Post*'s David von Drehle observed, Boyd's popularity at the well-attended gathering owed much to the fact that "[t]he story of his organization is one of the few clear successes lately in a party that took a drubbing last November and faces an uphill battle against a popular president." Boyd, like many other party activists, maintained that the Democratic Party needed to listen to the grass roots. As von Drehle summarized it, Boyd's position was that "progressive Democrats need to present an agenda beyond simple opposition to the Bush administration." "We need to stop playing defense," Boyd said.[10] Previewing the recurring intraparty conflict witnessed through 2006, the ultrahawkish Democratic Leadership Council attacked the focus of the conference. In a sniping "welcome note"–type statement, the DLC played its favorite "soft on terror" card. "We cannot regain the White House," the note stated, "if we deepen, rather than rebut, the lingering doubt . . . that too many Americans don't much trust us to protect them against terrorists and other threats to our national security. We're not convinced that your panel on 'Next Stages for the Peace Movement' will reassure the country on this count."[11] As a leader of both the peace movement and the Democrats' activist base, MoveOn would clash frequently with the DLC over the next few years. Soon after the conference, however, the group would help push a candidate not favored by the DLC to the front of the pack of contenders for the 2004 nomination.

Later in June 2003, MoveOn held another online plebiscite, in this case a presidential primary that promised to yield an early endorsement for 2004. If the winner received more than 50 percent of the vote, the group vowed to endorse that candidate, as well as to provide volunteers and to raise money. The timing of the primary was especially noteworthy. As the *Washington Post* pointed out, "It is an unusually early contest; most outside groups wait for a front-runner to emerge before even considering announcing their preferences." For MoveOn, the virtual event further solidified its position as a key player in the upcoming campaign—as the voice of the party's base. "Ordinary people, at the grass roots, often stand back until a lot of this is decided—and it doesn't make a lot of sense," Boyd told the *Post*, adding, "Why not play as much [of a role] as the folks who attend the rubber chicken dinners play?" Ostensibly, the primary would give all of the nine candidates then in the race an equal shot. Each candidate would receive a questionnaire—asking for his or her position on Iraq, the Patriot Act, Bush's environmental policies, and other issues—and the various answers would be posted on MoveOn's Web site before the voting began.[12] But despite the veneer of neutrality, one candidate clearly stood poised to seize the nomination.

Howard Dean had already made winning over the netroots a main component of his early campaign strategy. As the *American Prospect's* Harold Meyerson pointed out in a *Washington Post* op-ed, by the time MoveOn launched its primary, "[t]he former Vermont governor ha[d] clawed his way into the first tier of Democratic candidates in part through his campaign's unparalleled success in waging a candidacy online."[13] Dean had successfully used the Internet to raise money and to spread his antiwar message. Earlier in the year, Joe Trippi, at the time Dean's net-savvy campaign manager, discovered that a Web site called Meetup.com consistently helped to bring Dean supporters together for various events. Trippi began to utilize that site to help recruit volunteers and to raise money. As the *New Republic's* Ryan Lizza observed in early June, "Trippi seems to spend an inordinate amount of his time checking Meetup numbers, posting to liberal blogs, sending text messages to supporters who have signed up for the Dean wireless network, and otherwise devising ways to use the Internet to build what Trippi envisions as 'the largest grassroots organization in the history of this party.'"[14] Titled "Happy Days Are Virtually Here Again," a *New York Times* editorial now called the online primary "a glimpse into the politics of the future."[15] The Dean campaign's stylistic overlap with MoveOn's futuristic efforts made it the obvious front-runner in the primary. As Meyerson wrote, "Dean's legions are filled with highly educated, Internet-savvy young people, and that's a pretty good description of MoveOn's members as well."[16]

Seeing the handwriting on the wall, or perhaps scrolling across the computer screen, the other Democratic campaigns began to cry foul about the Internet primary. Some raised the issue of direct collaboration, since the Dean campaign had hired MoveOn's Zack Exley—who had joined the group after his bitingly satiric Web site gwbush.com gained notoriety in the 2000 campaign—as a technical consultant. That the timing of the primary announcement came just after Dean's official declaration of his candidacy seemed to lend credence to the collusion charge. Several campaigns also complained that MoveOn had distorted the voting by conducting a straw poll prior to the primary and then allowing the top three vote getters in that poll—Dean, Dennis Kucinich, and John Kerry—to send out e-mail messages to the group's members asking for their vote. Even one of the campaigns that had benefited from such access had no doubts about the outcome of the primary, though. As Kerry spokesman Robert Gibbs told the *Boston Globe*, "I think everyone believes Howard Dean is going to win."[17] In late June, just over 317,500 of MoveOn's 1.4 million members cast their ballots in the two-day voting, and Dean indeed prevailed, capturing 44 percent of the vote. While this showing indeed demonstrated the strong support of MoveOn's members, because it did not top 50 percent, it produced no official endorsement and no direct pledge of money or volunteers. Still, the popular perception became that MoveOn was squarely in Dean's camp.

More revealing than Dean's victory, perhaps, was the level of support for the second-place finisher, Dennis Kucinich, who received 24 percent of the vote. This essentially meant that nearly 70 percent of MoveOn's voters—or the most committed members of the activist group—supported an antiwar candidate for president. In celebrating his victory, Dean saw it as about more than just one issue, however. "This primary was participatory democracy at its finest," Dean declared. "Hundreds of thousands of ordinary Americans researched this race, voted and told their friends to vote."[18]

While it made sense for Dean to bask in the moment of triumph, his advantages in the race rendered his analysis just a bit hyperbolic. Meanwhile, Kucinich communications director (and FAIR founder) Jeff Cohen treated the vote as a referendum mainly on the war. As Cohen told the *Washington Post*'s von Drehle, "We're peeling the grass roots of the party away from other candidates. We connect to the base of the Democratic Party. That base is largely antiwar, anti–corporate trade deals, pro–cuts in military spending." [19] Ultimately, the meaning of the primary result was threefold: it gave Dean additional momentum; it showed the buzz that could be generated via Internet campaigning; and it demonstrated the leftward, antiwar sentiments of the netroots. The primary's third-place finisher, the Kerry campaign (which checked in at 16 percent), surely must have taken note.

The insurgency of both the Dean campaign and the MoveOn-led netroots augured trouble for the conservative leadership of the Democratic Party. In a front-page *Washington Post* article titled "Among Democrats, the Energy Seems to Be on the Left," von Drehle cited the Take Back America conference, the MoveOn primary, and Dean's emergence as clear signs of a battle over the future direction of the party. In their struggle to wrest control of the party from the centrist, Clinton-led New Democrats, the activist base, as von Drehle observed, no longer called themselves "liberals"—now, they were "progressives." And their main enemy was obviously the DLC. That group's president, former Clinton domestic policy adviser Bruce Reed—who earlier in the year had dismissively dubbed Dean "an elitist" from the "McGovern-Mondale wing" of the party—told von Drehle that "Clinton's 'New Democrat' approach was 'the most successful political and governing strategy in our lifetime.'" By contrast, FAIR's Cohen argued that "[t]he DLC strategy of waffling GOP-lite centrism has been a near total failure for the Democratic Party. I say 'near' total because of Clinton. Take away the unique charisma of that one politician, and the DLC strategy is a total failure." [20] With less than a year and a half to go before the next election, the activists appeared to have the momentum. MoveOn and other groups now faced the difficult task of sustaining that push while at the same time making sure that the issues they believed in did not get ignored or watered down by the party brass.

As it became a key player in the 2004 campaign, MoveOn also continued to keep the Iraq War on the front burner. Amid the fanfare over the primary, the group launched a petition drive that essentially accused Bush of lying in order to start the war. Along with Win Without War, MoveOn took out a full-page ad in the *New York Times* that called Bush a "misleader"; notably, the ad also echoed a soon-to-be familiar John Kerry line from the Vietnam era, as it concluded: "It would be a tragedy if young men and women were sent to die for a lie." Such an indictment of the Bush administration was far stronger than most mainstream Democrats were willing to put forth. At the time, Hillary Clinton and other leading figures in the party argued that prewar intelligence had indeed indicated that Saddam possessed weapons of mass destruction—which meant that the Bush administration was as deceived as Senate Democrats were by bad intelligence. At least one congressman, Jose Serrano from the Bronx, shared MoveOn's position, however. "One president said 'I did not have sex with that woman' and he got impeached," said Serrano. "Another president lied to the American people, to Congress, and to the United Nations about weapons of mass destruction, bombed a country and killed many people [and] he's some sort of hero. What gives?" [21] Yet while the voice of Clinton carried just a bit more weight than that of Serrano within the party, the petition struck a nerve with MoveOn's membership.

Just over a month after it was launched, the petition contained over 400,000 signatures from across the nation. More important, the campaign even appeared to be altering the course of the party's position on the war, as the Democratic National Committee released a TV spot accusing Bush of deception regarding the war. MoveOn also produced a commercial based on the petition, and it aired in Washington, D.C., and New York City. At the time, Henry Waxman, a liberal congressman from California, had been sponsoring legislation calling for an independent commission to investigate the Bush administration's prewar intelligence. In the week after MoveOn's ad appeared on television, the number of sponsors for Waxman's bill doubled to nearly fifty. Moreover, Waxman's chief of staff said that he expected "quite a few more [sponsors] directly as a result of the petition." Various co-sponsors of the bill even took to reading letters attached to the MoveOn petition on the House floor. According to Democrat Sherrod Brown of Ohio, who eventually became a U.S. senator, this action originated as a protest against the House Republicans' refusal to debate the subject of an investigation. Brown even vowed to read the letters every night until the upcoming August recess.[22] The antiwar statements made by MoveOn's members thus did more than float in cyberspace; instead, as in this case, they entered the venerable pages of the *Congressional Record*. And in the process, MoveOn's claims of transforming the Democratic Party began to seem like more than just hopeful rhetoric.

The impact of MoveOn and other netroots organizations captured the attention of nearly all blue media, new and longstanding. In "The Web Rewires the Movement," a lengthy feature story in the *Nation*, activist Andrew Boyd—co-founder of Billionaires for Bush, the satirical theatrical group—argued that the rise of the netroots marked a major transformation in both political activism and grassroots media. While none of MoveOn's multifaceted efforts "stopped the war," Boyd maintained that the group's work "did help put antiwar sentiment squarely on the political map—and made the case for how powerful the net can be in mobilizing social protest." The writer also endorsed what Eli Pariser characterized as MoveOn's "postmodern organizing model." "It's opt-in, it's decentralized, you do it from your home," Pariser explained. For Boyd, the model functioned as what he termed a "campaign aggregator," which brought members on board via their interest in one issue (e.g., the war), then got them involved in another (e.g., the deregulation of media ownership). In other words, what some would consider to be the group's weakness—its constantly shifting focus—seemed to be a strength, at least in the estimation of Boyd and Pariser. "We're helping to overcome the single-issue balkan-ization of the progressive movement," Pariser said. In Boyd's view, the direct line of communication between the group's leadership and its members, and the opportunity for the rank and file to shape the leadership's agenda, allowed MoveOn to serve as a vibrant source of alternative media. MoveOn, Boyd wrote, "is a grassroots answer to the corporate consolidation of media, which has enabled an overwhelmingly conservative pun-ditry to give White House spin real political momentum, and the semblance of truth, simply through intensity of repetition." Serv-ing as more than just an organizing network, the group has indeed helped progressives formulate their own mantras, much in the same way Fox News has done for the right.[23]

Through the late summer and into the fall of 2003, MoveOn continued its antiwar work while at the same time edging increas-ingly close to the Democratic Party. In early August, the group sponsored a high-profile speech given at New York University by Al Gore, in which the former vice president condemned the Bush administration for relying on discredited intelligence in making its case for the invasion of Iraq. Pariser's simple explanation of the alliance—"Gore basically said he felt MoveOn had played an im-portant role in involving people in a national conversation on these issues," he told the *Boston Globe*—suggested that the organi-zation was interested first and foremost in confronting the war, and would embrace high-profile figures who shared its opposition.[24]

But two of the group's next moves suggested that it was equally angling to curry favor within the Democratic Party. In late August, MoveOn launched a fund-raising drive to help fight the GOP-led redistricting battle taking place in Texas. Two days after its "De-fend Democracy" campaign got off the ground, the group had raked in nearly $800,000 to combat the redistricting of the Texas State Senate by the heirs to George W. Bush's state Republican

Party. In early October, just a few days before California's recall election of Governor Gray Davis, MoveOn entered the fray on behalf of the conservative Democrat. The group created a TV ad attacking Republican candidate Arnold Schwarzenegger for his past treatment of women. The spot featured images of women and a voice-over that stated, quite clumsily, "If you are a woman or your mother is a woman or your wife, or your daughter or your sister or there's a woman where you work, you cannot vote for this man because Arnold Schwarzenegger has a serious problem with women." As the *Sacramento Bee* reported, Schwarzenegger spokeswoman Karen Hanretty, quite predictably, "dismissed the commercial as 'clearly an effort to ensure that a Democrat stays in office.' "[25] Yet, in supporting Davis, a conservative and completely uninspiring figure, MoveOn again showed its willingness simply to carry water for the Democratic Party. By contrast, less than two weeks after the California effort, MoveOn resumed its role as the voice of the base. The group made headlines by taking out full page-ads attacking the Bush administration's "lies" about Iraq in newspapers in Ohio and West Virginia, both of which were predicted to be swing states in 2004.

In short, as the 2004 campaign began to get under way, MoveOn's actions revealed conflicting impulses: to stick to its principles regarding Iraq, and to make those positions part of the group's efforts to transform the Democratic Party; or to fight for the party's interest on every front, whether it be for a progressive cause—i.e., stopping right-wing redistricting in Texas—or simply for the sake of the party holding ground, as in the case of California. In any event, the group's potential to alter the outcome of the 2004 election was not lost on some key players in the progressive wing of the Democratic Party.

In mid-November 2003, liberal billionaires George Soros and Peter Lewis announced their support for MoveOn's efforts. At the end of October, MoveOn had launched its fund-raising drive for the 2004 campaign, with a goal of raising $10 million to help sway public opinion against Bush's reelection. Soros, whose fortune derived from international currency trading, and Lewis, head of Progressive Corporation, an auto insurance company, quietly got on board when the drive started, anteing up $1 million. In just a few weeks' time, MoveOn had raked in nearly $3 million in smaller contributions. The duo of benefactors then made public their pledge to match MoveOn's $10 million with a cool $5 million. (All told, by the end of the 2004 campaign, Soros gave just over $27 million to various liberal groups, while Lewis kicked in nearly $24 million—making them far and away the highest rollers against Bush.) As one Washington lobbyist explained to Lewis's hometown newspaper, the *Cleveland Plain Dealer*, in the world of car insurance, Lewis had been a "genius at redefining marketplaces. . . . [Now], what he is doing is redefining the political parties, and getting them away from the control of one or two elected officials." Accordingly, Lewis explained his actions by stating, "The MoveOn Voter Fund is an effective way to inform public opinion and bring new people into the game." [26] For his part, Soros emphasized the group's methods as the reason for his support. "I like what they do and how they do it," he told the *New York Times*. "They have been remarkably successful; I want to help them be even more successful." [27] The meet-up of the leading progressive donors with the most dynamic progressive group indeed seemed like a liberal match made in heaven.

The actions of Soros and Lewis did provoke some outrage from both the right and the center, however. To the group's delight, Bill O'Reilly began regularly attacking MoveOn as an "extremist organization," singling out its calls for a peaceful response to 9/11. (Only in the Orwellian world of Fox News could peace be termed "extremism.") A more temperate voice of criticism came from the editorial page of the *Washington Post*. It argued that large donors of any political stripe raised the problem of influence. The paper maintained that "[f]or Democrats thrilled with the Soros millions, imagine conservative financier Richard Mellon Scaife opening his bank account on behalf of Mr. Bush."

Moreover, Soros's high-minded disavowals of influence—"I do not represent any special interest. My contributions are made in the public interest," he had said—struck the *Post* as just a bit sanctimonious. The editorial thus wondered that while "Mr. Soros may not be seeking a rider on an appropriations bill, [who] is he to determine the public interest?"[28] Soros indeed seemed to fan the flames of criticism raging toward him. Born in Hungary, where he lived under the Nazi occupation during World War II, Soros attacked what he called the Bush administration's "supremacist ideology." Bush and the neocons' imperial vision, he said, contradicted the principles of "a free and open society, [in which] people are supposed to decide for themselves what they mean by freedom and democracy, and not simply follow America's lead."[29] While Soros could defend his contributions to groups like MoveOn by highlighting their participatory methods, his large-scale support nonetheless left open the question of how much influence he sought to wield.

Although it was now flush with big-donor money, MoveOn hardly toned down its antiwar message. Instead, it pumped the cash into TV ad buys attacking the Bush administration's war. In five battleground states, including Florida and Ohio, the group aired a spot that pointed out how the war in Iraq was squandering billions of dollars that could be spent on health care and education in the United States. "We could have built ten thousand new schools or hired almost two million new teachers," the voice-over stated. "Instead, George Bush wants to spend that $87 billion in Iraq. If there's money for Iraq, why isn't there money for America?"[30] MoveOn's angry ad appeared amid a flurry of political commercials that filled the airwaves that month, including several produced by Democrats attacking front-runner Howard Dean for allegedly being soft on terror. Ironically, MoveOn's strong message may have helped a war proponent and the eventual Democratic nominee, John Kerry, make what may have been his worst mistake during the campaign—he voted against continued funding for the war, thus providing substance to the "flip-flop" charge that the

Republicans so relentlessly leveled against him throughout 2004.[31] Still, MoveOn stayed consistent in its critique of the war. The group not only waged the ad campaign, but also helped promote and distribute the Robert Greenwald documentary about Iraq, which was released in December. As the 2004 campaign kicked into high gear, MoveOn—at house parties, on TV sets, via e-mail, and by many other means—sought to keep the war at the center of the Democratic attack on Bush.

The question of who would lead that attack remained to be answered, however. At the end of December, rumors began to circulate regarding Soros's preferences among the Democratic contenders. In his syndicated column, far-right gossipmonger Robert Novak reported that Soros had soured on Dean. According to Novak, "In conversations with political friends, Soros confided he has become alarmed by Dean's recent performance and wonders whether the former Vermont governor is capable of defeating George W. Bush. In one such chat, Soros suggested he is interested in retired Gen. Wesley Clark."[32] Ever since the June primary, MoveOn had appeared to be in Dean's camp. But now, with Soros and Lewis bankrolling MoveOn and several other groups, speculation centered on which candidate the financiers preferred, and how that choice would affect the actions of the various organizations they helped support. Exactly one week before the Iowa caucus, the first event of the Democratic primaries, Soros told the Carnegie Center for International Peace in D.C. (where he was promoting his new book, *The Bubble of American Supremacy*), "I am keen for Dean." Soros, however, further stated that he had yet to endorse any candidate, and that in addition to Dean, his views also seemed most in accordance with those of Clark and Kerry.[33] At the same time, the *Washington Post* reported that MoveOn was holding off on launching another virtual primary. As Wes Boyd explained to the *Post's* Brian Faler, the group's goal in holding the June primary was to counteract what he called the "money primary" happening at the time, in which candidates jockeyed for funding. In June 2003, Boyd said, MoveOn had felt compelled "to really inject some populism into the process." Now, with the actual primary season getting under way, he said that "there's no need for us to step in in any way." [34] On one level, this meant that MoveOn was content to be a follower, rather than a leader, in terms of shaping the campaign's message. On another, it suggested that the group was shying away from Howard Dean, who almost certainly would have won another MoveOn primary, likely by enough of a margin to carry the group's official endorsement.

By January 2004 MoveOn moved to the front line of the attack on Bush, and it began to bear the brunt of the right's reaction to that assault. As the new year commenced, Ed Gillespie, chair of the Republican National Committee, accused the group of "the worst and most vile form of political hate speech," a term that the right had appropriated from liberals and that it would repeatedly use to deflect criticism of the Bush regime during the campaign. Specifically, Gillespie referred to two commercials entered into a MoveOn-sponsored contest—called "Bush in 30 Seconds"—that compared Bush to Hitler. MoveOn had posted the ads on its Web site, along with many others among the 1,500 entries it received; although neither made it to the round of fifteen finalists, the right latched on to the pair of Hitler comparisons as "proof" of the group's alleged extremism. [35] (MoveOn did apologize and pull the ads from the group's Web site.) The controversy continued at MoveOn's much-hyped campaign kickoff and ad awards ceremony. Held at the Hammerstein Ballroom in New York City, the event featured an array of anti-Bush celebrities, including Michael Moore, Al Franken, Janeane Garofalo, Moby, Chuck D, and many others. Comedienne Margaret Cho served as one of the hosts, and at one point she addressed Gillespie's comments. Of the Hitler ads, Cho said, "I mean, out of thousands of submissions, they find two. They're like fucking looking for Hitler in a haystack. George Bush is not Hitler. He would be, if he fucking applied himself." Cho's pointed barb naturally became the focus of right-wing coverage of the event. Political gossip hound Matt Drudge stirred the pot on his Web site, the *Drudge Report*, with an entry titled "Raw Rage at Bush During MoveOn.org Awards."[36] Cho, in turn, reported that she received a slew of racist hate mail, while Moby went to bat for her "very irreverent and Lenny Bruce–style confrontational" humor.[37] The Hitler pseudo-controversy showed that MoveOn's prominence had caused the Republican attack machine to kick into overdrive against the group. It also demonstrated MoveOn's penchant for provocative advertising. And in the fall of 2007, MoveOn's print ad questioning the intentions of General David Petraeus would make an even larger splash.

Although far more cautious in tone than the Hitler spot, the ad that won the "Bush in 30 Seconds" contest sparked the next round of furor. A star-studded panel—consisting of entertainers including Moore, Franken, Garofalo, Moby, Cho, and Russell Simmons; and Democratic Party insiders including James Carville, Donna Brazile, and pollster Stan Greenberg—had judged the ads. The panel chose a commercial that targeted the budget deficit, rather than the Iraq War, as the winner. Titled "Child's Play," the spot showed children working in mostly low-wage jobs—as dishwashers, janitors, grocery store clerks, and so on—before asking: "Guess who's going to pay off President Bush's $1 trillion deficit?" That Bush's combination of a costly war and steep tax cuts for the rich had largely created that deficit was left unsaid. The victorious ad thus targeted an issue, the federal budget deficit, that was certainly of concern to voters, but that strayed from MoveOn's previous focus on the war. (Launched that week in several swing states, a different MoveOn-sponsored ad campaign, this one targeting prescription drugs for senior citizens, further departed from both the group's core issues and especially its base.) One factor in the "Bush in 30 Seconds" judges' decision was no doubt the organization's plans for what to do with the winning ad. At the Hammerstein ceremony, Pariser announced that MoveOn would now launch a $1.6 million fund-raising drive aimed at airing "Child's Play" during the Super Bowl. The strategy provided another example of MoveOn's recurring reliance on innovative means aimed at conventional ends. Symbolically, at least, airing an ad during the Super Bowl would be a clear statement that the New Blue Media had fully arrived. Indeed, as Michael Moore explained to *Alternet's* Deanna Zandt, "For years, progressives have been standing there with their arms folded over their chests, saying, 'Mainstream media is bad. We don't like it.' They've just been refusing to play the game. Well, it's time to play the game. This is where people get their information."[38] The media elite, however, had its own rules of entry.

In this case, the gatekeeper was CBS, the network that would broadcast the 2004 Super Bowl. Citing a long-standing company policy against airing commercials that took stands on public policy issues, CBS executives rejected MoveOn's ad (as well as one from People for the Ethical Treatment of Animals, which stood to really provoke football fans by arguing that eating meat causes impotence). As *New York Times* reporter Jim Rutenberg pointed out, despite such claims of neutrality, the network had "in the past and could again accept spots from the White House's antidrug office, raising questions about what is acceptable and what is not, and why."[39] While CNN broadcast the ad during the week of Bush's State of the Union speech, CBS held fast to its position, yet in so doing the latter generated what one paper called "a ton of publicity" for MoveOn. Pariser, of course, insisted that the group much preferred to run the ad rather than reap the rewards of free media coverage. Even so, less than one week into the controversy, he acknowledged that the attention "has been amazing. Over the past 24 hours, 40,000 more people have joined MoveOn." Betsy Gelb, a professor of marketing at the University of Houston, told the *Houston Chronicle* that MoveOn had actually gotten the "ideal outcome" from the CBS affair. "They didn't have to spend $2 million for the ad and still got tremendous publicity," Gelb said. "And they look like a big-time player trying to buy an ad for the Super Bowl."[40] At the same time, the controversy exposed the limits of the mainstream, corporate media. Although now owned by the media giant Viacom, CBS nevertheless still maintained a reputation for being the most "liberal" of the three major networks. But that same network now made sure that the most-watched television of the year would carry no political statements, even a fairly tame critique of the federal budget deficit.

As it tried to go mainstream with its message, MoveOn's antiwar leanings nonetheless stayed in the foreground. Shortly after the Super Bowl controversy subsided, the group began airing one of the other finalists in "Bush in 30 Seconds," a harsh indictment of the Bush administration's position on Iraq, in five swing states. Named "Polygraph," the ad showed only a lie detector test backed by a recording of Bush's 2003 State of the Union speech. The polygraph's needles jumped three times, responding to Bush's statements: "Saddam Hussein had an advanced nuclear weapons development program"; "Saddam Hussein recently sought significant quantities of uranium from Africa"; and "Saddam Hussein aids and protects terrorists including members of al Qaeda." Such a pointed critique prompted a hostile response from the Bush camp. "If MoveOn had its way," a Bush spokesman said, "the United States would not be fighting a global war on terror, and Saddam Hussein would still be the brutal dictator in charge of Iraq."[41] As MoveOn became a pivotal actor in the Democrats' effort to unseat Bush, the group's stance on the war remained far more radical than the party's. But no matter how hard it tried, MoveOn could not make the Democratic leadership embrace anything resembling an antiwar position.

Like many other key players in the campaign, MoveOn lined up quickly behind John Kerry once he became the front-runner. In the rush to join the "Anybody but Bush" bandwagon, the group moved from its de facto support of Howard Dean, an antiwar candidate, to openly back Kerry, who claimed that his Vietnam experience made him better prepared to fight the war than Bush. By March, MoveOn, along with the Soros-backed Americans Coming Together and several other groups, began airing TV ads attacking Bush in several states. Though not openly pro-Kerry, the ads were widely seen as benefiting the Democratic front-runner, prompting the Republicans to charge that the Kerry campaign was illegally coordinating its fund-raising efforts with MoveOn and other 527 groups. In any event, by mid-April, MoveOn was eagerly on board with Kerry. Most notably, the group launched a rather hokey "bake sale" event across the country. As Pariser explained in an e-mail to the group, "MoveOn members around the country will hold Bake Sales for Democracy in their neighborhoods to raise some dough, have some fun, and support our campaign to take back the White House and Congress and elect John Kerry." In a postscript, he also added the news, already reported elsewhere, that Zack Exley was leaving MoveOn in order to become director of online communications and organizing for Kerry. Pariser then added, rather unconvincingly, that since federal election law prohibited it, there would be no contact between Exley and MoveOn for the rest of the campaign.[42] Regardless, MoveOn was now clearly in Kerry's corner. And so the question through November and beyond would become, What did MoveOn get in return for its support?

Even as Kerry moved all over the map on the issue, the war stayed in the foreground of MoveOn's assault on Bush. Beginning with "Polygraph," MoveOn would launch no fewer than eight ad campaigns targeting the president on Iraq, six on TV and two on radio. Some ads aired in smaller local markets in swing states, including those found in Kentucky and Nevada; others were directed toward the opinion-shaping audiences in New York City and Washington, D.C.; and some were broadcast nationally, on both CNN and, yes, even the Fox News Channel. In March, as the invasion and occupation of Iraq neared its one-year mark, the group waged a multipronged assault: petitions to Congress, TV ads in New York City and D.C., and full-page print ads in the *New York Times* and *Washington Post*, all calling upon Congress to censure Bush for his "campaign of misinformation" in the run-up to the war. Although the censure campaign indicated that the group was still willing to travel outside of the orbit of the Democratic

Party's leadership, MoveOn's next statements about the war suggested that it was back in the fold. Timed to coincide with the
hearings of the 9/11 Commission, a pair of spots shown on CNN
spotlighted the views of Richard Clarke, Bush's former counter-
terrorism adviser, who argued that Bush could have done more to
prevent 9/11, and that the war in Iraq was a distraction from the
war on terror. (Clarke would publicly urge MoveOn not to run
the ads, telling the Associated Press that "I just don't want to be
used" or seen as a partisan.)[43] Clarke's positions would become a
central part of the Democrats' effort to make the party appear
strong on national security. In late April, MoveOn then produced
an ad in support of Kerry's attempt to make his "war hero" stature
a defining issue in the campaign. Using footage from *Brothers in
Arms*, a sympathetic documentary about Kerry and his crew in
Vietnam, the commercial questioned Bush's service in the National Guard. Shown nationally on Fox and locally in New York
City and D.C., the spot helped inflate the "war hero" issue, which
Karl Rove and the Swift Boat Veterans for Truth would so merci-
lessly, and scandalously, shoot down. Faulting MoveOn for having
failed to predict the backlash would not be a fair criticism. But in
even supporting the "war hero" argument in the first place, the
group opened itself to the charge that it was simply doing Kerry's
bidding. After all, Kerry's record during and after Vietnam in no
way led to the candidate taking a clear stance against the war in
Iraq.

There was no disputing where the activist base of the party stood
on Iraq, however. As discussed in the preceding chapter, in late
June, MoveOn helped promote and champion Moore's *Fahrenheit
9/11*. As Pariser explained to the group's members, "We launched
this campaign around *Fahrenheit 9/11* because to the media, the
pundits, and the politicians in power, the movie's success will be
seen as a cultural referendum on the Bush administration and the
Iraq war." The group took partial credit for the film's opening

weekend box-office success, and it also organized the "virtual house party" evening featuring a live conversation with Moore. Slightly more controversial was the letter-writing campaign it initiated in defense of the film. On its Web site, the group provided form letters that members could send to newspapers across the nation; the process was made even easier because the site also provided addresses for local media outlets. "I am shocked that many critics have denounced Michael Moore's new movie, *Fahrenheit 9/11*, as unpatriotic and anti-soldier," one letter began; another concluded that "Moore's movie raises extremely difficult questions that deserve our attention as we move toward the November elections." Such letters, in fact, were printed by more than a dozen newspapers, including the *Boston Globe*, the *Chicago Sun-Times*, the *Arizona Republic*, and the *Fresno Bee*. Critics who accused Moore of disseminating anti-Bush propaganda thus saw MoveOn as an obvious fellow traveler. Yet not only did the coordinated publicity strategy reciprocally help the efforts of both Moore and MoveOn to speak on behalf of the party's base, it also kept the Iraq War in the foreground of the campaign against Bush.[44]

Over the next few months, MoveOn took on other issues—especially outsourcing and the economy—but as the campaign began to heat up in August, the group maintained its dual position on the war: it kept championing Kerry's Vietnam record, as well as hammering away at the Bush administration on Iraq. At the Democratic National Convention in late July, Kerry had overeagerly reaffirmed that his war record would be the centerpiece of his campaign. He opened his acceptance speech by declaring, "I'm John Kerry, and I'm reporting for duty," and at the end of the speech his fellow Swift Boat veterans joined him on stage. In response, in early August, the Republicans initiated their notorious Swift Boat Veterans for Truth campaign, one of the slimiest character assassinations in the history of American politics. While Kerry struggled to respond to the unfounded accusations that he had lied about his war record, MoveOn went to bat on his behalf.

In the same four cities in Ohio, West Virginia, and Wisconsin where the Swift Boat Veterans ads appeared, the group countered with an ad on CNN that attacked Bush's National Guard service, or lack thereof. In MoveOn's spot, a voice-over stated, "George Bush used his father to get into the National Guard, was grounded and then went missing. . . . [Now,] he's allowing false advertising that attacks John Kerry." Kerry then strategically distanced himself from the MoveOn ad. He claimed to be doing so on behalf of John McCain, whose statement urging the Bush administration to condemn the "dishonest and dishonorable" Swift Boat ad was included in the counterattack on Bush. (McCain, for his part, maintained that MoveOn's spot was now repeating the same inappropriate line of insult regarding a candidate's war record.) In reality, Kerry spoke out against MoveOn's ad in hopes that he would make Bush look bad by not doing the same about the Swift Boat ad. Pariser, in turn, accepted Kerry's position, simply maintaining that "he's entitled to his opinion."[45]

At the same time that MoveOn waded into the Swift Boat fray, the group also announced the winners of another commercial contest it had sponsored. The "Real People" campaign asked contestants to explain how the Bush administration's actions had affected them personally. The winners were then interviewed by filmmaker Errol Morris, whose film *The Fog of War* (about Robert McNamara) had won the 2003 Academy Award for Best Documentary. As Joan Blades explained to the *San Francisco Chronicle*, of the sixteen thousand entries it received, MoveOn had chosen the forty finalists from the more than five hundred people who stated that they had supported Bush four years earlier; seventeen of these were then selected and placed on the group's Web site for a vote. One of the many finalists that focused on the Iraq War ended up winning the popular vote. It featured Lee Buttrill, a thirty-year-old from Denver who had been a marine sergeant in Iraq. Buttrill now stated, "We were given these ideas that there were weapons of mass destruction. . . . It was just a lie. That wasn't a proper use of American troops. It wasn't a proper use of my life, or my friends' lives, or the marines who I've seen die around me." A spokesman for the California Republican Party countered that such a view did not square with that of the "overwhelming opinion of voters or even that of John Kerry, who said that even if he had known there were not weapons of mass destruction, he would have voted in favor of the war." [46] In early August, Bush had indeed challenged Kerry on the war, asking whether he would still have voted for it, given the revelations regarding the lack of WMD; Kerry had said yes, an answer that the veteran left-wing columnist Robert Scheer and other observers viewed as one of the worst mistakes of the campaign. [47] The Buttrill ad, along with four others shot by Morris, would air during the Republican National Convention in nine battleground states. Yet, valiantly as MoveOn may have tried to keep the war at the center of the campaign against Bush, the group did not score much success in getting the Kerry camp to follow suit.

Throughout the homestretch of the 2004 race, MoveOn attacked on several fronts. It continued the ad campaigns, but now also put together a high-profile concert tour and ramped up its volunteer and fund-raising activities. The war issue continued to draw the most fire, however. In mid-September, the group debuted another commercial that delivered another harsh, but slightly modified, critique of the Bush administration's war. Airing in Iowa, Ohio, Pennsylvania, and Wisconsin, the new spot showed an American soldier sinking chest-deep into desert sand while he struggled to keep his rifle above his head. At the outset, the soldier ran toward the camera while the voice-over began, "George Bush misled us into war with Iraq, sending poorly equipped soldiers into battle. He said 'Mission Accomplished,' yet almost every day more soldiers die." The emphasis now seemed to shift from the war's dubious rationale to the president's mishandling of it. As the soldier sank into the sand, the text superimposed over his image reported that more than one thousand U.S. soldiers had been killed up to that point, and a voice-over then added that the United States had spent more than $150 billion in Iraq. "George Bush got us into this quagmire," the ad concluded, but "[i]t will take a new president to get us out."[48] The Republicans fired back, with Bob Dole leading the charge. Dole, chair of Bush's veterans' coalition, told the *New York Times* that "depicting an American soldier in effect surrendering in the battle against the terrorists is beyond the pale." Pariser responded, "Clearly, things in Iraq are heading in a very bad direction," and "It is irresponsible for the president to keep whitewashing the situation."[49] The Kerry camp denied having any input into the commercial, but hardly could have objected to it—after all, such strong messages kept Iraq in the spotlight without committing Kerry to a specific position on the war. MoveOn's efforts thus helped placate the large antiwar constituency in the Democrats' activist base. And they were compatible with those held by the group's major funder. In a two-page ad spread published in the *Wall Street Journal* in late September, Soros declared that the Iraq War had been "misconceived from the start."[50]

Yet as MoveOn began to mobilize voters and ground troops for election day, John Kerry continued to go back and forth on the war issue. In his initial debate with Bush, Kerry seemed in sync with MoveOn's position. The president, he said, had "misled" the nation into war, and by that time had spent "$200 billion that could have been used for health care, for schools, for construction, for prescription drugs for seniors." Kerry then said confidently, "I know I can do a better job in Iraq."[51] In the second debate, Kerry placed less emphasis on the causes and costs of the war than on the disastrous handling of the occupation. Bush, he said twice, had "rushed to war without a plan to win the peace."[52] By the third debate, Kerry's criticism was simply that Bush had "rushed" into the war, whereas he promised to "do a better job of waging a smarter, more effective war on terror and [I] guarantee that we will go after the terrorists." Moreover, "I will hunt them down, and we'll kill them, we'll capture them," the challenger vowed.[53] For a moment, Kerry had seemed to be edging toward a MoveOn-type antiwar position, only to then become a DLC-style hawk. Though his supporters cringed at the label, Kerry was indeed wishy-washy. Throughout the 2004 campaign, MoveOn, however, had been steadfast in its position on the war. Ultimately, the group gave far more—in terms of media work, money, volunteers, and overall commitment—than it got in return from a candidate who couldn't make up his mind about the most pressing issue of the campaign. As the grim reality of Bush's second term began to sink in, the question was, indeed, how the group itself would now move on.

5

NETROOTS II:
THE RISE OF THE BLOGOSPHERE

Amid the fallout from the November 2004 election, progressives across the nation grappled with the implications of Bush's victory, and MoveOn continued to stay at the forefront of the discussion. On a Sunday evening later that November, the group convened a series of 1,680 house parties at various locations around the country. The gatherings were linked together in an online conference centered on the question of what progressives should do next. In San Francisco, a handful of self-proclaimed "rabble-rousers" attended one such house party, held at a loft in upscale Potrero Hill. As reported in the *San Francisco Chronicle*, the activists on hand encountered an un–Bay Area–like computer problem that prevented them from joining the online conference, so they did the old-fashioned thing: talked over ideas with one another, face-to-face. Some of the proposals discussed fell well within the scope of conventional politics, such as the critique that "[w]e don't have a clear message and the team that won had three: anti-gay marriage, gun rights and God," or the notion that progressives should reach out to the Red States and show them that Democrats care more about their issues than Republicans. More radical proposals bandied about at the San Francisco gathering included the idea that future activism "has to be on the streets," and that progressives should lead a boycott of the ATM machines made by the same companies that built the disputed electronic voting machines used in Ohio. What did not emerge out of the nationwide conference, however, was a single message, a unified campaign strategy, or a specific plan for direct action. Instead, MoveOn embarked on an even more daunting task: a hostile takeover of the Democratic Party.[1]

The official declaration of war came in early December, when Pariser sent out an e-mail to MoveOn members on the eve of a Democratic National Committee meeting in which the process of selecting a new national chair would begin. In the widely publicized statement, Pariser threw down the gauntlet against the corporate interests and "professional election losers"—i.e., the high-priced Democratic political consultants—who controlled the party. "For years," said Pariser, "the party has been led by elite Washington insiders who are closer to corporate lobbyists than they are to the Democratic base." Yet the fund-raising success of MoveOn and other groups had now rendered that relationship obsolete. As Pariser stated, "In the last year, grass-roots contributors like us gave more than $300 million to the Kerry campaign and the DNC, and proved that the party doesn't need corporate cash." Speaking on behalf of not just MoveOn, but of the netroots insurgency in general, Pariser then declared: "Now it's our party: we bought it, we own it and we're going to take it back."[2]

In particular, Pariser's message had targeted outgoing DNC chair Terry McAuliffe, a Clinton loyalist known for prolific fund-raising in the corporate sector. While Pariser asserted MoveOn's desire to speak on behalf of the party's activist base, McAuliffe urged the party to adopt the Republicans' playbook. Addressing the DNC conclave held at Walt Disney World, McAuliffe argued that the Republicans had won because of terrorism and cultural issues. According to the *Washington Post*'s Dan Balz, McAuliffe further maintained that the party "must learn from Republican successes to become competitive." As Balz noted, MoveOn's attack on the current approach of the DNC was seen "as a blast at those Democrats who oppose former Vermont governor Howard Dean, who is considering a run for party chairman." But Pariser told Balz that MoveOn had not yet decided which of the many candidates to support for chair. As Pariser explained, "Our feeling is that there's a vacuum at the heart of the party and it's time to fill it with new energy, with people who have passion and who don't come from inside the Beltway." Such a position certainly suggested that MoveOn was leaning toward Dean, but the group, now obviously a recognized force within the party, initially shied away from an official endorsement.[3]

At the same time that MoveOn declared war on the Democratic Party leadership, its main backers hatched a strategy for building a long-term progressive movement. As first reported in the *Financial Times*, in December 2004 George Soros and Peter Lewis sat down in San Francisco with Herb and Marion Sandler, whose California savings-and-loan fortune had enabled them to become the third-largest contributor ($13 million) to the Kerry campaign. Together the entrepreneurs decided that they would underwrite a substantial "joint investment to build intellectual infrastructure." Their goal, according to the *FT*, was "to provide the left with organizations in Washington that can match the heft of the rightwing think-tanks such as Heritage Foundation and the American Enterprise Institute."[4] Along with several other liberal big-bucks donors, Soros and company threw their weight behind the Democracy Alliance, a group aimed at sponsoring such an infrastructure. The high rollers were heavily influenced by a Power-Point presentation by Rob Stein, a former Clinton administration official and now a member of the centrist New Democratic Network, who charted out the urgent need for progressives to match more than just the right's funding abilities.[5] As Michael Tomasky and other leading liberals would observe, the goal of such groups was to match the Republicans' "extensive idea-and-messaging network," which had been in place since the early 1970s. As outlined in the landmark "Powell Memorandum" (written by future Supreme Court justice Lewis Powell) in 1971, the right needed to rally in defense of the free-enterprise system, which Powell saw as "under broad attack."[6] Exactly what the wealthy liberal donors would fight for was a different story. As the *Nation*'s Ari Berman argued in an exhaustive critique of the Democracy Alliance's first year and a half of existence, "Unlike the money guys who underwrote the right, members of the Alliance seem to lack strong ideological conviction about what the future ought to look like. And they do not have the militant perspective of outsiders eager to disrupt and overrun the party establishment."[7]

Few would accuse liberal bloggers of lacking either strong convictions or a "militant perspective," although critics such as the *New York Times Magazine*'s Matt Bai would insist that they lacked an overarching vision.[8] Yet the rapid growth of this second leading component of the netroots occurred precisely as MoveOn, the Democracy Alliance, and many other progressive groups struggled to find a new direction for both progressive politics and the Democratic Party. Led by Markos Moulitsas, the blogger better known as Kos, this quite passionate and vocal element of the New Blue Media made its presence felt in the race for DNC chair, and it would relentlessly champion Dean's candidacy over the next few months. Dean, of course, ultimately prevailed, and Moulitsas and Jerome Armstrong, another leading blogger, celebrated that victory as a clear sign that the netroots had sent "a message to the D.C. establishment that they no longer had control over the direction of the Democratic Party." In *Crashing the Gate*, their provocatively titled 2006 book, Armstrong and Moulitsas explained that when John Kerry, Senate minority leader Harry Reid, and House Minority Leader Nancy Pelosi touted Iowa governor Tom Vilsack's candidacy for DNC chair, "It seemed to be business as usual—the leaders calling the shots, handpicking candidates for office and everyone else nodding in agreement." But a new day had dawned, and "this time, the party got a reality check from the netroots." Once essentially a backroom deal, the election for the party's committee chair now garnered considerable media attention and generated volumes of chatter from the blogosphere, which was perhaps emboldened by the fact that this was a race where, if nothing else, a Democrat was guaranteed to win.[9]

The blogosphere not only tracked the race closely, but also helped undermine what Armstrong and Moulitsas termed the "status quo" candidates. According to the pair, former Texas congressman Martin Frost's bid became toast after blogger Anna Brosovic (of *Annatopia.com*) reported that Frost had run campaign ads in 2004 highlighting his close relationship with Bush. Similarly, former Indiana congressman Tim Roemer, who seemed to be close to Reid and Pelosi, went down after bloggers exposed his leanings toward Social Security privatization and against abortion, as well as his vote against Clinton's 1993 economic plan. Roemer faced the music on ABC's *This Week*, when George Stephanopoulos told him that the party's activist base was "taking [its] cues from these Web logs, the blogs, that are, you know, engaged in this debate." [10] Such stumbling over the term "blog" by a mainstream political commentator suggested that the phenomenon had only begun to enter the national discussion. But Kos and his fellow travelers would soon become major players in Democratic Party politics, and more often than not, they held the party leadership's feet to the fire over the Iraq War. In addition to helping elect Dean as party chair, over the next few years the blogosphere would help put insurgent candidates like Paul Hackett, Ned Lamont, Jim Webb, and many others on the map, play host to an array of Democratic presidential hopefuls at its YearlyKos conventions in Las Vegas and Chicago, and continue to work with MoveOn and other netroots groups in trying to overhaul the Democratic Party. Along the way, the blogosphere would come under attack from the Democratic Party establishment as well as from the right. Such controversies only fed Kos and company's brash sense of their own importance. In the wake of the 2006 midterm elections, it appeared that the blogosphere—and the netroots as a whole—may not have crashed the gate, but they had certainly gained a place at the table.

Now a Democratic political consultant, Jerome Armstrong is credited for his pioneering work in building the blogosphere. Born in Los Angeles in 1964, Armstrong in the 1980s and 1990s was a Peace Corps volunteer and radical environmental activist arrested several times at both Earth First! and Greenpeace protests. In 2001, he started the Web site *MyDD.com*, which originally stood for the rather vague term "my due diligence"; in 2006, that was officially changed to its more common association, "my direct democracy." Beginning in the summer of 2001, the site provided a forum for interactive political discussion via "Web logs," or what would soon be known simply as blogs. The early *MyDD* bloggers' politics swung distinctly to the left, and it's no surprise that the first Web site supporting Howard Dean for president started at *MyDD* in April 2002. In December of that year, Armstrong's posting on the site, "Netroots for Howard Dean," not only provided an early sign of Dean's Internet-based campaign strength, but is also credited for initiating the term "netroots" (Armstrong, no doubt aware that his readers were other Web-based political activists, saw no need to define the term).[11] Armstrong would soon go to work for Howard Dean as a paid consultant, and he temporarily shut down MyDD in 2003. Meanwhile, Markos Moulitsas, one of the other bloggers who had first appeared on Armstrong's site, had already become the torchbearer of the new media.

Born to an ethnically Greek, middle-class family from El Salvador in Chicago in 1971, Moulitsas moved to El Salvador at age four and lived there until 1980, when the escalating civil war forced his family to return to the United States. After graduating high school in suburban Chicago, Moulitsas joined the U.S. Army, and from 1989 to 1992 he was stationed mainly in Germany; that experience would later shape his support for Democratic candidates with backgrounds in the military. After the army, Moulitsas did his undergraduate work at Northern Illinois and then earned a law degree from Boston University, before moving to the Bay Area in the late nineties in order to try his luck in the Silicon Valley. Arriving a bit late for the boom, Moulitsas was an unemployed Web developer when he began blogging for *MyDD* in 2002. His postings received a good response, prompting him to launch his own site, *dailykos.net* (now *dailykos.com*), in late May 2002. The name came from his army moniker, Kos, which rhymes with rose. The site's steady stream of left-leaning commentary quickly gained a large readership, and within one year, the *Daily Kos* could claim more than 1.6 million unique visits per month. By 2007, according to his own calculations, the number had grown to nearly 20 million; in terms of actual daily readers, the number translated to around 100,000.[12]

Like MoveOn, Kos operated from the Berkeley Hills, the obvious seeding ground of the netroots. In the 1960s, the Bay Area had wielded its influence over national politics as the home of both the New and radical Left; by the early twenty-first century, it had become the nerve center of the new progressivism, which was in sync with the Bay Area's high-tech, information-driven economy. By the early Bush II years, UC Berkeley linguist George Lakoff had established himself as a key intellectual figurehead of the new progressive movement. Written in reaction to the success of Newt Gingrich's "Contract with America" in 1994, Lakoff's *Moral Politics* (1996) began to outline the author's critique of political "framing"—which the *New Republic*'s Noam Scheiber has succinctly described as the "art" of "evoking metaphors that leave voters with favorable impressions of your positions."[13] Seeking new frames, though not necessarily new policies, influential liberal Democrats (led by South Dakota senator Byron Dorgan) began to solicit Lakoff's advice in 2003. The linguist would soon give frequent counsel to Howard Dean, who then wrote the foreword to Lakoff's slender but successful *Don't Think of an Elephant*, a bestseller published by the tiny house Chelsea Green of Vermont in September 2004. (Chelsea Green would also publish *Crashing the Gate*.) In a lengthy *New York Times Magazine* profile and analysis of what he termed the ensuing "Lakoffmania," Matt Bai showed how the linguist's theory could successfully explain the outcome of the 2004 election. For the Republicans, Kerry constantly remained a "flip-flopper," whereas for the Democrats, Bush was variously "a liar, a corporate stooge, a spoiled rich kid, [and] a reckless warmonger." Thus, Bai writes, "Bush was attacked. Kerry was framed." Critics on both the right and left would soon take on Lakoff, sparking what Bai depicted as "a debate about whether the party lacks only for language or whether it needs a fresher agenda."[14] In general, bloggers have tended to see themselves as op-ed columnists and media critics, and the short-form entries of most sites provided a convenient vehicle for debate over the future of progressive sloganeering. Within the Bay Area and well beyond, Lakoff's ideas soon provided another line of insurgent attack on the mainstream of the Democratic Party.

From the get-go, Kos had presented himself as both a dedicated progressive and a steadfast opponent of the Iraq war. In "Day 1," his initial entry on *dailykos.net* in May 2002, Moulitsas defined his political stance thusly:

> I am progressive. I am liberal. I make no apologies. I believe government has an obligation to create an even playing field for all of this country's citizens and immigrants alike. I am not a socialist. I do not seek enforced equality. However, there has to be equality of opportunity, and the private sector, left to its own devices, will never achieve this goal.[15]

Kos's definition of "progressive" sounded rather like that of the early-twentieth-century Progressives, who were reformers rather than socialists and who helped spawn the New Deal; in any case, such a view placed him at the left end of the Democratic Party. After his next entry, a de facto pro-socialist attack on the anti-Castro (and anti–Hugo Chavez) policies of the Bush administration, Kos took on Bush's plans for Iraq. Attention to spelling would not become a trademark of Kos or much of the blogosphere, but, to the world's misfortune, Kos's typo—"Iraq Invasion Loosing Steam"—served as an eerily accurate premonition.[16] As Kos would reiterate frequently over the next several months, he viewed a successful invasion as impossible, primarily from the standpoint of practical military strategy. The United States' lack of allies in the region or worldwide made it so. His own background in the army enabled him to speak with some authority regarding military issues, and as Bush and company began to beat the drums of war throughout the summer, Kos would apply his experience to his increasingly passionate opposition. In "Chickenhawks Push War," a late August 2002 posting, Kos explained that his unit had been preparing to serve in the first Gulf War, and he had spent a year training for chemical warfare, but he had never gone to the region because the war ended too early. Nonetheless, he observed:

> Make no mistake. We were ready to serve. In fact, we were eager to put our training into action, but we couldn't mask our fears. War is dangerous business, and death is final. It is impossible for non-veterans to fully understand. . . . Not only does war kill, but it destroys families, and scars survivors. Thus, war is ultimately a tool of last resort, to be used when the cause is just and all other options have been exhausted.[17]

Such caution, however, was not something that the "fools in the country's governing junta" (as Kos put it) could understand. Except for Rumsfeld, none of the leading warmongers among the neocons had served in the military, which, according to Kos, enabled them to view war simply as a "political tool."[18] Although Kos was not yet a recognized player, his emergence onto the scene suggested that the blogs might offer a new style of progressive politics. Like Kos, their creators would be passionate, declamatory, unfiltered by editors, and ready to shake up a Democratic Party that had no idea what to do about Iraq.

As his readership began to grow, Kos remained a steadfast opponent of the coming war. Throughout the fall of 2002, he consistently identified Bush's war agenda as a campaign strategy for the midterm elections. In early September, just after the announcement that Bush would seek a resolution authorizing war, Kos sniffed out the fact that the president's "Iraq obsession already reeks of politics. Pushing for a pre-election vote would only confirm the worst assumptions about Bush's motives."[19] While many leading Democrats tried, unsuccessfully, to triangulate between the administration's agenda and the antiwar sentiments of the party's base, Kos helped articulate the positions of the latter. In mid-September 2002, for example, he insisted that "[a] resolution allowing a unilateral and unprovoked declaration of war against a distant nation would be reprehensible."[20] He then began to slam the presidential hopefuls who decided to support the war. For Kos, the most problematic of the possible contenders to cast his lot with the Bush gang was neither Kerry nor Edwards, but Dick Gephardt. At that time, it was Gephardt, not Dean, who, "more so than any other of the Dems' presidential aspirants, appeals to the party's left wing." Yet even though polls showed that Democratic voters were against the war, Gephardt "instead of courting the peace wing of the Democratic Party . . . stabbed them in the back," wrote an angry Kos, who increasingly began to speak as a voice of the party's antiwar activists.[21] The untimely death of Paul Wellstone, for example, caused Kos to hope that "Wellstone's courage will inspire other Democrats to better uphold our party's convictions."[22] As he cut his teeth as a political player, Kos indeed seemed to fit comfortably in the party's Wellstone wing.

As the November election neared, Kos began to carve out another niche for the blogosphere—as a forum for political-insider gossip, poll watching, handicapping of the various races, and instant analysis. Such a role naturally lent itself to overheated predictions, which in this case included Kos's forecast that since the "Democrats are masters of GOTV," meaning getting out the vote on election day, they would defy the conventional wisdom that the Republicans would prevail in the midterms.[23] On the eve of election day, Kos further wrote that he was "getting tired of media stories talking about GOP chances of picking up the Senate, when no sane analysis of the political landscape should reach this conclusion."[24] When the final votes were tallied, however, the results showed that the Republicans had won the Senate by gaining three seats, including the one formerly held by Wellstone in Minnesota. Benefiting from his West Coast location, Kos was able to analyze the election results before the night was over. Whereas most of his more than thirty-five entries for election day 2002 were simply one-sentence updates about various races, Kos's last posting was quite substantial. In "Congrats to Republicans," he maintained that the outcome stemmed from the fact that the "Dems adopted a strategy of appeasement, and then watched Bush stab all of those Democrats that supported him on the tax cut, or on the Iraq war." Such a position would continue to place Kos and the party's base at odds with the Democratic leadership, and Kos concluded his entry by arguing that change needed to start at the top. Sounding a note at once upbeat and challenging, he declared, "The pendulum will swing back our way. But before that happens, the Democratic Party needs to clean house and start over, and it should start with Gephardt and McAuliffe."[25]

In the next few months following the midterm election, Bush's intention to go to war regardless of a coherent explanation became crystal clear, and Kos regularly took aim at the rogue regime in D.C. Postings such as his vituperative "The Bush Administration Is Out of Control" showed that the *Daily Kos* was increasingly becoming a site that generated significant chatter. Written as an early-December weapons-inspection deadline approached, the entry lambasted Bush and company for their claims that Saddam was winning the PR battle over the issue of inspections. In Kos's view, the United States was losing the battle, and Bush looked like "nothing more than a foaming-at-the-mouth war-mongering lunantic [*sic*]."[26] Kos's posting received 183 responses, an impressive number, suggesting that his audience was both growing and inspired to participate. (As blogs emerged onto the scene, one of their signature features remained their ability to allow readers to comment; but the tit-for-tat sparring so common among the respondents, most of whom use aliases or remain anonymous, rendered the actual content of such discussions of dubious historical value.)

That same December also saw one of the earliest examples of the impact the blogosphere could have on national politics. In this

case, some leading bloggers other than Kos—in particular liberals Josh Marshall and Atrios, and conservatives including Andrew
Sullivan and David Frum—kept alive a story first buried in the
national media about Mississippi Republican senator Trent
Lott. Poised to become Senate majority leader, Lott had told a
one-hundredth-birthday party for Strom Thurmond that "we
wouldn't have had all those problems" if then-segregationist Thurmond had been elected president when he ran in 1948, just as the
controversy over civil rights was about to reshape the South. The
relentless chatter on the blogosphere first kept the story of Lott's
nostalgia for segregation afloat, and it soon helped fuel the escalating pressure on Lott to step down, which he did (from his post as
party leader, not from the Senate) after two weeks in the headlines.
According to the New York Post's far-right columnist John Podhoretz, a tireless foe of the threatening new media, Lott's demotion
was "The Internet's First Scalp." [27] Having posted only a few entries late in the controversy, Kos could not claim to be a leading
member of the head-hunting party. But before too long, he would
be a whipping boy for leading Democrats and Republicans alike.

Adamantly opposed to both the war and the Democrats' inco-
herent position on it, Kos seemed to be edging toward Howard
Dean's camp. Armstrong had already expressed his support,
most directly with the "Netroots for Howard Dean" statement. An
initial signpost of Kos's stance came with the results of the
MyDD/Daily Kos poll, carried out in late December 2002. Still
largely unknown beyond Vermont, Dean finished first, winning 43
percent of the approximately two thousand votes cast (Kerry, with
28 percent, placed second, and Wesley Clark came in third at 11
percent). In his analysis of the results, Kos suggested that "[p]art of
Dean's support may be due to MyDD's strong backing of the candidate, but I doubt it," pointing to Dean's success in other polling
done by Democrats.com and other sites. Kos, however, seemed to
slough off the notion that such support automatically meant that
Dean was a viable candidate. He wrote, "So how does Dean trans-
late this nascent support into cold hard campaign cash? Beats me. If

I knew, I would be a highly paid political consultant."[28] Yet over the next six months Kos began to show his support for Dean—and make a foray into the lucrative world of political consulting.

As the next presidential race began to take shape in early 2003, Kos made his sympathies for Dean, as well as for another emerging candidate, increasingly clear. In his regular "Cattle Call 2004" entries, a *Racing Form*–type ranking of contenders, Kos at first seemed simply to lean toward Dean, voicing both praise ("Dean is poised for a breakout") and mild yet prescient criticism ("Dean's propensity for off-the-cuff speeches . . . while oftentimes fun to watch, can lead to . . . major pitfalls").[29] But "Dean Brings Down the House," a lengthy (by blog standards) late-February report about Dean's apparently successful performance at a national DNC meeting, saw Kos starting to cast his lot. "This will be a contest between Kerry, Dean, Edwards and Graham," Kos predicted, adding, "So long as they keep it clean, I'd be happy with any of them. But I must say, Dean has been looking *real* good lately. Seriously— Dean got the crowd on its feet, while the others got catcalls or chirping crickets."[30] At the same time he started touting Dean, Kos began to throw water on one of the other main antiwar Democratic candidates, Dennis Kucinich. On the basis of one story by another blogger, in late February Kos declared in an entry headline that it was "Time for Kucinich to Drop Out." Josh Marshall of the blog *Talking Points Memo* alleged that Kucinich had played the race card when he first ran for Congress in the early 1970s, presenting himself to Cleveland's white Slavic voters as a safe alternative to black power. Of dubious substance, the charge was not pursued by the media or other candidates. But for Kos, it was apparently enough to condemn Kucinich.[31] In subsequent editions of "Cattle Call," Kos continued to treat the long-shot challenger with utter condescension, at one point simply writing "ugh" about his chances.[32] Meanwhile, an as-yet-undeclared contender began to catch Kos's fancy. "Clark in 2004? I'm Leaning That Way" read the title of a late March posting. "Clark's criticisms of the current war effort are directly on target," maintained Kos, "and are a big reason the Chickenhawk neocons are suddenly on the defensive." Kos concluded his pitch for the retired general to run by stating that he was "having fantasies of either a Dean/Clark or Clark/Dean ticket. At this point, and considering the way the war is going, this ticket would probably offer the strongest challenge to Bush." [33] With only one member of his dream antiwar ticket officially in the race, by the spring of 2003, Kos was clearly edging toward Dean.

Kos openly revealed his leanings in his coverage of the California Democratic Party's convention in mid-March. The event was a milestone of sorts for the blogosphere, as it was reportedly the first time that bloggers—Kos and Armstrong of *MyDD*—had been granted press credentials to cover a political convention. Nearly all of the leading presidential candidates came to address the gathering. After noting that Kerry had been a "flop," Kos gave a glowing report of Dean's performance. Dean, he wrote, "started by blasting Bush's invasion [of Iraq], and the crowd was instantly hooked. It was electrifying. . . . [When he] uttered Wellstone's line: 'I'm here to represent the Democratic Wing of the Democratic Party[,]' [p]eople went wild. His speech was repeatedly interrupted by chants of 'we want Dean!'" By Kos's estimate, shortly into the speech more than half of the convention's 1,600 delegates were waving Dean placards. The event took place on the eve of the invasion of Iraq, the same weekend that Bush, after meeting with Britain's Tony Blair and Spain's José Aznar in the Azores, issued his cowboy ultimatum giving Saddam forty-eight hours to leave Baghdad. At the meeting of California Democrats, Kos said, every speaker—other than John Kerry and John Edwards—attacked Bush on the war (Joe Lieberman did not attend). This overriding sentiment was thus not unique to Dean, but, as Kos and Armstrong would later emphasize in *Crashing the Gate*, the former governor of Vermont had clearly captured it most forcefully. Moreover, Dean, they said, was combining his antiwar message with a "broad-based populism" that made full use of the netroots. [34] And so as the California convention came to a close, Kos stated, "I reserve the right to change my mind, but as of now, Dean's the one." [35]

In early June 2003, Kos announced that he was in fact signing on to work as a technical consultant for the Dean campaign. Titled "Full Disclosure," the posting would remain front and center on the *Daily Kos* Web site for the next several months. As Kos explained, he and Armstrong had formed their own political consulting firm, thus joining the ranks of the political guns for hire that they so often derided. In any case, his role with the Dean campaign would be "technical, not message or strategy," so despite his ties to Dean, he would keep blogging. "I won't turn this into a rah-rah for Dean site," he assured his readers. "That's just not my style." A bit defensively, Kos also tried to allay potential criticism. "Some of you may be upset," he wrote, "but there's nothing I can do about it. I have to make my living, and if I can do so helping Democrats win elections, I can't imagine anything more exciting and fulfilling." His commitment to the cause of sacking "King George" was such that he would "work [his] ass off" to get any Democrat— "even Lieberman"—elected. That said, there was a reason he had gravitated toward the Dean campaign. At the time, he maintained, there was "only one campaign that plays the game in my world— the virtual world—and [that] was a natural fit for the kinds of services I could help provide. The Dean campaign wants to prove that the Internet can and will change the way campaigns are organized and run. I want to help prove them right." Kos received a flurry of mostly congratulatory comments in response to his announcement. But he also posted replies to some mild criticisms of his new role. One skeptic wrote, "Who cares what is proved by the way the battle was won and what computer/communications technologies were involved in spreading its message?" To this Kos insisted, "I care—the Dean campaign is . . . empowering the grassroots— giving them a direct stake in the candidacy. LISTENING to them. And technology is the enabler." While elsewhere Kos stressed Dean's antiwar message, here he pushed the candidate's effort to become the champion of the new medium. When someone asked him how this move toward Dean affected his stance toward Wesley Clark, he stated simply, "I got tired of waiting. I'll be pushing hard for a Clark VP, though." [36] Kos's comment here implied that he hoped to play a more active role in the campaign than simply that of a "technical consultant." It also suggested that the coverage of the early stages of the presidential campaign found on the *Daily Kos* would be compromised.

Regardless of his personal leanings, Kos could take credit for helping make a new medium, the blogosphere, a dynamic addition to the political scene. In mid-2003, it was not yet a recognized player, either by most conventional media outlets or by most political strategists other than Joe Trippi. But its passionate participants knew that they were onto something. In some respects blogs were akin to the invention of the Internet, or the advent of Web sites and e-mail as leading contemporary forms of communication. Obviously, only a small portion of blogs covered politics, and of that type, a much smaller number leaned to the left. But with his blog generating millions of hits, and receiving hundreds of comments, Kos felt comfortable in his role as the pied piper leading the chattering masses. In early June 2003, just before he revealed his connections to the Dean campaign, Kos observed, rather prophetically, "The passion we demonstrate for politics is making waves. The Dean people are pioneers in this regard, but by [the] next cycle all campaigns will be 'working' the blogs." The buzz around Dean had already started to take off, and at the end of June he would win the MoveOn poll, making Dean's ascent and the rise of the netroots inseparable. "Indeed," Kos asked his readers, "do any of you think Dean would be where he is without the power of the weblog? The other candidates, thanks to their techno-ignorance, have ceeded [sic] this entire territory to Dean. You better believe no one will make that mistake in future campaigns." [37] Though clearly ahead of the curve from a technological standpoint, the Dean campaign would stumble on the old-fashioned stump come primary season. But led by Kos, the blogosphere had only just begun to fight.

At the same that he was beginning to become an influential new member of the Democratic Party, Kos also started to outline his vision of what he hoped would be its future direction. In "What I Will Tell McAuliffe," a blueprint he wrote in mid-June 2003, Kos took aim at the interest-group coalition that made up the party's base. Ostensibly directed at the head of the DNC, the piece took more swipes against unions, environmentalists, and all the other traditional Democratic groups "organize[d] around narrow issues" than it did against McAuliffe. Naming the AFL-CIO and the Sierra Club as his only specific examples, Kos offered a sweeping indictment of the various interest groups, arguing that they "no longer represent anything remotely resembling the grassroots. Those organizations are riven by turf battles, thirst for political power and access, and are compromised by egos, unable to work together for the common good of the party and the people it represents." Such petty squabbling stood in sharp contrast to the emerging blogosphere, he said. Instead of unions or advocacy organizations, in Kos's view, the blogosphere was now "the true grassroots—working on behalf of a greater political movement, taking a 'big picture' approach to politics." Kos then tried to temper such hyperbole with a dose of realism. The blogosphere, he conceded, was still "small" in number; conspicuously, he left out how its largely white, middle-class demographic makeup rendered it unlike the labor movement or most other traditional liberal grassroots constituencies. Yet while "we don't wield much influence at this point," he continued, "we are growing, and with numbers comes strength—in financial donations, in raw manpower, in an activist community organized to promote the Democratic Party and its agenda." On this last account, he urged McAuliffe and the party to take cues from the Dean campaign. Unlike the party, or its leading figures, the Dean campaign had "embraced the blogosphere" and was thus "listen[ing] to the grassroots." Kos urged McAuliffe to make the rest of the party follow suit.[38]

As the 2004 campaign took shape in the middle of 2003, Kos had already outlined his causes: building the blogosphere, helping elect Dean, and ending both the war in Iraq and interest-group dominance over the Democratic Party. It was no small agenda, especially for a newcomer to the political scene. On only one of these scores—making the blogosphere a force in national politics—would Kos find success by the end of the 2004 campaign. That influence within the world of Democratic Party politics grew precisely in relation to the new sector's ability to raise money. On a smaller scale than MoveOn, but still at an impressive level, the *Daily Kos* became a source of Internet fund-raising that tapped into the wallets of the party's base. All told, by the end of 2004, Kos raised more than $500,000 for the thirteen congressional candidates he supported, and upwards of $100,000 each for both the Kerry campaign and the Democratic Party. Such totals provided a glimpse of the blogosphere's potential to back up its tough talk with cold, hard cash for its candidates. Though the new media had not yet become a major player, Democratic strategists, led by Joe Trippi and Howard Dean, saw the blogosphere as a flowering plant to be nurtured. And the Democrats failure to defeat George W. Bush in 2004 merely proved to be the blogosphere's gain. As progressives figured out their next move, Kos and company surged to the forefront of the effort to transform the party.

In the homestretch of the 2004 election, Kos served as a columnist covering the American political scene for the *Guardian*. Here he outlined what would become another of his rallying cries: the need for the Democrats to fight back against the "Rightwing Noise Machine." In his debut column at the end of September 2004, Kos described it as "the multiple think tanks and a well-oiled message machine that has a stranglehold on American discourse. From the *Weekly Standard, Wall Street Journal, Drudge Report* and Murdoch's Fox News, to (more recently) the mindless drones in the rightwing blogosphere, the right enjoys the ability to control entire news cycles, holding them hostage for entire elections." In the 2000 campaign, that machine had routinely pilloried Al Gore. Even though Gore had won the election, Kos maintained that the Democrats were "outmanoeuvred in Florida, legally and rhetorically. [And we] looked around for a 'liberal media,' yet found nothing of the sort." The 2000 debacle was thus a "wake-up call" for Kos and many others. But he was careful not to give too much credit to the blogosphere. While the "seeds of a liberal media blossomed on-line," Kos noted that he and other like-minded bloggers had lots of company—from the Dean campaign, liberal think tanks, Air America, MoveOn, Americans Coming Together, and Berkeley's Lakoff. The prospects were hopeful, but the right had spent three decades building its infrastructure and, Kos said, "We can't be expected to counteract that in one year."[39] Absent from Kos's analysis here was the role of the party. Even though it at times attacked the party for ideological backsliding, the right's noise machine had long been on good terms with the Republican leadership. Matching up the left-liberal base of the Democrats with the party's conservative centrist brass would be a more difficult task.

Even in the wake of Bush's victory that November, Kos nonetheless remained hopeful. Like Michael Moore and MoveOn's Pariser, he quickly found silver linings in a very dark cloud, and urged his shock troops not to lose their momentum. In a column posted on the *Guardian*'s Web site on Wednesday, November 3, Kos first ripped apart the Republicans' line of attack. Bush and company had won, he said, "by demonising an entire group of people—gays and lesbians. By cynical appeals to religion. By slandering a true war hero. And, most importantly, by scaring people." Such a benighted message had been faithfully transmitted, of course, by the right-wing noise machine. The "explosion in the blog world," growth of a "liberal radio network," and other noble attempts to fight back were no match for the machine powered by Fox News. Although never openly stated, "God, guns and gays," Kos noted, was a powerful mantra for the Republicans. But in response, there emerged a "great resurgence in progressive activism," and "[n]one of these new activists heeded the call to arms only to abandon the fight today." The big-money donors like Soros and Lewis would help build the new progressive infrastructure. Meanwhile, "The blogs will continue to grow, as will our new radio personalities. The seeds of a genuinely liberal media have been planted and will continue to bear fruit." Like a halftime speech from a coach whose team had already lost, Kos's pep talk contained both platitudes and insight into why his side had been defeated. To extend his metaphor, the New Blue Media had formed a productive small farm, but the right-wing noise machine was still the giant agribusiness next door. "The United States," he told his *Guardian* readers, "is a bitterly divided nation, at war with itself." While he further assured them that progressives "will be training our forces, re-evaluating our tactics, [and] marshalling our strength," what he didn't mention was that the next front in this war would be a struggle for control of the Democratic Party.[40]

As Armstrong and Kos triumphantly recounted the story in *Crashing the Gate*, the netroots led the charge to make Dean the new chair of the DNC. The battle pitted the Deaniacs versus the party establishment, the latter inextricably bound to the pro-corporate legacy of outgoing chair Terry McAuliffe. According to Armstrong and Kos, "The bloggers, just about the only regular source of regular information on the DNC chairman race, became a go-to source for news by party enthusiasts and insiders. And we trained our guns on anyone in the way of the reform candidates." (Armstrong and Kos were also friendly with New Democratic Network president Simon Rosenberg, a lesser-known but well-connected player who eventually wrote the foreword to *Crashing the Gate*.) The bloggers first made a splash at the meeting of state party chairs in Orlando in December 2004. There Armstrong and his comrade Matt Stoller were "tossed out of the convention hall for blogging the event." Such hostility merely fueled the fire against the party establishment. The *Daily Kos* and *MyDD* first took aim at candidate Leo Hindery, a cable TV tycoon and major party benefactor supported by McAuliffe, Gephardt, and Tom Daschle. According to Armstrong and Kos, once their blogs exposed Hindery's role in helping bankroll the notorious Iowa TV spot that linked Osama bin Laden to Howard Dean, Hindery saw the handwriting on the wall and dropped out of the race.[41] In a postmortem analysis of what he termed Hindery's "absurd candidacy," the *New Republic*'s Ryan Lizza also noted various bloggers' work in revealing that Hindery, a former Republican, had greased various GOP candidates even after becoming a Democrat.[42] After sending Hindery away on his private jet, the bloggers then issued their aforementioned takedowns of former congressmen Martin Frost and Tim Roemer. Among other results, such assaults indicated that the blogosphere was indeed changing the pace of insider politics—with many thousands of investigative reporters working around the clock, no longer could the contradictory and/or shady pasts of obscure candidates be shielded from media scrutiny.

When it came time for the 447 members of the Democratic National Committee to finally vote on the new chair in February 2005, Dean was for all intents and purposes the last candidate standing. The bloggers most certainly had been at the forefront of the attacks on rival candidates. Dean's own efforts to win over the so-called 447 had been widely successful, however. Dean had told them of his plan to reinvigorate the state Democratic parties, and of his desire to make the Democrats compete in all fifty states—a departure from the national party leadership's recent strategy of writing off many Red States. With its implication of more funding and more organizers for each state, such a message was surely music to the ears of the many party representatives who had been ignored over the years. Yet when combined with his provocative style and antiwar positioning, this decentralizing move only increased the opposition to Dean by the party's brass. As Lizza noted, "From the congressional leadership to the governors to the Clintons, top Democrats were all terrified of a Dean victory. They believe he will turn what is essentially a low-key fund-raising and management position into a lightning rod for GOP attacks." According to Lizza, "one of the most inept attempts" to undermine Dean came from Nancy Pelosi, who went so far as to back Roemer, a candidate who favored the privatization of Social Security and opposed abortion. That the whole affair was clearly a victory for both Dean and the insurgent netroots was perhaps captured best by James Carville, the ubiquitous stalking horse for the conservative party leadership. Carville told Lizza that the controversy and attention surrounding the DNC race made the Democrats seem "pathetic." After all, "This is supposed to be a rigged deal. You think the Republicans would do it this way?"[43] The party's attempt to conduct business as usual, of course, had produced figures such as McAuliffe, whose track record was one of continued failure. In leading the charge for Dean, the netroots were helping create the possibility of future success. Score one for the insurgency.

Dean's message to the leadership of the state parties went beyond simply declaring his intention to make the Democrats compete in every state. He also vowed to help move the party away from an interest-group coalition, in hopes of creating a big-tent political party like the Republicans, who had managed to hold together a spectrum of constituents ranging from libertarians to flat-earth evangelicals. In his presidential campaign, Dean had sparked controversy by proclaiming his desire "to be the candidate for guys with Confederate flags in their pickup trucks." In early November 2003, Dean, then the front-runner, made that statement in an interview with the *Des Moines Register.* He continued by explaining, "We can't beat George Bush unless we appeal to a broad cross-section of Democrats." Such a position provoked a flurry of "outrage" from candidates including John Kerry, Dick Gephardt, Joe Lieberman, and Al Sharpton, who kept the issue alive.[44] However, Dean had first made such a statement the preceding February—at a meeting of the Democratic National Committee. According to CNN, at that event, the 447 cheered loudly when Dean told them, "White folks in the South who drive pickup trucks with Confederate flag decals on the back ought to be voting with us, and not [Republicans], because their kids don't have health insurance either, and their kids need better schools too."[45] Dean's main point, that class issues could expand the party's base, was a good one; but his choice of symbolism to describe his target audience—Confederate-flag-waving southerners—was obviously poor judgment. In any case, as the 447 well knew, making the

Democrats competitive in every state required the embrace of a range of issues beyond those put forth by the liberal interest-group coalition that had dominated the party for the past two decades.

For Armstrong, Kos, and other leading voices of the netroots, Dean's position was the right one. In *Crashing the Gate*, Armstrong and Kos recalled an April 2005 gathering of leading progressives held in Monterey, California, where they joined Joan Blades and Wes Boyd from MoveOn as well as leaders of various liberal organizations, including Kim Gandy of the National Organization for Women and Maggie Fox of the Sierra Club. According to the authors, the war between the big-tent advocates and the "single-issue dogmatists" escalated throughout the weekend. The primary example Armstrong and Kos cited was Gandy and the abortion-rights crowd's success in forcing Congressman Jim Langevin to withdraw his challenge to Senator Lincoln Chafee, a liberal Republican in the nation's most Democratic state. Langevin, a Democrat, on most issues had a very progressive record, which included a vote against the war and against the amendment banning same-sex marriages, as well as high marks from labor, seniors, and a host of other liberal groups. But Langevin had also voted to restrict abortions, whereas Chafee had remained solidly prochoice (at least in his own direct votes on the issue; he had supported the nomination of anti-choice judges including Janice Rogers Brown and Samuel Alito). In May 2005, NARAL actually gave Chafee an early endorsement. For Kos and Armstrong, such dogmatism on the part of the abortion-rights wing of the party was sinking the Democrats. "What candidate passes every single litmus test?" they asked. "The fact remains that Langevin would never have gotten a chance to vote against abortion in a Democratic-led Senate, and otherwise would've been a huge boon to the larger progressive cause."[46] In retrospect, neither side won this debate. Sheldon Whitehouse, a prochoice liberal Democrat, ended up defeating Chafee in the 2006 campaign. The lesson for both the single-issue advocates and the big-tent adherents proved to be one of patience. At least in a state as Blue as Rhode Island, there was no need for

NARAL to back Chafee, nor for the netroots to line up behind Langevin. Whitehouse's victory showed that the party need not necessarily concede too much ground on issues dear to its base.

At the same time, the Democrats' choice of a challenger to archconservative Senator Rick Santorum in Pennsylvania threatened to exacerbate the rift between the big-tent adherents and the abortion-rights advocates. Led by Chuck Schumer and Hillary Clinton, the party's brass had chosen State Treasurer Bob Casey Jr., son of the former Pennsylvania governor, as their preferred candidate. Antichoice, anti-same-sex marriage, and pro-war, Casey could only be considered progressive because of his good relationship with labor and his proconsumer background; during the campaign, his support for the nominations of John Roberts and fellow Pennsylvanian Samuel Alito to the Supreme Court further illustrated his antiprogressive bias. His backing of Alito prompted former NARAL president Kate Michelman, a resident of the Philadelphia area, to consider a primary challenge to Casey. "As a Pennsylvanian, I am particularly appalled that local and national Democrats would hand our Senate nomination to someone who openly supports giving *Roe* an Alito-induced death," Michelman stated. Michelman never made a bid, presumably because the Alito controversy occurred in February 2006, just three months before the state's primary. As John Nichols noted in the *Nation*, another progressive candidate, former treasurer Barbara Hafer, had dropped out a year earlier. According to Nichols, Pennsylvania activists had "watched national Democrats elbow out" the prochoice Hafer (the state's governor, Ed Rendell, had also pressured Hafer to drop out, in order to pave the way for Casey). As Kathy Miller, outgoing president of Pennsylvania's NOW chapter, observed regarding abortion rights, "A lot of women feel ignored, like the boys decided that this is a throwaway issue." Pennsylvania progressives were thus left with one candidate in the race, college professor Chuck Pennachio.[47]

Quixotic as its challenge to Casey may have been, Pennachio's campaign posed a real challenge for the netroots. Would the new legions of activists stick to their principles, even if it meant backing a losing horse? Or would they play ball with the party's leadership by supporting insider candidates like Casey, who shared few of the activists' progressive ideals? This particular primary campaign saw the leaders of the netroots split, with Kos sticking with Pennachio and MoveOn lining up very early behind Casey. A blogger with the handle of "Chuck Pennachio for US Senate" regularly contributed to the *Daily Kos* site. The posts documented the long-shot campaign's need for money, volunteers, and simply attention. As Pennachio explained to Nichols, Pennsylvania's recent electoral history—victories for Gore and Kerry, and the repeat elections of prochoice Republican Arlen Specter to the Senate and Democrat Ed Rendell as governor—showed that there was no need to compromise on abortion. Pennachio also made his opposition to Iraq and support for universal health care his top priorities. Such solid progressive credentials apparently meant little to MoveOn, however. In June 2005, or almost one year before the primary, the MoveOn PAC took a poll of its members in the Keystone State regarding the contest between Casey and Pennachio. As Gwen Shaffer reported in the *Philadelphia Weekly*, the group seemed to stack the deck in favor of Casey. "Most political observers believe Casey has a lock on the Democratic nomination, and we tend to agree," MoveOn's e-mail missive read. "But we wanted to check with MoveOn's Pennsylvania members before we endorse anyone." Absurdly, the e-mail's bio of Casey failed to mention his antichoice position or his support for the war in Iraq, and it provided a favorable quote about Casey from Howard Dean, which Pennachio said was taken out of context. Such a rigged poll produced its desired result, with Casey garnering two-thirds of the vote. MoveOn followed up with a fund-raising letter in late June, and within twenty-four hours, it had raised $150,000 for Casey. It is no stretch to suggest that a fair presentation of the rival candidates' views could easily have produced the opposite result in terms of votes and money, thus putting the Pennachio campaign on the map.[48] But, one year before the primary, MoveOn chose to back a pro-war, antichoice candidate, asking nothing in return. Score one for the party brass.

Yet in the summer of 2005, the netroots soon seemed like the vanguard again, when bloggers spearheaded the unexpectedly high-profile campaign of Iraq War veteran Paul Hackett. Hackett challenged Republican Jean Schmidt in an off-year special congressional election in suburban Cincinnati, a longtime Republican stronghold. Against the conservative Schmidt, leader of a Greater Cincinnati "Right to Life" group and strongly pro-war, Hackett ran as a libertarian Democrat, who memorably called Bush a "chicken hawk" and a "son of a bitch" for his handling of the war. Hackett said that he had been opposed to the war, but had volunteered to fight because of his loyalty to fellow marines. By the summer of 2005, he had adopted a moderate position on what to do next. "We need to develop an exit strategy and execute it," Hackett told the *Cincinnati Inquirer*. "That strategy must commit 100% of our efforts to training the 140,000 Iraqi soldiers to do the jobs that the United States is doing now. We cannot again falsely declare victory."[49] Led by Chris Bowers and Jerome Armstrong of *MyDD*, the netroots began to champion Hackett after he easily won the five-way primary in June (Kos was a latecomer to this campaign). As David Goodman reported in a lengthy recap of the race in *Mother Jones*, the Democratic Congressional Campaign Committee (DCCC) initially showed little interest in Hackett, because he had not yet raised $100,000. When the netroots raised more than $150,000 by mid-July, the national leadership got interested and brought in some big guns to raise money and work on behalf of Hackett, including James Carville, Wesley Clark, and Max Cleland.[50] Hackett's campaign quickly gained national attention, garnering a front-page story in the *New York Times*. Hackett was narrowly defeated (52–48 percent) in early August. But if not for the netroots' work on Hackett's behalf, his campaign would never have gotten off the ground. Writing for *TomPaine.com*, Armstrong said that the campaign's near success echoed "what Howard Dean first tapped into—the growing movement within the Democratic Party willing to take the Republicans head on about the direction of this nation," and called for more direct collaboration between the netroots and the DCCC.[51]

Like MoveOn, Armstrong, and nearly all other netroots figureheads, Kos made no secret of his desire to win back Congress for the Democrats at all costs. In a lengthy profile in the *Washington Monthly* in early 2006, Benjamin Wallace-Wells portrayed Kos as more of a tactician than a strategist. Kos, the writer observed, possessed a "relentless competitiveness, founded not on any particular set of political principles, but on an obsession with tactics —and in particular, with the tactics of a besieged minority, struggling for survival: stand up for your principles, stay united, and never back down from a fight." Kos concurred with the analysis, telling Wallace-Wells, "They want to make me into the latest Jesse Jackson, but I'm not ideological at all. . . . I'm just all about winning." Although they may not have agreed with him on which issues would carry them forward, many party leaders surely respected such determination on Kos's part. The profile indeed carried a number of favorable comments about Kos from non-DLC party officials (in August 2005, Kos had declared, but never executed, a "secret plan to destroy the DLC" because of the group's relentless support for the war). The DCCC's John Lapp called the rise of liberal blogs like the *Daily Kos* "a signal event in political history, like the Kennedy-Nixon debates, in how it gets people involved." Meanwhile, the New Democratic Network's Simon Rosenberg insisted that "frankly I don't think there's anyone who's had the potential to revolutionize the Democratic Party that Markos does." What these and other players wanted from Kos, though, bore no resemblance to a "revolution." Rather, Kos and the rest of the netroots offered new life for the party.[52] The bloggers stirred up the younger generation, got people to write checks and volunteer, and encouraged their many readers to fight both the Republicans and the right-wing noise machine. For the party, because of both his reach and his volatile temperament, Kos was (and is) worth having on your side.

With the first annual YearlyKos convention in June 2006, Kos became a familiar name and face to audiences well beyond the blogosphere. Held at the Riviera Hotel in Las Vegas, the event drew over nine hundred bloggers and around a hundred journalists, many from the leading print and broadcast outlets (or the "MSM," blogger shorthand for mainstream media). Aided by his own personal media team, Kos was the star of the show, signing autographs and rallying the troops. "These have been heady days for the People Power Movement, and it's only four years old," he reminded a cheering ballroom crowd.[53] Many leading figures in the Democratic Party, including Harry Reid, Barbara Boxer, Howard Dean, Wesley Clark, Bill Richardson, and Mark Warner, showed to up to curry favor. "The netroots is key to giving people the courage to stand up for what is right," Boxer told the gathered legions in a keynote speech.[54] The event gave various print outlets the opportunity to consider the rise of the liberal blogs. Not surprisingly, right-wing magazines like the *Weekly Standard* and the *National Review* covered the convention with a cynical eye, emphasizing the upstarts' self-congratulatory delusions of grandeur. Less expected, perhaps, were the views found in the *New York Times.* The paper's often-surly lead national politics reporter, Adam Nagourney, who was on friendly terms with the party's leadership, actually seemed impressed. With "bloggers, Democratic operatives, candidates and Washington reporters" all rubbing shoulders, Nagourney noted, "it seemed that bloggers were well on the way to becoming—dare we say it?—part of the American political establishment."[55] Yet for the "iconoclastic" columnist Maureen Dowd, however, the bloggers were a bunch of wannabes—"Even as Old Media is cowed by New Media, New Media is trying to become, rather than upend, Old Media," she wrote.[56] (Never one to mince words, Kos told a blogger from Seattle's *Stranger,* "Maureen Dowd is an insecure, catty bitch.")[57] The *New Republic's* Ryan Lizza provided more in-depth analysis than Dowd. Previewing the critique of Kos and company that Matt Bai would make in his book *The Argument* (2007), Lizza observed that "while the bloggers and their readers are obviously liberal, they aren't like any other party interest group. . . . There is no single issue that binds them together, and they have no discernible agenda." [58] They may not have had a fully coherent agenda, but their goal—influence over the party's direction—was becoming apparent in the attention the convention received from broadcast media, in particular *Meet the Press*. As Kos told Tim Russert, the blogosphere had created "a place where good, strong, progressive voices can get together, and we can talk, and we can motivate each other, and we can organize, and we can do and plan the kind of hard work that it takes to win elections." [59] Now a fixture in MSM political conversation, Kos and company clearly had arrived.

In order to show that they did more than generate hype and funding for campaigns, the liberal blogs needed to show that they could actually help win elections. In the fall of 2005, Kos began to assemble his own slate of candidate, the so-called Fighting Dems. His work paralleled the efforts of the Democratic Congressional Campaign Committee to recruit a similar set of candidates for 2006, but Kos doggedly asserted his independence from the DCCC. Inspired by Hackett's campaign, this group consisted of military veterans running for office who were not incumbents. Eventually headlined by Jim Webb, who won a Senate seat in Virginia, the roster at its height included more than eighty-five candidates. Thirty-one either dropped out or lost in the primaries, in some cases to other Fighting Dems; by the fall of 2006, the group included sixty-one candidates for national office, plus four other parents of Iraq War veterans. Beginning in October 2005, Kos interviewed one candidate each week for Sam Seder's *Majority Report* show on Air America (prior to the weekly slot, Kos had already been a frequent guest on the show). The slate offered the chance for Democrats to counteract the right's post-9/11 charge that they were weak on national security. It also gave Kos a chance to try his hand at becoming a power broker, in the process enhancing his own rep as a tough-minded vet who looked out for his fellow soldiers. "I wouldn't be who I am today without my service to

my nation," he wrote in late 2005, as the ranks of the Fighting
Dems began to grow.[60] But even as Kos remained solidly against
the war, the same could not be said for all of the Fighting Dems.
The Web sites of forty-five of the sixty-one candidates in the final
group expressed clear statements against the war, but only thirty-
two of them proposed some form of imminent withdrawal. Of the
remaining sixteen, only two expressed open support for the war.
But the others were surprisingly (or perhaps tactically) unclear
about any position, a stance made even more conspicuous given
that these candidates were billed as Fighting Dems. In the end, just
six of the sixty-one candidates emerged victorious, five in the
House (three from Pennsylvania) and Webb in the Senate; two of
the parents of vets won in the House as well. As Garance Franke-
Ruta observed in a postelection analysis in the *New Republic*, many
in the group "never had a chance. They were political novices
challenging incumbent Republicans in traditionally red districts
and states. All things considered, it should come as no surprise that
so many of them went down in flames."[61]

In one of the more high-profile races of the 2006 campaign,
Kos actually backed a Fighting Dem against a more progressive
opponent in the Democratic primary. In Illinois, archconservative
Republican Henry Hyde had announced his retirement. As
Nicholas Jahr reported in the *Brooklyn Rail*, Christine Cegelis,
who had turned in a strong showing in 2004 (44 percent) against
the veteran incumbent Hyde, was the preferred choice of the
activists; Kevin Spidel, deputy director of the solidly antiwar Progressive Democrats of America, had agreed to manage Cegelis's
campaign. But led by Rahm Emanuel, a Clinton loyalist and head
of the DCCC, the party made a strong push for Tammy Duckworth, a vet who had lost both legs and the use of her right arm in
Iraq. Duckworth's identity as a courageous wounded vet, however,
was far more inspiring than her actual position on the war. While
Cegelis called for "a comprehensive timetable for withdrawal of
the majority of our combat troops at the earliest possible date,"
Duckworth maintained that "we can't simply pull up stakes and

create a security vacuum."[62] With the party's support, Duckworth prevailed by just a thousand votes in the Democratic primary in March. For his part, Kos was officially "neutral" in the race for the suburban Chicago district where he grew up (and once worked for Hyde). Yet even as he deplored Emanuel's party-boss maneuverings against Cegelis, and said that both were "stellar candidates," Kos clearly pushed for Duckworth. He featured her in one of his Air America Fighting Dem profiles in mid-January, just as the primary race began to take shape. Typically, Kos previewed each week's segment with a short entry on his site. His Duckworth preview, though, was unusually lengthy, and in it he poured the praise on thick, calling her a "woman of incredible courage and accomplishment," truly representative of a group that was already "fight[ing] back against those in DC that are getting our men and women killed in un[n]ecessary wars."[63] Despite the best efforts of both Kos and the DCCC, Duckworth went down to defeat that fall (and in the process, sparked a war between the DCCC's Emanuel and the DNC's Howard Dean over funding for Duckworth's campaign). More to the point here is that Kos's loyalty to his fellow veterans was apparently so strong that he was ready to excuse their lack of opposition to the war.

By contrast, Jim Webb's Senate triumph in Virginia became one of the biggest victories for the netroots, and here the candidate ran on a platform more in sync with Kos: he pitched himself as a Fighting Dem strongly opposed to the war. A long shot early in the campaign, Webb—a decorated Vietnam vet and former secretary of the navy under Reagan, with a son in the marines—sprang to life in August, helped by both his opponent's now-classic bumbling and his friends in the liberal blogosphere. On Friday, August 11, 2006, Virginia's incumbent Senator George Allen, then considered to be a future contender for the 2008 Republican nomination for president, made a campaign stop in the town of Breaks, near the Kentucky border. One of the people in the gathering of a hundred or so, an Indian American named S.R. Sidarth, was there as a Webb volunteer to videotape the event for the campaign's

Web site—work more commonly known as video-blogging. As recorded by Sidarth, Allen first told the crowd that he was "going to run this campaign on positive, constructive ideas," before launching into his fifteen seconds of infamy. Pointing to Sidarth, Allen said, "This fellow here, over here with the yellow shirt, macaca, or whatever his name is. He's with my opponent. He's following us around everywhere. And it's just great." At that, many of the Allen supporters chuckled. After briefly referring to Webb's support from "a bunch of Hollywood movie moguls," Allen then said, "Let's give a welcome to macaca, here. Welcome to America and the real world of Virginia." Seamlessly, the senator then shifted into a discussion of the "war on terror."[64] What might have been politics as usual—a Confederate-flag-loving Virginia politician stoking the knee-jerk, xenophobic sentiments of his base—soon morphed into something far greater. Allen indeed became the buffoonish poster child who illustrated the ability of blogs to transform politics.

Allen's downward spiral did not exactly happen overnight, but it did begin over the weekend. The Webb campaign first posted the video on YouTube. That Sunday, August 13, a Virginia-based blogger named "Not Larry Sabato" (whose name referred to the University of Virginia's ubiquitous political prognosticator) then called attention to it on his blog. By late Monday afternoon, other blogs including *Wonkette* had picked up on it; the webmag *Salon.com*, a forerunner of sorts to blogs, followed suit. Blogger ChrisNYC posted the YouTube video on the *Daily Kos* later that day, and late in the evening, the *Washington Post*'s Web site ran what would be a front-page story in the following morning's paper. Headlined "Allen Quip Provokes Outrage, Apology," staff writers Tim Craig and Michael D. Shear's story provided rich details of the incident. "Depending on how it is spelled," they wrote, "the word *macaca* could mean either a monkey that inhabits the Eastern Hemisphere or a town in South Africa. In some European cultures, macaca is also considered a racial slur against African immigrants, according to several Web sites that track ethnic slurs." That

Sidarth, whose parents were from India but who was born and raised in Fairfax County and was now a student at the University of Virginia, fit none of those descriptions made Allen's choice of words all the more ridiculous. The senator further continued to stumble when pressed to explain the term "macaca." "I don't know what it means," he told Craig and Shear; he did suggest that it sounded like "Mohawk," the nickname his staff had given to Sidarth (because of his haircut). Regarding his "Welcome to America" comment, Allen claimed that he was really saying welcome "to the real world. Get outside the Beltway and get to the real world."[65] Comfortably ahead at the time, Allen would quickly begin to slide in the polls. And though it occurred in the dog days of August, the incident stayed in the news cycle throughout the fall campaign.

Given Allen's eventual loss to Webb that November, the question that arises is this: To what extent can the liberal blogosphere claim that it influenced the race? The best answer may be that both the Allen camp and Webb himself agreed that blogs indeed shaped the outcome. "I have never seen a campaign that was more driven by liberal bloggers," an Allen strategist told *National Review* editor Rich Lowry.[66] Meanwhile, as quoted by a gleefully victorious Kos, Webb stated that "[t]he netroots have been a tremendous help to my campaign and a huge inspiration to me personally. I am where I am in large part because of their support."[67] Such pronouncements referred to far more than just the blogs' role in highlighting and keeping alive the macaca incident. In retrospect, that moment appeared to be only Webb's point of departure. From there, he suddenly became a viable candidate, and Kos and Armstrong led the charge, helping raise nearly $200,000 for Webb. Kos posted regular entries on Webb throughout the fall campaign, calling special attention to the campaign's announcement that Webb's son, Jimmy, an infantry lance corporal in the marines, was being sent to Iraq. "Here's something not a single Republican in the Senate has to worry about," Kos said by way of introducing a letter from Webb's campaign manager on the upcoming deployment.[68] Ultimately, the blogosphere could not take full credit for Webb's victory, but the candidate's success showed quite clearly that Kos and company were a force to be reckoned with. The work of the bloggers on behalf of Webb seemed even further vindicated a few months later, when the freshman senator delivered a stirring antiwar, economically populist rebuttal to Bush's 2007 State of the Union message. With a real Fighting Dem as the new face of the liberal wing of the Senate, Kos surely could be happy.

Even more dramatically than the Webb example, it was Ned Lamont's campaign to unseat Joe Lieberman that most galvanized the netroots and illustrated their emerging ability to influence Democratic Party politics. Lieberman, the former Democratic vice-presidential nominee, had angered many in the netroots base because of his dogged support of the Iraq War and willingness to back the Bush administration on many other issues. Yet the relative suddenness and initial success of Lamont's challenge showed that the most entrenched politicians could no longer take incumbency for granted. As 2006 began, Lamont, a Greenwich cable TV businessman, was neither an official candidate nor even a familiar name for most Connecticut voters. But word of his potential candidacy had been floating around insider circles for a while, and in early January 2006, Kos reported that Lamont would be throwing his hat into the ring. "The big questions," Kos wrote, "are whether DFA [Democracy for America] and MoveOn [will] get involved as they've been threatening the past couple of months." [69] In an initial assessment of whether the blogosphere should focus its energies on the race, *MyDD*'s Matt Stoller cautioned against taking on a Democratic stalwart. An insurgent campaign, he argued, would encounter opposition from both the state and national party, as well from various interest groups (e.g., labor) that had a good relationship with Lieberman. Surprisingly, especially given the senator's manifest views of the war, Stoller also feared that "in picking this fight against Lieberman, we're not really running 'on' something. I see no thread of articulated principles here that would justify a Lieberman challenge."[70] A flurry of blogger responses quickly suggested to Stoller that there were plenty of principles at stake, most dramatically Lieberman's support for Bush's war. And so less than a month later, Stoller came back with another posting called "Ned Lamont, Political Entrepreneur." He had spent time with Lamont in Connecticut, and beyond just the candidate's progressive belief in universal health care and his opposition to the war, Lamont, in Stoller's view, represented a new breed of politicians. "What we face as a country is systemic corruption, not a few bad apples," Stoller wrote. "And the way to shift that system is through a new crop of entrepreneurial leaders who seek to occupy and create new political space, not to swell on the legacy of the New Dealers. Ned Lamont is one of these leaders."[71] A media exec who was new media–friendly, and a candidate with progressive positions but not beholden to liberal interest groups, Lamont indeed seemed to be the netroots' ideal figurehead.

The Lamont campaign brought together the two main components of the netroots: the blogosphere, led by Kos; and the organizers, driven by Democracy for America and MoveOn. Kos initially helped frame the battle as the next front in the war for control of the party, labeling it "Old world politics versus new. Insurance and corporate interests versus people-power. A Fox News Democrat versus a real one."[72] Through the winter and spring, the *Daily Kos* paid steady attention to the race, helping to raise media interest in, as well as volunteers and cash for, the campaign. When things began to heat up in mid-May, Kos appeared in a TV commercial for Lamont. Then, when the "blogfather" came to New Haven for what was supposed to be a stop on his book tour for *Crashing the Gate*, the event essentially became a Lamont rally, with the candidate himself showing up, and Kos wearing a Lamont T-shirt and a button showing Lieberman's now-infamous kiss with Bush. Meanwhile, Democracy for America, the group headed by Jim Dean, Howard's brother who lived in Connecticut and had long been involved in local politics there, threw its support behind Lamont. "Ned Lamont has been loud and clear about America's

position in Iraq and world affairs, one of the most important concerns for voters," Dean said.[73] That same week in late May,
MoveOn polled its 50,000 members in Connecticut. The vote
took place in a twenty-four-hour time frame, so only 5,500 members weighed in; but of that number, more than 85 percent backed
Lamont. In reporting the endorsement to MoveOn's e-mail list,
Eli Pariser quoted one local member who stated that "Lamont is
exactly the sort of candidate MoveOn should support: a true progressive running against the forces of Beltway conventional wisdom and accommodation of the Radical Right."[74] The MoveOn
endorsement now made the Connecticut campaign national
news. And as Scott McLean, chair of the political science department at Quinnipiac University, the polling source, told the *Los Angeles Times*, MoveOn's nod "shows the grass-roots and money
[donors] . . . that there is something behind Ned Lamont. "It's big.
It's huge," he said.[75] Like a start-up Internet company in the late
1990s, in just three months, Lamont's campaign had fully taken off.

In taking on Lieberman, the netroots had declared war on a favorite candidate of the DLC, and as usual, that group's figureheads
responded to the challenge by sounding the alarm bells. "A very
simple thing happened that changed Democratic politics dramatically, and that was that the war turned bad," stated Al From, who
would continue to support Bush's war well beyond the 2006 elections. "There's a group in our party that makes a lot of noise and I
don't think they've ever won an election," he declared. Now,
"They're trying to take out one of the great statesmen our party
has and that's wrong."[76] Indeed, "This is a fight for the soul of the
Democratic Party," DLC fellow Marshall Wittmann told the *Los
Angeles Times*. "It will have repercussions for the 2008 presidential
campaign and whether centrists will feel comfortable within the
Democratic Party."[77] The DLC's statements seemed mild when
compared to the outrage expressed by members of the Beltway
punditocracy, many of whom were good friends with Lieberman.
David Brooks of the *New York Times*, who had recently attacked
Kos as a "Keyboard Kingpin" backed by "Kossack cultists," spear-

headed the assault.[78] "What's happening to Lieberman can only be described as a liberal inquisition," Brooks said. For Brooks, the Lamont campaign represented nothing less than an attempt by "the upscale revivalists on the left [to] reduce everything to Iraq, and all who are deemed impure must be cleansed away."[79] On ABC, Beltway insider Cokie Roberts predicted that a Lamont victory would be a "disaster" for the Democrats, a telltale sign of "liberal blogs and all that taking over the party."[80] The *Washington Post*'s longtime columnist David Broder attacked Lamont's "elitist insurgents" who were pushing the party "toward a stronger antiwar stand," which Broder said would hurt the Democrats in the midterm elections.[81] And *Newsweek*'s Jonathan Alter stated that the bloggers who had "noisily intervened" in the campaign did so because they "brook no dissent" on Iraq. In so doing, Alter said, the netroots had created "a cannibalistic distraction" within the Democratic Party.[82] Come November, the DLC and the Beltway pundits could take comfort in their pal Lieberman's reelection (as an independent). But these same insiders' "certainty" about the way in which the war issue would damage the Democrats' chances in the midterms ultimately proved to be nothing but hot air.

In terms of both style and substance, Lamont's effort indeed shook up the political establishment. In a lengthy article just prior to the primary, the *New York Times* assessed the Lamont campaign's reliance on blogs to spread its message and to attack its rival. (The *Times*, it should be noted, had climbed aboard the Lamont bandwagon with a somewhat surprising endorsement before the primary.)[83] Written by Mike McIntire and Jennifer Medina, the story began by explaining how after Lieberman had scored points by showing how Lamont held stock in Halliburton, a blog named *Firedoglake* had exposed the fact that Lieberman also held stock in Halliburton, a revelation that the Lamont campaign then circulated widely. McIntire and Medina cited this as just "one example of how the Lamont campaign [has] tried to harness the energy, anger and muckraking zeal of an expanding network of blogs in its effort to unseat Mr. Lieberman, the three-term senator." At the time, Lamont's Web site carried links to seventeen sympathetic blogs, and the *Times* reporters further said that the campaign's consultants "communicate daily with as many as 150 bloggers who offer advice, pass on intelligence, encourage campaign contributions and sometimes leave their computers long enough to pester Mr. Lieberman at campaign events." A bit belatedly, other candidates, including Lieberman and Hillary Clinton, had begun to catch on, hiring their own bloggers. *Firedoglake's* founder, Jane Hamsher, who worked on the Lamont campaign (a tie that Lieberman tried to play up), downplayed the role of blogs. "My sense is that most people in Connecticut today don't know what a blog is," Hamsher told the *Times*.[84] Similarly, in the wake of Lamont's victory in the primary, MoveOn's political director, Tom Matzzie, told the *Nation's* Ari Melber, "I bet 70 percent of people who voted for Ned don't know what a blog is." Instead, Melber maintained, the "public agrees with the netroots views about Iraq, Bush and the confrontational nature of national politics today."[85] Yet Lamont was indeed in sync with the netroots, and with the help of the money brought in via the Internet (as well as his own deep pockets), he was thus able to bring that antiwar message to a larger audience. While the average voter probably paid little attention to blogs, the influence of the new media cannot be underestimated. By generating money, buzz, and mainstream media attention, the netroots in 2006 showed that they have the ability to help make (e.g., Lamont) or break (e.g., George Allen) a campaign.

As the midterm election returns came in on November 7, the netroots couldn't claim a clean sweep, as Lamont lost to Lieberman and the bulk of the Fighting Dems went down. But several progressives supported by the netroots, led by Webb in Virginia, Sherrod Brown in Ohio, and Jon Tester in Montana, had helped the Dems win back the Senate. More important, the issue that most helped the Democrats win back both houses, the debacle in Iraq, had been pushed strongly by the netroots ever since the war began. With a few exceptions—MoveOn's embrace of Bob Casey, Kos's support for Tammy Duckworth and some other Fighting Dems—

the netroots had stuck to its guns in opposing the war. Even as the DLC and its candidates held fast to its support of the Bush administration, some party leaders, notably Chuck Schumer and Rahm Emanuel, belatedly latched on to the issue of the war. The netroots, meanwhile, were far more in sync with DNC chair Howard Dean, who saw the party's success reclaiming the House as vindication of his fifty-state strategy. That the netroots were now an instrumental player in the party was most evidenced by Senate minority leader Harry Reid's election-day message that he posted on the *Daily Kos.* Complete with a YouTube video of him making the short statement, Reid assured Kos's readers that "you got us here." Following up on his address to the YearlyKos convention earlier that year, Reid said:

> [I]t was only five months ago when I asked you for three things: 1. Call Republicans and their friends in the media on their crass and hypocritical political games. 2. Make it clear where Democrats stand. 3. Never give up. Thank you for doing all of this and more. Because of you, no attack went unanswered. Because of you no lie avoided the truth. Because of you no distortion became a distraction to Democrats.[86]

In addition, Reid stressed the fund-raising ability of the netroots, which brought in more than $1.5 million on the ActBlue page sponsored by *MyDD* and Kos. "Blogging," Reid said, "is here to stay. It's part of our American life. It's only going to become more important in years to come. Keep up the good work."[87] By the end of 2006 campaign, it was clear that the netroots had begun to make an impact on the party, helping it move in a progressive direction. But, as the moderate Reid's statement suggested, the danger of the netroots being swallowed up by the party establishment remained palpable.

6

THE SUCCESS OF *THE DAILY SHOW–COLBERT REPORT*

More than any other outlet, *The Daily Show* best captures the sensibility of the New Blue Media. One of its creators, Lizz Winstead, helped found Air America; the show's producer during its ascendancy, Ben Karlin, came to it from the *Onion*. Nearly all of the progressive voices discussed in the preceding chapters have appeared as guests on *The Daily Show* or its spin-off, *The Colbert Report*. Jon Stewart, who took over as *The Daily Show*'s host in 1999, quickly became a familiar media figure well outside of political circles, serving as host of the Academy Awards in 2006 and likely again in 2008. Stephen Colbert, who launched his own show in the fall of 2005, would experience an even faster rise to media celebrity, partic-ularly after his appearance at the White House Correspondents' Association Dinner in the spring of 2006. Beginning with its "Indecision 2000" coverage of that year's presidential election, *The Daily Show* would win television's top awards, including several Emmys and a Peabody, over the next few years. In 2004, John Edwards, the Democrats' eventual nominee for vice president, would first officially declare his candidacy to Stewart's viewers. And after the notorious Swift Boat assault in August 2004, the party's presidential nominee, John Kerry, chose to make his initial appearance on national television on *The Daily Show*. As the favorite programs of many progressive political junkies, and the leading news sources for a younger generation of TV viewers, Stewart's and Colbert's shows would become a prominent feature of the media landscape of the Bush years.

Such prominence was especially revealing of the era's sensibility in that neither show presented itself as serious political coverage. Stewart preferred to call his show a "fake news" program, and Colbert's character parodied Bill O'Reilly and the right-wing cable talk show format. Yet despite their claims to be simply "comedians," both Stewart and Colbert have often been treated as serious political commentators. Each came under attack from conservative voices in the mainstream media. Stewart's memorable showdown with Tucker Carlson on the set of CNN's *Crossfire* in October 2004 prompted a flurry of charges from the right that Stewart was hiding behind the label of comedian. Instead, Carlson and others said, Stewart was actually an advocate for progressive views. Colbert's biting assault on President Bush in front of the president and the Beltway elite at the correspondents' dinner similarly aroused the ire of Beltway moderates and conservatives alike. While Stewart claimed to be simply a comedian, and Colbert stayed in character as a right-wing talk show host, their actual worldviews and positions on issues often came through loud and clear. As illustrated by the opinions, both real and satirical, they offered, the guests they spoke to, and the issues they parodied, Stewart and Colbert established themselves as two of the leading progressive foes of the Bush regime in the media. At the same time, they continually offered up a trenchant left-leaning critique of the mainstream political media's subservience to the Bush regime itself.

The Daily Show debuted on Comedy Central in 1996, as the brainchild of Madeleine Smithberg, a TV producer, and Lizz Winstead, a comedienne who an *Esquire* writer said "was known for her feminist, issue-oriented humor."[1] (To this day, the program would hardly be considered "feminist"-oriented.) The original host was Craig Kilborn, a former ESPN sportscaster; as the *New Yorker's* Tad Friend observed, Kilborn was "a blow-dried blond anchor mocking blow-dried blond anchors."[2] In the original format, Kilborn told topical jokes about the news; a variety of "correspondents" (including Stephen Colbert, who started in 1997) then parodied mainstream television news coverage; and this was followed by a variety of guests, mainly culled from the entertainment world. The correspondents tended to spoof oddball human interest stories more than national politics. Indeed, for the first two years, *The Daily Show* seemed like *Saturday Night Live*'s longstanding "Weekend Update" segment matched with the late-night talk show format. In early 1998, the jocular Kilborn created waves when he told *Esquire* that Winstead was "an emotional bitch who over-reacts to him" and that she should perform Monica Lewinsky–style sexual favors on him.[3] A power struggle ensued, with Kilborn being suspended from the show, only to return, which caused the rightly offended Winstead to quit. Kilborn paid little for his chauvinism, and in the spring of 1998 he was offered a slot as host of the *Late Late Show* on CBS, a transition that would occur the following January. The departures of both Winstead and Kilborn paved the way for Jon Stewart to take over in January 1999, as both host and architect of the show's future direction.

Stewart at the time was an emerging figure in the TV world. Born Jonathan Stuart Liebowitz in 1962 in New York City, but raised in Lawrence Township in southern New Jersey, he graduated from the College of William and Mary in 1984 with a degree in psychology. After college, Stewart worked at a variety of jobs, including as a bartender at City Gardens, a rock club in Trenton. He moved to New York City in 1986, where he started to do stand-up comedy at the Comedy Cellar and other venues. Early in his career, Stewart explained to *Rolling Stone*, his comedy was not particularly political, and instead it examined what he termed "the holy trinity of comedy: sex, religion and death." During the Gulf War, his comedy started to become more topical. "They were afraid this was going to be another Vietnam," he observed of the three-day ground war, "and it turned out it wasn't even another Woodstock." In 1993, Stewart scored his own talk show on MTV. It achieved modest success—within a year, it was syndicated. The format was that of a fairly straightforward talk show, with Stewart interviewing midlevel celebrities from the entertainment world.

Stewart said on several occasions that he never felt comfortable in that setting, and the show fizzled out in 1995. Over the next few years, Stewart's various gigs included serving as a guest on the *Late Late Show*, acting on the *Larry Sanders Show* on HBO, and doing stand-up on Letterman.[4]

By the time he was named the new host of *The Daily Show* in the summer of 1998, Stewart had become immersed in politics, and he had also begun to form his own critique of the media world he inhabited. In noting Stewart's new role, *Newsweek* asked how he planned to change the show. "Hopefully it won't be defined by my neuroses but the targets we go after and the attitude," Stewart said, adding that he nonetheless "ha[d] a lot of hostility . . . [for] the news media. I have more trouble with the commentary on Clinton's affair than Clinton's affair. The self-righteousness is embarrassing." He also expressed his intention to move the program "out of the celebrity realm."[5] Stewart's newfound interest in politics augured a change in direction for the show and helped shape what would become *The Daily Show*'s signature style. Another central figure in defining that style was Ben Karlin, who became the show's head writer in 1999. From 1993 to 1996, Karlin, who majored in history at the University of Wisconsin, was the editor of the *Onion*. Just as the *Onion* parodied the *USA Today* approach to politics, *The Daily Show* would now deploy a similar sensibility in its send-ups of the political news coverage found on broadcast television. In his lengthy 2002 *New Yorker* profile of Stewart, Tad Friend described what was then a close working relationship between the host and head writer. "Stewart and Karlin finish each other's jokes and are in near-perfect synch," Friend observed. "But, while Karlin tends to push for fiercer barbs, Stewart often goes for big laughs, a quantity reverentially known among the show's staff as 'the funny.'"[6] Such a healthy give-and-take, perhaps, helped keep the show's satire from becoming too didactic—the death knell of both comedy and often of progressive politics.

How, exactly, one would define *The Daily Show*'s brand of comedy has remained an open question. Like most media reporters, Comedy Central has most frequently characterized the show as a "fake news" program. In August 2004, a Comedy Central billboard across from Madison Square Garden, site of the Republican National Convention, called *The Daily Show* "the most trusted name in fake news." (A Fox News billboard hung beside it.) While Stewart himself has frequently used the term, when pressed, he has acknowledged that it may not be entirely accurate. "It's not fake news," Stewart explained to Howard Kurtz, media critic for the *Washington Post* and CNN. "We are not newsmen, but it's jokes about real news. We don't make anything up, other than the fact we're not actually standing in Baghdad."[7] Indeed, the opening several minutes of the show generally consist of a series of clips compiled from "real" news coverage of actual events. Herein, politicians, reporters, and others say ridiculous things, and Stewart pokes fun at them. One of the "correspondents" then riffs on some aspect of the actual event—usually a dubious statement from President Bush or some other political figure about world events. This segment often becomes a parody of the spin put forth by White House correspondents, the travails of war reporters, or the silliness of media coverage of calamitous events, such as when reporters "brave" hurricanes. The middle segment of the program most often is a "feature" segment, where correspondents first dupe a media-hungry rube into believing they are real reporters, then pose unexpected, zany questions (a style that Sacha Baron Cohen would perfect in his 2006 film *Borat*). In the final segment, Stewart interviews his guests—a range of politicians, authors, entertainers, et al.—and asks mostly serious questions. While "fake news" is catchy shorthand, it doesn't account for the substantial nonfiction component found in each edition of *The Daily Show.*

A handful of leading commentators have more closely identified the exact nature of *The Daily Show*'s style. In the summer of 2003, Stewart sat down with Bill Moyers on the latter's *Now* program on PBS. A former White House press secretary under LBJ, since the 1960s Moyers has been a leading liberal voice in the mainstream media, and from the outset of the conversation, he

clearly showed that he was a fan of Stewart's program. "When future historians come to write the political story of our times,"
Moyers began his introduction, "they will first have to review hundreds of hours of a cable television program called *The Daily Show.*
You simply can't understand American politics in the new millen-
nium without *The Daily Show.*" Moyers then began the interview
with what he called a "confession." It pertained to Moyers's own
confusion regarding how to characterize Stewart's program. "I do
not know whether you are practicing an old form of parody and
satire . . . or a new form of journalism." Elsewhere, Stewart usually
responded to such weighty questions with a dismissive joke about
his lack of serious intent, but here, his response to Moyers illustrated his underlying sincerity. Referring to Moyers's suggestion
that the program blended satire and journalism, Stewart said:

> Well then that either speaks to the sad state of comedy or
> the sad state of news. I can't figure out which one. I think,
> honestly, we're practicing a new form of desperation.
> Where we just are so inundated with mixed messages from
> the media and from politicians that we're just trying to sort
> it out for ourselves.[8]

Stewart, in other words, essentially acknowledged that the show is
an ongoing work of political and media criticism. Such intellectual
labels would never be adopted by a network called Comedy Central, but nonetheless the shoe still fit. At the *New Yorker* Festival in
the fall of 2006, David Remnick offered a similar perspective.
Stewart, Remnick said by way of introduction to a public conversation, is "probably the most astute press critic there is."[9]

It's not just the marketing department at Comedy Central
that would reject such a label, of course—Stewart, in fact, most
often calls himself a comedian. When Bill Moyers asked Stewart
whether he saw himself as a "social critic" or a "media critic,"
Stewart flatly said "no" both times (to the media critic reply, Moyers said, "You don't?"). Stewart then explained, "I think of myself

as a comedian who has the pleasure of writing jokes about things that I actually care about. And that's really it."[10] At times, he has tried to engage directly in serious discussion, most notably in the *Crossfire* exchange with Carlson (discussed below). But in reflecting on that debate, Stewart told Howard Kurtz, "I am far more comfortable in my role as comedian."[11] While that is in fact his primary role, such a designation removes the intellectual burdens that go along with being either a media or political critic. As a comedian, Stewart does not have to explain his positions or advocate specific ideas. Maureen Dowd, in a lengthy fall 2006 *Rolling Stone* cover story about Stewart and Colbert, tried to press the issue. Dowd stated, "I don't understand why you always say, 'I'm just a comedian,' because from Shakespeare to Jonathan Swift, humor is the best way to get through to people." For his part, Stewart explained that his brand of satire does not imply "an agenda of social change. We are not warriors in anyone's army. . . . I don't view us as people who lead social movements."[12] Even as his humor has both implicitly and explicitly made political statements—as well as exposed the mainstream media's complicity in enabling the Bush administration to advance its far-right agenda—Stewart has held fast to his position that he is first and foremost a comedian trying to make his audience laugh. The record suggests a far deeper level of engagement, though. *The Daily Show*, in fact, has been fully immersed in the political controversies of the Bush era.

In spoofing both national politics and media coverage of it, Stewart joined a small but distinguished tradition in American pop culture history. While liberal comedians like Steve Allen and Stan Freberg had become fixtures on television (and radio) in the 1950s, NBC's program *That Was the Week That Was*, debuted in 1964, was the first TV program devoted entirely to lampooning the news. A product of Chicago's legendary Second City improv comedy troupe (as *The Daily Show*'s Steve Carell and Stephen Colbert later would be), the weekly show struggled to find advertising and ran into political conflicts with NBC's president, Robert

Kintner, who was an ally of LBJ's administration. The program lasted only two seasons, and—although jokes and sketches about politics would crop up in the many variety shows popular later in the decade—it was not until the 1970s that political satire became prominent on television.[13] Inaugurated in 1971, Norman Lear's classic series *All in the Family* proved that there was indeed a large, sophisticated audience for political satire; Archie Bunker would be a spiritual forerunner to Stephen Colbert's mock right-wing character. Four years later, *Saturday Night Live* made a considerable splash. In the show's regular "Weekend Update" segment and elsewhere on the program, Chevy Chase memorably mocked Gerald Ford for being the first bumbling president. *SNL* was by no means devoted exclusively to political satire, but it did regularly parody mainstream media coverage of national affairs. Second City Television, which ran in the late 1970s and 1980s, also was particularly sharp in its send-ups of the *60 Minutes* formula. Originating during the rise of 24/7 cable news and the era of TV punditocracy, *The Daily Show* now had many more targets than its predecessors.

Stewart's revamped version of *The Daily Show* first gained critical acclaim for its yearlong "Indecision 2000" coverage of that fateful presidential race. Not only was the name of the regular segment prescient, given the eventual debacle in Florida and the Supreme Court decision awarding the election to Bush, but the coverage also put *The Daily Show* on the map in the political world. Bob Dole, the 1996 Republican presidential nominee, served as a regular guest. Dole represented the Republican side, while former Clinton labor secretary Robert Reich and a range of others—most often Stewart—took the Democratic side. "Indecision 2000" garnered *The Daily Show* a prestigious Peabody Award that same year. The official Peabody announcement of the award noted that "[o]ut of the convoluted sameness of media coverage of the last presidential election sprang the irreverent and inventive" *Daily Show* critique of the campaign.[14] On the eve of that summer's Republican National Convention in late July, Stewart perhaps best summarized his view of the race. Choosing between that year's edition of Al Gore and George W. Bush, he told the *San Diego Union-Tribune*, was like "asking me to choose between flossing and a Water Pik. I've met Gore. I think it might have been a cutout. I have not met Junior. I never played for the Texas Rangers and I've never been on death row in Texas." [15] The show's election coverage gained more than just critical success, however. Clips from the previous night's program frequently cropped up on the *Today* show and other major network programs. And on election night, the live broadcast of "Indecision 2000" captured nearly as many viewers (435,000–459,000) as Fox News in the eighteen-to-thirty-four age range. Amid the frenzied aftermath of the actual election, the program captured even more media attention. "It's like they've handed over the reins of commentary and reporting to comedians because we're the only ones who can make sense of it; because our currency is one of insanity," Madeleine Smithberg told the *New York Times*. [16]

The next pivotal moment in *The Daily Show*'s rise came with the program's response to 9/11. Stewart and company described their reactions to the calamitous event to Tad Friend for his February 2002 *New Yorker* profile. "I live downtown," Stewart said. "I felt sick. I didn't want to eat." Karlin's response was more directly political. "We all felt that our lives were meaningless," Karlin told Friend. "Because of the virulent hatred toward the West, you're suddenly aware that we're just disgusting consumers: twenty-five per cent of the world's energy consumption, with five per cent of the world's population." [17] The show stayed off the air for more than a week, until Thursday, September 20. That night, it opened with an utterly sincere monologue from Stewart—one that contained little of the critique of the West that Karlin outlined (or that got Bill Maher fired at ABC). Visibly shaken, Stewart looked straight into the camera and detailed his fear and grief, but said, "I do not despair," pointing to the bravery of the firefighters and rescue workers at Ground Zero. He concluded his nine-minute statement by stating, "The view from my apartment was the World Trade Center. Now it's gone. . . . But you know what the view is now? The Statue of Liberty." And "You can't beat that," he said with a smile. Honest and patriotic, Stewart's monologue showed that he was capable of presenting both comedy and straight talk. The Bush administration's jingoistic attempt to capitalize on 9/11 would soon become the target of both.

During the buildup to the war in Iraq, Stewart displayed a keen bullshit detector. The deceptions of Bush or then–White House spokesman Ari Fleischer provided constant fodder for the opening segment of news clips. Stewart also debated the war with many of his guests, who in the fall of 2002 and winter of 2003 included war supporters ranging from Oliver North and Chuck Schumer to war opponents including *Nation* editor Katrina vanden Heuvel and columnist Eric Alterman. In one particularly memorable exchange, Stewart sat down with Clinton insider and now ABC host George Stephanopoulos in late September 2002. Stewart opened the interview by asking, "What should we do about Iraq?" Parroting the White House rationale, Stephanopoulos quickly shot back, "The real question is what should we do about Saddam Hussein's weapons of mass destruction?" Stewart seemed caught off guard by Stephanopoulos's aggressive advocacy of the Bush administration's line, and the interview fizzled from there.[18] In some respects, it was a "Welcome to the big leagues" moment for Stewart—i.e., if one wants to play ball with the Beltway elite, one must be ready for high, inside fastballs under the chin. But Stewart's manifest skepticism toward Bush's war aims would ultimately prove correct. And in his chronicles of the mainstream media's complicity in the disaster, he enacted his own brand of revenge.

Before and after the invasion and during the subsequent occupation, Stewart and his colleagues repeatedly lampooned both the Bush administration's zeal and the media's cheerleading. Media critics Laura Miller of *Salon* and Frank Rich of the *New York Times* noted many of the better examples of *The Daily Show*'s war-related coverage. In Stewart's estimation, the attempt by Bush and Colin Powell to bully the UN into supporting the war boiled down to the following: "Unless the UN authorizes the use of force against

Iraq for disregarding its guidelines, the U.S. will unilaterally attack Iraq, thus disregarding the UN's guidelines." Such an attack, Stewart repeatedly suggested, was based on dubious premises. In an exchange with "senior UN analyst" Stephen Colbert, Stewart, in the comedic role of the straight man, said, "I'm confused. We think [Hussein] has weapons, but if he doesn't . . ." To which Colbert replied, "Jon, don't confuse him actually having them with the threat posed by our thinking he has them. Just imagine what Saddam could do if he did what we're imagining he'll do. It's almost unimaginable." Such back-and-forth banter was not only funny, but its antic spirit also captured the lunacy of the Bush administration's position regarding WMD. Shortly after the war began, Miller noted, Stewart and Colbert teamed up again for a similarly incisive satirical critique of the media's complicity in the war. "What should the media's role be in covering the war?" Stewart asked Colbert, now billed as a "senior media analyst." The following exchange ensued:

COLBERT: Very simply, the media's role should be the accurate and objective description of the hellacious ass-whomping we're handing the Iraqis.

STEWART: Hellacious ass-whomping? Now to me, that sounds pretty subjective.

COLBERT: Are you saying it's not an ass-whomping, Jon? I suppose you could call it an ass-kicking or an ass-handing-to. Unless, of course, you love Hitler.

STEWART [*stammering*]: I don't love Hitler.

COLBERT: Spoken like a true Hitler-lover.

The sparring soon continued:

STEWART: Isn't it the media's responsibility in wartime . . .

COLBERT: That's my point, Jon! The media has no responsibility in wartime. The government's on top of it. The media can sit this one out.

In just three minutes of comedy, Stewart and Colbert had shred-ded the wide swath of pro-war coverage found everywhere in the mainstream media, from the front pages of the *New York Times* to Fox News. And as Miller observed, *The Daily Show*'s parodying of TV war reporting was "a far better way of needling the mindless-ness of mainstream journalism than to simply rail against them for kowtowing to popular sentiment."[19]

In the estimation of the *Times*'s influential Sunday columnist Frank Rich, *The Daily Show* became the most successful television program—late-night or otherwise—covering the war, precisely because its satire was both humorous and nonideological. One month after the invasion, Rich wrote, "Throughout the war, Mr. Stewart has turned his parodistic TV news show into a cultural force significantly larger than any mere satire of media idiocies." To illustrate what he viewed as Stewart's nonpartisanship, Rich sin-gled out the host's comments on the day that the United States toppled the Hussein statute and claimed victory in Baghdad. Stew-art was clearly moved by what appeared to be a powerful statement of victory by the Iraqi people over a brutal dictatorship (but what later was revealed to be an event carefully stage-managed by the U.S. Army). "If you are incapable of feeling at least a tiny amount of joy at watching ordinary Iraqis celebrate this, you are lost to the ideological left," Stewart said. At the same time, "If you are inca-pable of feeling badly that we even had to use force in the first place, you are ideologically lost to the right." And "both of those groups to leave the room now," he declared. Rich saw this position as capturing the conflicted views of many Americans regarding the war at the time. "The coordinates of [Stewart's] comedy, falling somewhere between the poles of left and right," Rich argued, "may delineate the precise location of the ambivalence and anxiety that many, if not most, Americans have felt about their first pre-emptive war."[20] This was by no means the first time that Stewart claimed no allegiance to either the left or right, however. Two years earlier, Stewart had told the *New Yorker*'s Friend that the show's sensibility reflected that of "[t]he disenfranchised center . . .

upset that the extremes control the agenda."[21] But as *The Daily Show*'s scathing coverage of the occupation continued to suggest, Stewart's stated position is best viewed as a tactical one. As Bill Maher had found out, to survive in commercial television, it is best not to wear one's politics on one's sleeve.

As the "triumphant" invasion quickly became a disastrous occupation, *The Daily Show*'s critiques became razor-sharp. From the beginning of May 2003, all the way through the following year's Republican National Convention and beyond, clips of Bush's ludicrous "Mission Accomplished" media stunt aboard the USS *Abraham Lincoln* would surface repeatedly in the show's coverage of the war. By the summer of 2003, the program notoriously began to headline its recurring segments regarding Iraq "Mess O' Potamia"—a witty but poignant summary of the situation. In his July 2003 *Now* interview, Bill Moyers observed that Stewart was "the first to call attention, if I remember correctly, to the fact that the war in Iraq was over as far as the media were concerned." To illustrate the point, Moyers then showed a clip in which Stewart spotlighted the broadcast media's obsessive focus on the Martha Stewart trial, contrasting that event to the war in Iraq. Opening with clips of the media circus surrounding the trial's verdict, Stewart asked what the "fanfare" was about. Stewart speculated that it could be because "the president is in the Middle East trying to jumpstart the peace process. Or they finally found those weapons of mass destruction we've heard so much about." This was followed by rapid-fire clips of TV reporters' breathless coverage about the Martha Stewart outcome. In the eighth and last of those clips, a reporter stated, "After terrorism this is the number two priority for the Justice Department." The host then shot back, "Yes! [They] finally captured Martha Stewart. You know, with all the massive and almost completely unpunished fraud perpetrated on the American public by such companies as Enron, Global Crossing, Tyco and Adelphia, we finally got the ringleader. Maybe now we can lower the nation's terror alert to periwinkle."[22] This was indeed a representative clip, capturing as it did the perspective that shaped Stewart's brand of political and media criticism. Obsessed with celebrities and pulp, the mainstream media ignored bigger questions, from the debacle in Iraq to rampant corporate corruption at home. Yet by keeping "Mess O' Potamia" in the foreground, Stewart and company were far ahead of the curve in terms of public opinion, which over the next few years would increasingly turn against the war. More immediately, heading into the upcoming election year, *The Daily Show*, like MoveOn and the emerging blogosphere, helped keep Iraq at the center of the New Blue Media's critique of Bush.

The Daily Show's steady rise in both its audience—more than 700,000 viewers by early 2002, up to over 1 million by the fall of 2003—and, equally important, its critical recognition from the media and political elite, ensured that it would be a key player in the 2004 campaign. The first telltale sign of the program's importance came in mid-September 2003, when John Edwards formally announced his candidacy for president to Stewart's viewers. While he was already one of the nine candidates taking part in the Democratic presidential debates, Edwards had not yet made an official declaration that he was running. The candidate thus stood to score some free publicity, while at the same time reaching a politically savvy audience; the program, meanwhile, stood to gain in stature. An excited Stewart thus led off his September 15 show with Edwards's announcement, a departure from the program's standard format, in which the guests appear last. He prefaced the candidate's statement by showing a clip of an interview that had appeared on the show in late October 2002. Stewart had asked Edwards if he planned to run for president, as was widely rumored at the time. When the North Carolina senator said he had not yet made up his mind, Stewart jokingly responded, "Do you think one of the first people you'll tell is me?" Edwards seemed to surprise the host when he said that he "most certainly" would—and "On this show, as a matter of fact." True to his word, the candidate came back the following September, declaring: "I am here to keep my promise. I

am announcing my candidacy for president on your show, today."
After making Edwards say it again, so that it could be accompanied
by heraldic brass music in the background, Stewart only half jokingly offered him some advice. "We're a fake show, so I want you to
know, this may not count," Stewart said.[23] Such a "true" statement
by a presidential candidate nevertheless illustrated how *The Daily
Show* blurred the line between comedy and news. The show also
became an increasingly popular outlet for politicians—Democrats
and Republicans alike—seeking to curry favor with younger audiences. In the fall of 2006, Edwards appeared on the show, and while
he didn't declare his candidacy for 2008, he effectively eliminated
any doubts that he would indeed run by telling Stewart's viewers
to keep "an eye on my Web site" in the near future.[24]

Stewart did not openly declare his support for any of the long
list of Democratic contenders in 2004, and the name of the show's
campaign-coverage segments—"Race from the White House"—
suggested that Stewart and company cast a jaundiced eye toward all
of the candidates. But at one pivotal stage of the campaign, the
show chose a rather timely guest and implicitly made a statement
of support. On the night of the Iowa caucus, held on January 19,
2004, the "Dean Scream" had taken place. Even though by all accounts it was quite loud at Dean's headquarters that night, and the
candidate had done nothing more than try to exhort his troops,
Dean's frantic demeanor caused the punditocracy to react in uni-
son against the former Vermont governor. Slammed by the Kerry
campaign and the party insiders in the Iowa vote, and now pilloried in the mainstream media, Dean's campaign was suddenly on
the ropes. Stewart, however, traveled to New Hampshire, the site of
the following week's primary, and interviewed Dean on the campaign trail. It was unusual for Stewart to leave the studio and go on
location, and in trying to act as a conventional campaign reporter,
he appeared to be rather uncomfortable. But unlike nearly any
other national media outlet at the time, *The Daily Show* actually
gave Dean a fair shake, letting the candidate define his own positions. The segment then aired on Monday, January 26, the night

before the New Hampshire primary. If not an actual endorsement, Stewart's coverage was a clear sign of support for the only one of the leading candidates who was attacking the Bush administration on Iraq. For both Dean and Stewart, it may have been too little, too late, but the nod on Stewart's part certainly put him in sync with the party's activist, antiwar base.

As *The Daily Show* became an increasingly recognized political media outlet, a variety of analysts measured the program's impact. An oft-cited Pew Research Center study released in mid-January 2004 found that 21 percent of young adults (ages eighteen to twenty-nine) said they "regularly learn something" about the presidential campaign from comedy shows, meaning *The Daily Show* and *Saturday Night Live*; that number trailed only slightly behind those who said they followed the race through both nightly network news and daily newspapers (23 percent each). Cable news networks (37 percent) and the local news (29 percent) still led, but comedy shows, along with the Internet (20 percent), were clearly fast-rising news sources for younger audiences. The Pew study did find that those who relied on comedy programs were "poorly informed about campaign developments," citing high levels of incorrect responses to relatively basic questions regarding the backgrounds of candidates Wesley Clark and Richard Gephardt. But in September 2004, a study by the Annenberg Center for Public Policy at the University of Pennsylvania reached a different conclusion. According to the press release from the Annenberg National Election Survey, the study found that "[v]iewers of late-night comedy programs, especially *The Daily Show with Jon Stewart* on Comedy Central, are more likely to know the issue positions and backgrounds of the presidential candidates than people who do not watch late-night comedy." The show may not have provided the same information as regular news programs, but its viewers weren't exactly ill-informed (nearly half, in fact, said that they followed politics "all the time"). The study, conducted between mid-July and mid-September 2004 (thus spanning both party conventions), also recorded some important demographic infor-

mation about *The Daily Show*'s viewers. Asked to define their political positions, 43 percent responded "liberal," 38 percent called
themselves "moderate," and 18 percent said they were "conservative." Given the stigmatization applied to the term "liberal" in
American politics since the Reagan era, it is safe to assume that a
significant portion of the moderates could be termed as left of center. To say that at least half of *The Daily Show*'s million-plus viewers
could be labeled as progressive political junkies is not a stretch.[26]

For Democratic Party insiders, the most telling of all the statistics regarding *The Daily Show*'s audience pertained to the number of viewers ages eighteen to twenty-nine who watched the
program's coverage of the Democratic National Convention in
Boston at the end of July. That number exceeded 500,000, a number far greater than the viewers in that age group for any of the
cable news channels in the same time slot. *The Daily Show*'s entire
audience for its four nights of DNC coverage did not exactly wit-
ness a flattering portrayal of the Democrats, however. Stewart and
company indeed dished out plenty of zingers regarding Kerry's in-
coherence and the party's lack of a meaningful blueprint for a new
direction. In one particularly hilarious bit, Stephen Colbert lampooned many of the convention speakers' attempts to score points
by talking about their humble origins—John Edwards as "son of a
mill worker," Barack Obama as son of a "goat herder," etc. In describing himself as the son of a "Virginia turd miner" and the
grandson of a "goat ball licker," Colbert thoroughly demolished
one the Dems' favorite ways of showing the masses that they were
on their side. Stewart also kept the war in play, particularly during
a conversation with Senator Joe Biden. He asked Biden, a supporter of the invasion and a good friend of Kerry, why the war's
dubious justifications, including WMD and the alleged links between Iraq and al Qaeda, had not become issues Democrats used
against Bush. When Biden suggested that even though 70 percent
of the intelligence community disputed the administration's
claims, the other 30 percent supported them, thus providing cover
for Bush. Not missing a beat, Stewart said, "Do you think the next

time we go to war, it can at least be sixty-forty?" Kerry, meanwhile, was thoroughly skewered by the program in a biopic that
mocked the actual one that Steven Spielberg had helped create for
the convention. Its title alone, "John Kerry, He's Not George W.
Bush," got the point across. The segment's opening quotes came
from an array of Democratic convention delegates who said they
were really voting for "Anybody but Bush." Narrated by Colbert,
who adopted a pitch-perfect "serious documentary" tone, the series of clips then showed how Kerry, from Skull and Bones
through the present, was more similar to Bush than most Democrats wanted to believe. *The Daily Show*'s many jabs at the Democrats, in short, came from the left.[27]

During the week following the DNC, the Swift Boat Veterans
for Truth launched their notoriously sleazy TV ad campaign. Full
of dubious allegations that Kerry had lied about his war record, the
effort sparked a wave of coverage and a fair amount of outrage
across the mainstream media. But, to the consternation of many
supporters, the Kerry campaign remained conspicuously silent
about the attack—an especially surprising response given that
Kerry had spotlighted his war hero status at the DNC. Finally, after
going over two weeks without being interviewed on national television, Kerry chose to sit down with Jon Stewart on *The Daily
Show*, a coup of sorts for the program. In explaining the choice, a
Kerry spokeswoman told the *Washington Post*'s Lisa de Moraes that
"Jon Stewart understands perfectly all the important issues facing
this country right now," adding that the show was an excellent way
to reach a younger audience. Another Kerry staffer invoked the
example set by Bill Clinton in 1992, when he appeared on the *Ar-
senio Hall Show* and played his saxophone. According to Ben Karlin, the Swift Boat controversy was very much on everyone's minds
at *The Daily Show*. All of the staff "are just blown away by the turn
the campaign has taken," Karlin said. "We cannot believe that this
is what is being talked about at this juncture."[28] Sure enough, when
Kerry came onto the program, Stewart wasted no time bringing
up the controversy. After exchanging some initial pleasantries,

Stewart said, "[H]ow are you holding up? This has been a rough couple weeks. I watch a lot of the cable news shows. So I understand that apparently you were never in Vietnam." To this Kerry replied, "That's what I understand, too. But I'm trying to find out what happened."[29] Throughout the campaign, Stewart regularly mocked Kerry for being both wooden and indecisive. But on the show, Kerry seemed unusually relaxed and good-spirited, and his performance rightly earned him favorable notices in the press. To nobody's surprise, the Bush campaign repeatedly declined Stewart's invitation to the bumbler in chief to appear on the program. Meanwhile, Kerry scored one of the few successes of his campaign in his *Daily Show* visit.

Held in New York City, formerly the capital of liberal America, the Republican National Convention provided several prime targets for *The Daily Show* to lampoon. Stewart led off the show's first night of coverage with by saying that "Madison Square Garden had not seen this many white people since . . . the last Rangers game," adding that the RNC delegates were a "milkier, creamier kind of white." Correspondent Rob Corddry then stood before footage showing large NYPD vans outside the Garden; the Republicans' message that they had made America "safer," he said, was illustrated by the "freedom vans" and "concrete liberty hurdles" protecting the convention. Several all-too-accurate jokes about the city being a "police state" and under "martial law" followed. Stewart then zeroed in on the Republicans' shameless exploitation of 9/11. He first mocked Rudy Giuliani's repeated invocations of September 11 simply by showing clips of the former mayor's repetition of the date in his opening-night speech. "Senior convention analyst" Stephen Colbert next provided keen insight, observing that "9/11 and its aftermath bring to mind a time of unprecedented national unity, when from the crucible of an unthinkable tragedy, there arose a steely patriotism transcending ideology and partisanship. That stuff kills in the swing states. Those NASCAR dads suck it down in a feeding tube." The "overall theme" of the convention, Colbert noted, was "a time for unmitigated gall," and the closing-night message would be "Fuck you, what are you going to do about it?"[30] Where most of the mainstream media failed to even suggest that the Republicans were shamelessly trading on the tragedy of 9/11, Stewart and Colbert shredded the GOP's crass efforts to do so.

Ruthless throughout the four nights of coverage, *The Daily Show*'s critique of Bush came through loudest and clearest in the utterly devastating biopic of Bush that aired on day two. "George W. Bush, His Words Speak Louder Than His Actions" directly contradicted the message of the film actually shown at the RNC about Bush, which stressed his handling of the war on terror. In a seamless series of real clips, many of them unfamiliar footage, the film captured Bush first vowing that "we'll get bin Laden," but then announcing that "the objective is not bin Laden" because "Saddam Hussein is a threat to peace" and "you can't distinguish between al Qaeda and Saddam when you talk about the war on terror." Next came a rapid-fire list of dubious accusations by Bush regarding Iraq and WMD. "Scared shitless, the country rallied, and victory was proclaimed," stated Colbert, the narrator, segueing into Bush's "Mission Accomplished" speech. The film then interspersed Bush's claims to be making "progress" in Iraq with actual footage of explosions and combat in Baghdad and elsewhere. When the truth about Iraq's lack of WMD came out, Bush then altered his words to say that the findings still showed that Iraq had initiated "weapons of mass destruction–related program activities." As triumphant music played in the background, Colbert excitedly said, "The president had courageously modified the war's justification." Rather than listen to "the facts, listen to the words," Colbert intoned. In just three minutes, *The Daily Show* had thoroughly demolished Bush and all of his deceptions regarding Iraq and the war on terror. Painful to watch even a few years after the fact, *The Daily Show*'s spot-on satire here verged on tragedy.[31]

Stewart's growing popularity, critical acclaim, and identifiable political slant began to arouse the ire of right-wing media figures. When the Pew study came out, there had been some hand-wringing from mainstream commentators about the growing number of young people who acquired their news from a comedy show. When Stewart appeared on *Nightline* during the DNC, Ted Koppel stated, "A lot of television viewers—more, quite frankly, than I am comfortable with—get their news from . . . *The Daily Show.*"[32] (The pair quickly patched things up, and Koppel appeared on Stewart's program during the RNC.) In mid-September 2004, Bill O'Reilly seemed even less comfortable with Stewart's growing popularity—which now included a satirical history textbook, *America (the Book): A Citizen's Guide to Democracy Inaction*, that soon became a runaway bestseller. When Stewart went on *The O'Reilly Factor* in mid-September, the host instantly went after him. "You know what's really frightening?" O'Reilly began. "You actually have an influence on this Presidential election." In his familiar self-deprecating manner, Stewart responded, "If that were so, that would be quite frightening." The Fox News stalking horse then issued his own memorable description of Stewart's audience. "[Y]ou've got stoned slackers watching your dopey show every night," O'Reilly declared. He repeated the phrase "stoned slackers" several times throughout the interview, and also added that no less than "87%" of Stewart's viewers "are intoxicated when they watch" the program. As an example of his guest's rising influence, O'Reilly referred to Kerry's appearance on Stewart's show. "John Kerry bypassed me and went right over to you," said O'Reilly, who then continued to pepper Stewart with questions about exactly why the Democratic candidate wanted to reach *The Daily Show*'s audience. Stewart refused to return any of the fire, answering mainly with jokes and insisting that his show was just comedy. His lighthearted demeanor here effectively contrasted with that of the venomous O'Reilly; at one point, Stewart simply laughed at one of O'Reilly's rants against the French.[33] But in his next, even more memorable showdown, Stewart adopted a decidedly different tone.

On Friday, October 15, 2004, Stewart sat down with CNN's

Crossfire hosts Paul Begala and Tucker Carlson. The bow-tied Carlson had long been a butt of Stewart's jokes on *The Daily Show*, and in the 2003 interview with Moyers, Stewart also offered up his critique of *Crossfire*, one of the most long-standing cable news talk shows. When Moyers asked, "Which is funnier, *Crossfire* or *Hardball?*" Stewart replied, "Which is more soul-crushing, do you mean?" Adopting the role of media critic, he then explained that both shows were "equally dispiriting" because "political discourse has degenerated into shows that have to be entitled *Crossfire* and *Hardball*." For Stewart, such programs effectively removed any nuance from political debate, pitting two rival camps squarely against each other. In particular, *Crossfire*, he said, "is completely an apropos name. It's what innocent bystanders are caught in when gangs are fighting." The viewers of *Crossfire* thus became the innocent bystanders, and serious discussion of the issues proved to be the main casualty. "It's so two-dimensional," Stewart maintained, "to think that any analysis can come from, 'It's the left and it's the right and well, we've had that discussion and that's done.' "[34] *Crossfire*, of course, never pitted "left" versus right in any meaningful sense. In addition to Begala, a Clinton adviser, DLC front man James Carville also regularly hosted the show, meaning that *Crossfire* presented the conservative Democratic position as the "left." But Stewart's point about the two-dimensionality of the debate on such shows was well founded, and when he came on the show with Begala and Carlson, he was determined to get his message across.

From the outset of the interview, Stewart showed that he was there to challenge his hosts. He opened by asking the duo, only half jokingly, "Why do we have to fight?" He then pleaded with Carlson to say a kind word about Kerry and with Begala to say something nice about Bush; both hosts mustered halfhearted compliments. Carlson then tried to get Stewart to make a negative comment about Kerry, specifically by asking the guest whether he thought Kerry was the "best the Democrats can do" and "the most impressive" of the Democratic contenders. His anger rising, but the show's audience behind him, Stewart said that he actually found the Reverend Al Sharpton "very impressive." As he explained why, he began to launch his direct critique of *Crossfire*. "I enjoyed [Sharpton's] way of speaking," Stewart said. "I think, oftentimes, the person that knows they can't win is allowed to speak the most freely, because, otherwise, shows with titles such as *Crossfire* or *Hardball*, or 'I'm Going to Kick Your Ass,' " will attack that figure. The battle now fully joined, Stewart then issued his primary challenge. He acknowledged that in the past he had said that *Crossfire* was "bad." That night, however, he advanced the critique: "It's not so much that it's bad, as it's hurting America. . . . I wanted to come here today and say . . . Stop, stop, stop, stop hurting America." The show's hosts were startled by the criticism, and perhaps even more surprised when Stewart kept pounding away. "Right now, you're out there to help the politicians and corporations. And we're left out there to mow our lawns," Stewart told Begala and Carlson, whom he soon labeled "partisan hacks."[35]

Carlson fought back by trying to smear Stewart as a liberal. Earlier that week, Stewart had openly declared that he intended to vote for Kerry, thus angering *Crossfire's* voice of the right. Like O'Reilly, Carlson also seemed peeved that Kerry had gone on Stewart's show, rather than his. The bow-tied host then suggested that Kerry had done so because the candidate knew that Stewart would only throw him softballs; he cited a few examples of Stewart's questions to Kerry, such as "How are you holding up? Is it hard not to take the attacks personally?" Isolated from the Swift Boat controversy, such questions did make Stewart seem like a pushover. But Carlson then slammed Stewart by stating, "Why not ask him a real question, instead of just suck up to him?" Instead of completely devolving into name-calling, the debate actually turned to the comedy versus news issue. After saying that he didn't "realize" that news outlets expected hard-hitting coverage from a Comedy Central show, Stewart stated, "If your idea of confronting me is that I don't ask hard-hitting enough news questions, we're in bad shape." Begala tried to intervene, arguing that *Crossfire* was designed to foster debate. But Stewart, pointing to Carlson's bow tie as evidence of the staged quality of the show, then insisted that "you're doing theater, when you should be doing debate." From that moment forward, things did get ugly. Carlson called Stewart Kerry's "butt boy" and then said, "Wait. I thought you were going to be funny. Come on. Be funny." "No. I am not going to be your monkey," shot back Stewart, who would later call Carlson a "dick."[36] Stewart had come on the show with the intention of making a statement about the negative influence of *Crossfire*-type programs on political discussion. In the end, he had got caught up in the crossfire—a tit-for-tat exchange where the name-calling threatened to outweigh any serious discussion of the issues.

Stewart's performance on *Crossfire* nevertheless earned him plaudits throughout the political media, both new and traditional. According to the Web trade magazine *Search Engine Journal*, Stewart's "humiliation" of Carlson was the "most popular blog story of 2004"; the statistic was based on the number of blogs that linked to the story. (Christopher Hitchens's slam against Michael Moore ranked second.)[37] Based on the show's audience's reaction, Kos wrote, "I think Stewart won . . . and Carlson is ridiculous for thinking it was Stewart who looked ridiculous." Kos also noted that iFilm reported that over 400,000 viewers downloaded its clip of the Stewart-Carlson battle in the weekend after the Friday debate alone (by the spring of 2007, the number had reached nearly 4 million).[38] *New York Times* TV columnist Alessandra Stanley concurred, writing that "[t]here is nothing more painful than watching a comedian turn self-righteous. Unless of course, the comedian is lashing out at smug and self-serving television-news personalities." For Stanley, the "surprise attack" was "so satisfying" because in this instance Stewart exchanged his "usual goofy teasing for withering contempt."[39] Stories in the local press across the country tended to agree, although the *New York Post* proved to be a not-surprising exception. Reversing the more common headline, the *Post*'s story, "CNN Host Rips Cranky Comic," declared Carlson the victor, and said that Stewart stuck around for half an hour after the show in order "to continue haranguing" Carlson and Begala.[40] On the following Monday's edition of each show, the war of words continued. "Let me say something about Jon Stewart. I don't think he's funny. And I know he's uninformed," said *Crossfire*'s far-right Robert Novak; "I think he's funny," replied Carville, a figure not known for his modesty. "I just think he's a pompous ass."[41] For his part, Stewart observed that "they said I wasn't being funny. And I said to them: But tomorrow I will go back to being funny, and your show will still blow."[42]

In many respects, Stewart emerged triumphant in the dustup with Carlson. Liberal bloggers and mainstream media critics celebrated his ability to deflate the pretensions of a "serious" news program. Stewart's position was further solidified just a few months later, when incoming CNN president Jonathan Klein fired Carlson and ended *Crossfire*. "I guess I come down more firmly in the Jon Stewart camp," Klein explained to the Associated Press (although the show was hardly garnering good ratings).[43] But all the fanfare surrounding his exchange with Carlson also marked a change in Stewart's popular reputation. As both the critics and Stewart himself acknowledged, he wasn't "being funny" in his comments about the sorry state of the American political media. The host of a "fake news" program had become quite a serious commentator indeed.

As the 2004 campaign wound down, the prominence of both Stewart and *The Daily Show* continued to rise. After reaching the top in early October, *America (the Book)* remained number one on the *New York Times* bestseller list for nearly four months. A parody of a high school American history textbook, the book managed to stir up a small, but telling, bit of controversy. On October 21, Wal-Mart decided not to sell the book in its stores. The company's official explanation centered on the one page of nude photographs in the book; in an entry called "Dress the Supreme Court," all of the nine justices stood completely disrobed. A company spokeswoman told the *New York Times* that Wal-Mart "felt [that] a majority of our customers may not be comfortable with that image."[44] The right-wing, antiunion retailer may have made the unusual decision not to sell a number one bestseller because of the work's final section as well. While the "Election 2004" supplement included at the end of the book contained a number of slams against both candidates, the spoofs of Bush and the Republicans were much harsher. A mock boxing poster that promoted the November 2 match pitting "Skull" (Kerry) versus "Bones" (Bush) carried the phrase "Every Citizen Guaranteed a Vote," but in the fine print added "Vote not guaranteed to count." It was followed by a "Tale of the Tape" that made Bush appear like a real hick. After several cracks about the president's lack of intelligence and drinking habits, the final category assessed the war on terror. Specifically, it contrasted where each figure stood on "Defying International Community and Invading Another Country Based on Questionable Military Intelligence Without Practicable Exit Plan, Ultimately Invoking Wrath of Entire Arab World." Bush had the clear advantage here.[45] "Neutral" as any other history text, America (the Book) was hitting the president hard on the eve of the election. It was thus not surprising that Wal-Mart would keep it off its shelves.

Although clearly sympathetic, neither Stewart nor The Daily Show ever seemed to fully champion Kerry, however. As seen in the convention coverage and throughout the homestretch, Stewart, like many progressives, viewed Kerry as stiff, indecisive, and vague, and as lacking a compelling vision. The Democratic candidate's appearance on the Dr. Phil show in early October seemed to be a particularly illustrative moment for Stewart. On The Daily Show, after a clip that showed Kerry, incredibly, managing to "flipflop" on a question as simple as "Which one of your daughters reminds you more of yourself?" the camera cut back to an obviously miserable Stewart, his head dejectedly in his hands. In retrospect, Kerry did seem to be a "hopeless" candidate indeed.[46] But by election day, he still appeared to have a real chance of defeating Bush. The Daily Show's live election-night coverage captured both the frustration with Kerry and the anxiety that he might lose felt by his supporters. "Senior correspondent" Samantha Bee "reported" from Kerry campaign headquarters that his staffers believed that "with all the focus on election results, tonight is the perfect night for their man to lay out his vision of America to the voters." Fellow "senior correspondent" Ed Helms, meanwhile, reported from Bush headquarters that even with the polls still open, the president had "taken decisive, preemptive electoral action" and declared himself the winner. As he announced real-time results, Stewart offered some trenchant analysis of his own. In his estimation, Kerry's decisive victory in New York showed that the "people most damaged by 9/11 didn't vote to protect their own security. New Yorkers have no idea who makes them safer." Like the eight nights of convention coverage, *The Daily Show*'s election-night program was as insightful as that found anywhere in the broadcast media. Stewart and company's entire "Indecision 2004" series rightly won another Peabody Award.[47] Yet for Stewart, such a prize was no substitute for the actual outcome of the 2004 election. According to the *New York Daily News*, Stewart was in a "real bad mood" at the show's election-night party, and he left early.[48] Progressives everywhere shared a similar sentiment.

In the spring of 2005, Comedy Central announced that Stephen Colbert would split off from *The Daily Show* and host his own program, which would debut the following fall. That *The Colbert Report* would come on immediately after *The Daily Show* made perfect sense; in the past few years, the network had not found a successful follow-up to Stewart's program. It also had seemed only a matter of time before Colbert, who had often hosted *The Daily Show* in Stewart's absence, would get his own program. As *New York Times* media reporter Jacques Steinberg pointed out, in breaking up Stewart and Colbert, Comedy Central was "risking diluting a recipe that has made [*The Daily Show*] so popular." But at the same time, if Colbert's program could flow naturally from Stewart's show, the network stood to gain by effectively creating a one-hour version of the duo. The main question thus involved the format that the new show would adopt. According to Steinberg, Colbert explained that his program "will lampoon those cable-news shows that are dominated by the personality and sensibility of a single host. Think, he said, of Bill O'Reilly and Chris Matthews and Sean Hannity." While Colbert would be far and away the driving force behind his show, Stewart helped define it, and Ben Karlin would serve as its original executive producer. "In the way 'The Daily Show' is kind of a goof on the structure of news, this is more of a goof on the cult of personality-type shows," Stewart told Steinberg.[49] For one hour on Monday through Thursday nights, Comedy Central thus promised to match the programming of cable news networks. And pairing Stewart's "fake news" with Colbert's "fake views" proved to be a successful formula, indeed.

As *The Colbert Report*'s October debut approached, its format slowly began to take shape. "If 'The Daily Show' is faux evening news, 'The Colbert Report' will be faux Bill O'Reilly," *New Yorker* editor David Remnick observed in a friendly "Talk of the Town" miniprofile of Colbert.[50] Remnick also noted that Colbert would likely draw on his training in improv comedy in Chicago. (Born in 1964 in D.C. but raised in Charleston, South Carolina, Colbert studied acting at Northwestern University before joining Chicago's legendary Second City comedy troupe.) Colbert's left-leaning political perspective had surfaced repeatedly in his *Daily Show* bits; although as a guest host of the show in July 2004, Colbert, while interviewing Ralph Nader, he did sincerely state that he was a Democrat.[51] In playing a "faux Bill O'Reilly," Colbert thus needed to start swinging from the right. But he carefully avoided party labels. As he explained to the *Times*'s Steinberg in October, "I don't think he's necessarily a Republican or Democrat. He is part of the 'Blame America Last' crowd. Mostly, he just wants to get those bastards—whoever they are. They know who they are, and they know they're going to get gotten."[52] Such knee-jerk faux populism played well in the real world of cable news, and its main practitioners likewise refused to identify themselves by party affiliations. Despite his sympathetic three-part interview with Bush in late September 2004, O'Reilly repeatedly claimed that he was independent; trying to peg the party identifications of other "populist" cable news hosts such as Chris Matthews and Lou Dobbs proved to be a more difficult task. Newcomers might be fooled, but anybody who had watched Colbert on *The Daily Show* knew that his attempt to join the crowd of right-leaning cable news hosts would be pure contrivance.

Initially slated for an eight-week trial run, *The Colbert Report* debuted to considerable critical acclaim in mid-October 2005. In assessing the program's first week, Alessandra Stanley of the *Times* maintained, "There was never much chance that Stephen Colbert would bungle his own show." Stanley continued her glowing review by arguing that Colbert's persona of a "smug, bombastic and ultrapatriotic cable news commentator" successfully delivered a heaping dose of "wit and acid commentary in 22 minutes." From the get-go, the show conveyed the sophisticated nature of Colbert's satire; in effect, he began to mock right-wing commentators from the inside, adopting their language and style while delivering damning criticisms of their positions. A regular feature called "The Word" spoofed O'Reilly's "Talking Points Memo" as well as other political commentators' attempts to deliver simplistic messages. On the premiere episode, "The Word" was "truthiness," a neologism coined by Colbert to describe the "divide between those who think with their head, and those who *know* with their *heart*." To illustrate the point, Colbert showed a clip of Bush trying to refute the strong doubts about the qualifications of his longtime counsel Harriet Miers, whom he had nominated to the Supreme Court; "I know her heart," Bush insisted. Similarly, the host noted that while there may have been a "few missing pieces to the rationale for war[,] doesn't taking Saddam out just *feel* like the right thing?" Repeatedly, Colbert vowed to "feel the news" to his viewers, and to speak straight from the "heart," "gut," or any body part other than the brain.[53] In a rare moment of straightforward comment, Colbert later told the *Onion* that "Truthiness is tearing apart our country." [54] A razor-sharp critique of the antirational politics of both Bush and the right-wing media, the term "truthiness" caught on like wildfire. It would be lauded by the American Dialect Society and *Webster's*, and it was frequently invoked by the *Times's* Frank Rich and many other commentators across the land.

Colbert also established early on that, in contrast to *The Daily Show,* the interview portion of his program would be a noteworthy component. Where Stewart tended to be a bit fawning toward his guests, Colbert became far more combative; he did so while remaining in character, however. During the first week, *60 Minutes* mainstay Lesley Stahl came on the show amid the controversy over Valerie Plame, in which Bush officials outed Plame as a CIA agent in retaliation for her husband's publicly questioning the WMD evidence. When Stahl compared the scandal to Watergate, Colbert asked, "What's the big deal about this particular case? I mean, all that they are saying is that somebody in the White House had to do what they had to do to get the war they wanted." [55] Pushing the right's argument to its unstated but logical extreme proved to be a recurring technique applied by Colbert. Such a style alone required the guests on the show to be both highbrow and willing to spar. Like those on *The Daily Show,* Colbert's guests generally tended to be fairly prominent figures from the worlds of politics, entertainment, media, and publishing, but he also saw fit to bring on some lesser-known figures to talk about relatively obscure subjects. One memorable example of such an exchange occurred in the summer of 2006, when Colbert asked Barnard cosmologist Janna Levin whether studying theoretical physics was comparable to studying "unicorn husbandry." [56] Such was hardly the stuff of "real" pseudo-populist talk shows. When sitting down with hosts who fit that description, though, Colbert proved to be equally at ease. In the January 2007 appearance by CNN's nativist host Lou Dobbs, Colbert—shown in an infrared light—used a wire cutter to get through the barbed-wire fence that enclosed the show's interview area. The host then accused Dobbs of being soft on illegal immigration because he would not support "trenches filled with flames" along the border.[57] It took a "faux populist" to expose the far-right politics of one of the mainstream media's ascending populist figureheads.

The multiple levels of satire present in Colbert's character helped make him an overwhelming success among the critics, who were starved for such intellectual forms of entertainment. Colbert's insights about both Bush and the media, however, hit pretty close to home at the White House Correspondents' Association Dinner at the end of April 2006. Ordinarily, the comedians invited to the event traveled in the same political orbit as the president; during the Clinton years, for example, Al Franken appeared twice, and Stewart did once, while Colbert's predecessors in the Bush years included right-winger Jay Leno. But at the 2006 dinner, carried live on C-Span, Colbert served up a biting critique of the president, which was brazen not simply for breaking the protocol regarding "light-hearted" humor but also because Bush sat just a few feet away from the podium where Colbert spoke. Either in disbelief or perhaps due to his lack of understanding, Bush good-naturedly laughed at many of Colbert's jokes. But the messages behind most of them were not really funny at all. Colbert's deep digs at Bush included:

- (Looking directly at Bush) We're not so different, he and I. We get it. We're not brainiacs on the nerd patrol. We're not members of the factinista. We go straight from the gut, right sir?
- I believe the government that governs best is the government that governs least. And by these standards, we have set up a fabulous government in Iraq.
- I've never been a fan of books. I don't trust them. They're all fact, no heart. I mean, they're elitist, telling us what is or isn't true, or what did or didn't happen.

Colbert's "jokes" encapsulated why liberal-leaning Americans everywhere loathed the president—he was uninformed, anti-intellectual, and ideologically blinkered. As a result of Bush's trust in his own "gut," the United States had launched its increasingly nightmarish occupation of Iraq. But perhaps even more damning were Colbert's cracks to the gathering of the White House press corps and others in the mainstream media and their complicity in allowing Bush to advance his agenda:

- Now, I know there are some polls out there saying this man has a 32% approval rating. But guys like us, we don't pay attention to the polls. We know that polls are just a collection of statistics that reflect what people are thinking in "reality." And reality has a well-known liberal bias.
- Fox News gives you both sides of every story: the president's side, and the vice president's side.
- Over the last five years you people were so good—over tax cuts, WMD intelligence, the effect of global warming. We Americans didn't want to know, and you had the courtesy not to try to find out.
- Here's how it works: the president makes decisions. He's the Decider. The press secretary announces those decisions, and you people of the press type those decisions down. Make, announce, type. Just put 'em through a spell check and go home . . . [and] [w]rite that novel you got kicking around in your head. You know, the one about the intrepid Washington reporter with the courage to stand up to the administration. You know—fiction![58]

Undaunted by the crowd's sometimes frosty reception, Colbert soldiered on. With White House press secretaries past (Scott McClellan) and present (Tony Snow, formerly of Fox News) to his left, Colbert then presented his own version of a White House press conference. In it, playing the part of a press secretary, he spoon-fed the press corps heaping helpings of BS. He then closed with a skit featuring the venerable Helen Thomas, whom Colbert, Stewart, and other media watchers held in high esteem because of her willingness to challenge the administration. The message of Colbert's twenty-four-minute takedown was loud and clear: A dangerous president had been able to carry out his disastrous agenda in large part because the mainstream political media had not done their job.

The response to Colbert's performance illustrated the power of new media to counter old. Reflecting the views of Beltway insiders toward the breach in the event's protocol, a number of columnists in the *Washington Post* hammered Colbert. According to the paper's TV critic Lisa de Moraes, "Comedy Central's faux news show host Stephen Colbert stupidly delivered a stingingly satirical speech about President Bush and those who cover him."[59] In the Tuesday paper following the Saturday-night event, a pair of *Post* gossip columnists claimed that the "reviews were in," and "the consensus is that President Bush and Bush impersonator Steve Bridges stole Saturday's show—and Comedy Central host Stephen Colbert's cutting satire fell flat because he ignored the cardinal rule of Washington humor: Make fun of yourself, not the other guy."[60] (The initial *New York Times* coverage of the event also highlighted the Bush-Bridges bit, angering Colbert's fans.) A more influential figure in the political media, *Post* columnist Richard Cohen, also seemed offended. "Colbert was not just a failure as a comedian but rude," he wrote. The veteran moderate pundit maintained that Colbert "is representative of what too often passes for political courage, not to mention wit, in this country. His defenders—and they are all over the blogosphere—will tell you he spoke truth to power," but in Cohen's view, the routine was full of "lame and insulting jokes," and Colbert was a "bully."[61] Yet as Cohen's reference to the blogosphere's strong support of Colbert suggested, the Beltway elite could no longer make or break popular political opinion. For liberal blogs, Colbert was now their hero and Cohen became the enemy. In his column the following week, suggestively titled "Digital Lynch Mob," Cohen reported that he had received over 3,500 e-mail messages attacking him for his criticisms of Colbert.[62] Progressive audiences everywhere could not get enough of the performance. Three weeks afterward, Apple's iTunes store reported that an audio version of Colbert's speech ranked number one on its charts, beating out new releases by Pearl Jam and Paul Simon, among others.

Colbert's rising stature in the progressive world had been confirmed by the response to his takedown of Bush. Meanwhile, leading figures of the New Blue Media and their allies in the political world have been well represented on *The Colbert Report*. Earlier in April 2006, Kos came on to discuss *Crashing the Gate*. Colbert played the part of the yokel, stating at the outset, "You are a blogger, on the Internet. I don't know what either of those terms means." Pressed to clarify the book's title, Kos explained that it referred to his goal of making the "Democrats stop losing, and . . . listen to the people." Colbert in general went pretty easy on Kos, hitting him with only sympathetic jabs. He then closed the interview by extending an invitation of sorts. "If the Democrats do take back the Congress, come back and be a guest," he told Kos, before adding, "My fear is, my friend, I will never see you again."[63] On Monday, July 31, the netroots hero Ned Lamont appeared on the program, exactly eight days before the Connecticut Democratic primary. Colbert introduced his guest by declaring that while Lamont believed that "Joe Lieberman is in bed with the president[,] I say they're in a ménage à trois with America." Early in the interview, Colbert showed the footage of Bush kissing Lieberman that had been a staple of Lamont's campaign. The host's questions then directly opened the door for the challenger to address the incumbent's various attacks, including those on Lamont's experience, whether he was a one-note candidate, and, as Colbert asked, "Who's a greater friend of Israel, you or Joe Lieberman?" Colbert concluded the amiable discussion by focusing on Lamont's blue-blood background. "You're rich," said the host, "so why aren't you a Republican?"[64] When Eli Pariser came on the program just a few days after Lamont's victory in the primary, Colbert issued more friendly fire. After initially asking why MoveOn wanted to "destroy America," the host, in discussing the Lamont victory, later stated, "I want to thank you for destroying the Democratic Party." Pariser countered, with some foresight, that Lieberman represented the "status quo" on Iraq that would be defeated in November. Firmly in his right-wing character, Colbert cited "Papa Bear" O'Reilly (his frequent name for him), who had called MoveOn "extreme left-wing smear merchants." Colbert then averred, "You smeared Joe Lieberman by saying he should not be reelected. That is a vicious attack."[65] It was no surprise that Lieberman rejected Colbert's offer to come on the show. Bluster aside, Colbert's actual sympathies clearly lay in the party insurgents' camp.

In early 2007, Colbert finally got to square off with his "mentor," Bill O'Reilly, as each agreed to appear on the other's show on the same night in mid-January. Taped first, *The O'Reilly Factor* was relatively tame stuff, with the host making a number of unsuccessful cracks about the "French" origins of Colbert's last name (in fact, it's Irish). Confessing that he did indeed seek to emulate O'Reilly, Colbert explained that his goal was "to bring your message of love and peace to a younger audience—to people in their 50s and 60s."[66] When "Papa Bear" went over to *The Colbert Report*, the gloves came off a bit, though. Colbert opened with a series of clips in which O'Reilly told his guests to "shut up" or interrupted them; then Colbert talked over O'Reilly talking over a liberal guest. The pair then sat at the interview table, with a red, white, and blue "Mission Accomplished" banner behind them. O'Reilly explained that his current book, *Culture Warrior*, was about the battle between "secular progressives" like Colbert and Jon Stewart and "traditionalists" like himself. The host responded by asking O'Reilly if he had ever "gone undercover as a secular progressive," before holding up a Photoshopped picture of a gay leather man with O'Reilly's head superimposed on it. The Fox News warrior then claimed that his tough-guy demeanor was only "an act," to which Colbert brilliantly replied, "If you're an act, then what am I?"[67] The contrast between the two figures could not have been clearer: O'Reilly unapologetically stoked the fires of the culture war, whereas Colbert knew his rival's act was bullshit. But rather than simply say that, Colbert showed it. Opting for satire over didacticism, but nonetheless still delivering a real message, *The Colbert Report* had become far and away the most sophisticated critique mustered by the New Blue Media.

CONCLUSION

2008 AND BEYOND

As the 2008 election began to heat up, many leading players of the New Blue Media stayed at the forefront of partisan controversy. In mid-September 2007, MoveOn made its now-infamous statement questioning the credibility of General David Petraeus, commander of the U.S. forces in Iraq. Over the preceding eight months, the Bush administration had been putting off any decisions about changing course in Iraq until Petraeus delivered his "progress report" on the troop surge to Congress—conveniently enough for the White House, the general's two days of testimony were scheduled to coincide with the anniversary of September 11th. On Monday, September 10, as Petraeus prepared to deliver his utterly predictable warning to the Senate against pulling out of Iraq, MoveOn took out a full-page ad in the *New York Times*. Beneath a large photo of the general speaking to reporters, the ad's headline read "General Petraeus or General Betray Us?" The subtitle stated "Cooking the Books for the White House," and the text of the ad proceeded to explain why Petraeus should not be treated as a neutral observer but instead as a Bush partisan.[1] As the *New York Times*'s Paul Krugman had repeatedly pointed out, there was plenty of evidence to support the latter contention.[2]

Nonetheless, a torrent of hyperbole and hypocrisy instantly rained down on MoveOn inside the Beltway and beyond. That the Republicans, the same party responsible for shamelessly smearing decorated veterans including Max Cleland and John Kerry, cried foul was not especially surprising. Neither was Joe Lieberman's insistence that "we must reject the slander of this brave soldier and patriot," or that General Petraeus would sit down for an hour-long interview with Brit Hume on Fox News the same night that the ad appeared.[3] (As Salon's Glenn Greenwald observed, Hume's "interview," which allowed the general to show the U.S. military's charts and graphs on a flat-screen TV in the Fox studio, could have been "conducted with a Soviet General by Pravda."[4]) A bit more surprising was the response of John Kerry, who called the ad "over the top," explaining, "I don't like any kind of characterizations in our politics that call into question any active duty, distinguished general who I think under any circumstances serves with the best interests of our country."[5] Because of the influence of Fox News and the rest of the right's attack machine, the high ground that Kerry valiantly sought out no longer existed. The Swift Boat Veterans' campaign showed that the right would stop at nothing in attacking an opponent's credibility. MoveOn's ad was a similarly combative provocation, but unlike the attack on Kerry, it was rooted in facts: Petraeus was not a neutral observer.

What happened next illustrated that the New Blue Media has a long way to go before it can match the power and influence of the right's noise machine. Republican senator John Cornyn, a right-winger from Texas, sponsored an amendment that in essence (if not in actual wording) condemned the MoveOn ad. President Bush weighed in, calling the ad "disgusting" and suggesting that Cornyn's measure was not receiving full support in the Senate because "most Democrats are [more] afraid of irritating a left-wing group like MoveOn.org . . . than they are of irritating the United States military." Eli Pariser, in turn, fired back, declaring, "What's disgusting is that the president has more interest in political attacks than developing an exit strategy to get our troops out of Iraq and end this awful war."[6] The Senate then debated both Cornyn's amendment and a countermeasure sponsored by progressive Barbara Boxer, which included a condemnation of the Cleland and Kerry smears—but in the process, Boxer's measure also explicitly denounced the MoveOn ad as an "unwarranted personal attack." Most leading Democratic senators, both progressive (including Barack Obama, Patrick Leahy, and Jim Webb) and centrist (led by

Hillary Clinton, John Kerry, and Chuck Schumer) cast a vote for at least one of the amendments repudiating MoveOn's ad.[7]

Such weak-kneed support for MoveOn contrasted sharply with Republicans' backing for Rush Limbaugh. As first reported by Media Matters, amid the Petraeus controversy, Limbaugh on his radio show called Iraq War veterans who now advocate withdrawal "phony soldiers."[8] Harry Reid and forty other Democrats (including all of the above) issued a statement denouncing Limbaugh, an action that Bill O'Reilly claimed was "engineered by the far left to divert attention away from the MoveOn Petraeus ad."[9] Aside from John McCain, few members of the GOP spoke out against Limbaugh, and a House Republican, Jack Kingston of Georgia, even sponsored a resolution aimed at commending Limbaugh's "tireless public support for American troops and their families through radio broadcasts, fundraising and other public support."[10] The lesson of the MoveOn/Petraeus flare-up was simple: for the Democrats, the New Blue Media remained useful but expendable; whereas for the Republicans, the noise machine continued to play an instrumental role.

Several leading figures from the New Blue Media nonetheless seemed destined to become even more prominent on the political scene throughout the 2008 campaign. Al Franken, for example, established himself as a serious challenger against Republican senator Norm Coleman in Minnesota. In seeking what the *Nation*'s John Nichols called the "Wellstone Seat" in Minnesota, Franken carried some baggage from his days at Air America and elsewhere. As Nichols observed, "After initially accepting some of the Administration's arguments for invading Iraq, Franken emerged several years ago as a vocal critic of the war." As seen in Chapter Two, that criticism focused mainly on the White House's disastrous handling of the occupation; now, as Nichols explained, even as the Democratic challenger maintained that "Congress should use the power of the purse to bring the troops home," Franken, like Hillary Clinton, was "still a little murky on the precise timing of the withdrawal process." Such vagueness left the former comedian open to attacks from fellow Democratic challengers Mike Ciresi and Jack Nelson-Pallmeyer, a professor of justice and peace studies at the University of St. Thomas, whom Nichols characterized as an "antiwar champion." But the right also found plenty of ammo in Franken's long record of trash-talking against Republicans. In the fall of 2007, the Minnesota GOP already began using Franken's hostile barbs—e.g., that Republicans are "shameless dicks"— against him.[11] Franken was more like the 2004 contender Howard Dean (a "fighter") than the 2008 challenger Barack Obama (a "unifier"), and it remained to be seen whether the free-swinging style would carry him into the Senate. Air America, meanwhile, promised to play ball with the mainstream Democrats. Mark Green, the network's CEO, assured readers of the *Huffington Post* and the *New York Daily News* that—despite the party's inability to change the direction of the war since 2006—Iraq was the number one reason why "a perfect storm is gathering force that will likely decimate Republican strength in federal and state races."[12] The numbers (1.5 million listeners each) for the network's two leading hosts, Randi Rhodes and Thom Hartmann, remained steady, though not spectacular.[13] And in general, Air America promised to play a supporting, rather than leading, role for the Democrats in the coming election.

Stephen Colbert, though, seemed destined to remain in the spotlight. In late October 2007, his book *I Am America (and So Can You)* reached number one on the *New York Times* bestseller list. At the same time, he tried to throw his hat into the ring for president, announcing that he would officially add his name to the ballot in his home state of South Carolina, running as both a Democrat and a Republican. Colbert's foray was a publicity stunt to drive book sales and TV ratings, as well as a reflection of an improv comedian's instinctive desire to play a character to the extreme. But like everything Colbert now did, the short-lived effort captured significant mainstream media attention. In mid-October, Maureen Dowd turned over her Sunday column space in the *Times* to Colbert, allowing the fledgling candidate to state, "I am not ready to announce yet—even though it's clear that the voters are desperate for a white, male, middle-aged, Jesus-trumpeting alternative."[14] The following Tuesday, October 16, Colbert visited *The Daily Show*, where he "announced" to Jon Stewart that he had "decided to officially consider whether or not I will announce that I am running for president of the United States," adding that he would make that declaration "very soon—and preferably, on a more prestigious show."[15] That show, of course, was the same night's edition of *The Colbert Report*, where, from his news desk, he declared "I am doing it!" as red, white, and blue balloons poured down. Touting himself as a "native son" in his home state, Colbert averred, "I am from South Carolina, I am for South Carolina, and I defy any candidate to pander more to the people of South Carolina—those beautiful, beautiful people."[16] Yet it soon became clear that the fake talk-show host was sincere in his desire to actually run. As Jacques Steinberg reported in the *New York Times,* three weeks prior to announcing his bid, Colbert had contacted the offices the Democratic Party in South Carolina, asking about filing dates, and he had also called the state's Republican headquarters.[17] As blogger Chris Bowers (now writing for *Open Left*) first noted, a late October poll of voters in the state revealed that Colbert was the favorite choice of 13 percent of voters in the state (among those between eighteen and twenty-nine years of age, the number was 28 percent),[18] while a national poll placed him in front of established candidates, including Bill Richardson and Dennis Kucinich.[19] Though he never actually made it onto the ballot, Colbert's poll numbers showed that satire was no longer just one of the leading styles of New Blue Media coverage—it was now making inroads into actual American politics.

Kos and the liberal blogosphere, meanwhile, struggled to find a winning horse to back. For Kos, the war remained an issue of paramount importance, and in his critiques of the initial candidates, Iraq was always at the foreground. Never a fan of DLC favorite Hillary Clinton, Kos kept hammering away at the front-runner even as she appeared to gravitate slightly toward an antiwar position—"You gotta give the Clinton team credit for bamboozling the public on her Iraq stance," Kos wrote in mid-2007.[20] After Joe Trippi came aboard the Edwards campaign as a senior advisor that April, Kos indeed seemed to be in the former VP nominee's camp. Earlier in the year, even as he praised Edwards for being the "sharpest voice in the race," Kos had wondered if the candidate would be "better served running for governor (NC has an open seat in 2008), setting himself up for that presidential bid with a bit more heft in his resume." (Kos also noted that he tends to "like my politicians a little on the raw side [e.g. Dean, Tester, and Webb], and Edwards is very polished.")[21] Yet in late May, Kos rightly became quite angry at the Senate Democrats over their feeble opposition to Bush's latest budget allotment for the war—which, in Lakoffian terms, Kos and others characterized as the "Iraq Capitulation Bill." Kos paid special note to the candidates' varying positions on the measure, noting, "Edwards is currently the strongest anti-war voice, unafraid to take a strong stance against the Iraq Capitulation Bill (unlike Clinton and Obama, who were afraid to state an opinion on it until after the vote)."[22] A few days after this posting, the Democrats met for a debate in New Hampshire. There, taking a cue from Kos, Edwards quickly went on the attack against Clinton and Obama, slamming both for their failure to show "leadership" in opposing the Iraq spending bill.[23] Heading toward the primary season, Edwards remained on solid footing with the Kos crowd—but that support was not strong enough to counteract the hostility that the candidate, running as a populist, encountered in the mainstream media. Even so, the rising influence of the liberal blogosphere was illustrated in early August 2007, when all of the Democratic candidates chose to go to the YearlyKos convention in Chicago and none attended a gathering of the DLC held that same week in Nashville (Bill Clinton, however, went to the latter). Although certain to support the 2008 Democratic ticket, no matter who led it, Kos and company would also focus their energies on supporting progressives running for the Senate and the House.

The *Onion* showed that it would continue to march to the beat of its own drums, unafraid to lampoon others in the New Blue Media. "John Edwards Vows to End All Bad Things by 2011," read a lead story in the summer of 2007. The piece poked fun at the relentlessly upbeat Edwards, who vowed that if he were elected, "Racism will soon be a thing of the past. Same goes for being picked last for playground athletics, AIDS, robbery, not having enough spending money, and murder." But it also took a swipe at the support the candidate received in the netroots. The story quoted a fictional *Daily Kos* contributor named "BitchingPoints" who complained that because Edwards did not "mention poisonous snakes, nasty red wine stains on rugs, trolls, and noisy neighbors," he had "left the door wide open for a rival candidate to outflank him on his own issue by introducing a comprehensive plan that fills these gaping holes." [24] The relentlessly earnest instapunditry of the blogosphere certainly lent itself to such easy ridicule, and the *Onion* was always ready to burst bubbles. Any doubts about whether the paper's politics had fundamentally changed would be erased the following week, when the lead story declared, "Study: Iraqis May Experience Sadness When Friends, Relatives Die." In the piece, a number of experts speculated on whether "Iraqis are exhibiting actual, U.S.-grade sadness." [25] The paper also memorably poked holes in a leading Republican's rallying cry, declaring "Giuliani to Run for President of 9/11," [26] which *Times* columnist Thomas Friedman later used as the basis of an attack on the Republican front-runner. [27] In a simple headline, the paper later demolished one of the GOP's sacred tenets: "Reaganomics Finally Trickles Down to Area Man." [28] While the *Onion's* political satire remained sophisticated, the same could not be said for much of the paper's college-dude humor. But the publication nonetheless seemed certain to provide plenty of good zingers throughout the 2008 campaign and beyond.

As the upcoming campaign took shape, it seemed unlikely that either Michael Moore or Jon Stewart would again play a starring role, but the presence of both figures was still felt across the political media. Increasingly popular among progressive media watchers, Keith Olbermann combined Moore's sledgehammer style with Stewart's playful but critical approach. In an October 2007 cover story for the *Nation*, TV critic Marvin Kitman argued that Olbermann's nightly show *Countdown* is "very absurd but serious, very angry, very stupid, very silly, very snarky, very much about pop culture." On his program, which debuted just after the Iraq War began in March 2003, Olbermann delivers both wry observations and blunt commentaries about American politics. In his Fourth of July "Special Commentary" in 2007, the host shredded the Bush administration:

> I accuse you, Mr. Bush, of lying this country into war. I accuse you of fabricating in the minds of your own people a false implied link between Saddam Hussein and 9/11. I accuse you of firing the generals who told you that the plans for Iraq were disastrously insufficient. . . . I accuse you of subverting the Constitution, not in some misguided but sincerely motivated struggle to combat terrorists, but to stifle dissent.

Olbermann also keeps a close eye on O'Reilly, whom he regularly crowns as the "Worst Person in the World," as well as the rest of the right-wing media. Kitman and others compare Olbermann to Edward R. Murrow, the legendary CBS newsman and McCarthy foe, but most TV viewers today are too young to have ever watched Murrow.[29] Instead, Olbermann's rising success is best explained by his ability to combine the styles of Michael Moore, Jon Stewart, and others in the New Blue Media.

In general, the terrain of the New Blue Media is quite expansive. The impact of the new outlets often can be seen in the national conversation, but the popularity of the new media is also self-sustainable and not dependent on mainstream media attention. As just one case in point, consider the success of Glenn Greenwald, a left-wing blogger for *Salon*. Even though both of his two recent books, *How Would a Patriot Act? Defending American Val-*

ues from a President Run Amok (2006) and *A Tragic Legacy: How a Good vs. Evil Mentality Destroyed the Bush Presidency* (2007), received scant coverage in the mainstream media, both became *New York Times* bestsellers and reached number one on Amazon.com. Greenwald's success further illustrates that the havoc wrought by the Bush regime has produced a sizable audience for all manner of dissenting media. If Bush were to be succeeded by Rudy Giuliani, Mitt Romney, Mike Huckabee, or another Republican, that audience will surely continue to grow. But for 2008 and beyond, the question remained: how would the New Blue Media interact with the Democratic Party?

Until just before the primary season actually began, Hillary Clinton appeared certain to become the Democratic candidate. Her relationships with most of the New Blue Media had never been strong, and she was especially unpopular with the netroots. As Chris Bowers (then of MyDD.com) observed, based on a 2006 survey, "The more frequently a netroots activist read[s] blogs, the less likely s/he is to have a favorable opinion of Hillary Clinton." [30] Early in the 2008 campaign, Clinton tried to curry favor with the netroots. In mid-April 2007, MoveOn hosted a "virtual town hall" meeting about Iraq, in which the eight Democratic hopefuls connected via Internet video to MoveOn members gathered at house parties across the country. While other candidates used their closing statements to stake out clear policy positions, Clinton simply heaped praise on MoveOn. [31] Few of the group's members bought it, though, and the New York senator placed a distant fifth, with 11 percent of the vote. Barack Obama, who had opposed the war and was now backed by George Soros, came in first, at 28 percent, while Edwards, who had supported the war, admitted his mistake, and now stridently questioned Clinton's commitment to ending the war, tallied 25 percent. In late September 2007, the Democratic front-runner again showed her willingness to play ball with the neocons. Alone among the party's candidates, Clinton voted in favor of the Bush administration measure (co-sponsored by Joe Lieberman) declaring the Iranian Revolutionary Guard to be a foreign terrorist organization. The hawkish action seemed likely "to intensify America's continuing confrontation with Iran," observed Helene Cooper in the *New York Times*. As Cooper further explained, Clinton's embrace of the neocons' drumbeating against Iran suggested that she "had already shifted from primary mode, when she needs to guard against critics from the left, to general election mode, when she must guard against critics from the right."[32] Both cynical and premature, such calculations suggested that the New Blue Media and the antiwar base would not wield much influence in a Clinton White House.

By contrast, Barack Obama's appeal to young voters and continued opposition to the Iraq War suggested that he would remain on solid footing with the new progressive outlets. Released just before the Iowa caucus in early January 2008, a MoveOn survey of its membership showed Obama trailing John Edwards by only a slender margin (22 percent versus 23 percent) as the group's leading choice for president. Clinton was not far behind (19 percent), but, when combined with the tally for Dennis Kucinich (17 percent), the numbers for Edwards and Obama again revealed MoveOn members' abiding support for candidates with strong antiwar positions.[33] At the same time, as the populist Edwards warned, the Illinois senator's repeated calls for bipartisanship threatened to move another favorite progressive position—corporate regulation and accountability—to the back burner. Over the last seven years, the New Blue Media have been most effective when sticking to their principles, rather than when cozying up to the Democratic Party leadership. And if the New Blue Media creators and participants want to remain a dynamic presence on the American political scene, they must continue to keep a vigilant eye on the actions of both the pro-war and pro-corporate wings of the Democratic Party.

NOTES

Introduction: The Rise of the New Blue Media

1. Eric Alterman, *What Liberal Media? The Truth About Bias and the News* (New York: Basic Books, 2004); Jeff Cohen, *Cable News Confidential: My Misadventures in Corporate Media* (Sausalito, CA: PoliPointPress, 2006). Also see Robert W. McChesney, *The Problem of the Media: U.S. Communications Politics in the Twenty-First Century* (New York: Monthly Review Press, 2004).
2. Stephen E. Kercher, *Revel with a Cause: Liberal Satire in Postwar America* (Chicago: University of Chicago Press, 2006), 242–43.

1. Reading the *Onion* Seriously

1. Zoe Williams, "The Final Irony," *Guardian*, June 28, 2003.
2. For the *Onion*'s early history, see Jim Cryns with Kathy Buenger, "Area Man Sells & Tells," *Greater Milwaukee Today*, January 19, 2004.
3. Liesl Schillinger, "Award-Winning Local Journalists Reflect Own Self-Hatred Back on Nightmarish World," *Wired*, March 1999.
4. Ibid.
5. "Nation Trying to Fix Up Ralph Nader with a Date," *Onion*, September 6, 2000.
6. "Gore Wondering If Latest *Doonesbury* Is About Him," *Onion*, September 27, 2000; "Bush Horrified to Learn Presidential Salary," *Onion*, October 18, 2000.
7. "Bush or Gore: 'A New Era Dawns,'" *Onion*, November 8, 2000. Kolb quoted in Jane Ganahl, "Satirical Paper Comes to Town. Hundreds Die Laughing," *San Francisco Chronicle*, May 17, 2005.
8. "Bush: 'Our Long National Nightmare of Peace and Prosperity Is Finally Over,'" *Onion*, January 17, 2001.
9. Ibid.
10. See the *Nation*, November 13, 2000, artwork by Brian Stauffer.
11. Numbers drawn from Onion Media Kit 2007, www.mediakit.onion.com.
12. "Holy Fucking Shit—Attack on America," *Onion*, September 26,

2001; Siegel quoted in Daniel Kurtzman, "The Return of Irony," *Alternet*, September 10, 2002.

13. Roger Rosenblatt, "The Age of Irony Comes to an End," *Time*, September 24, 2001; *Onion*, September 26, 2001; "Shattered Nation Longs to Care about Stupid Bullshit Again," *Onion*, October 2, 2001.

14. "Military Promises Huge Numbers for Gulf War II: The Vengeance," *Onion*, March 13, 2002.

15. Card quote cited in John R. MacArthur, "The Lies We Bought: The Unchallenged 'Evidence' for War," *Columbia Journalism Review*, May/June 2003.

16. "Bush Won't Stop Asking Cheney If We Can Invade Yet," *Onion*, September 11, 2002.

17. For an analysis of the *Times* and the war, see MacArthur, "The Lies We Bought."

18. "Bush Seeks U.N. Support for 'U.S. Does Whatever It Wants' Plan," *Onion*, October 2, 2002.

19. "Bush on Economy: 'Saddam Must Be Overthrown,'" *Onion*, October 16, 2002.

20. "Bush on North Korea: 'We Must Invade Iraq,'" *Onion*, January 15, 2003; "Bush Offers Taxpayers Another $300 If We Go to War," *Onion*, March 5, 2003.

21. "Bush Bravely Leads 3rd Infantry into Battle," *Onion*, March 26, 2003; "Dead Iraqi Would Have Loved Democracy," *Onion*, March 26, 2003.

22. "Bush Thought War Would Be Over by Now," *Onion*, April 2, 2003.

23. "Bush Visits U.S.S. Truman for Dramatic Veterans Benefits-Cutting Ceremony," *Onion*, June 4, 2003.

24. "Gen. Tommy Franks Quits Army to Pursue Solo Bombing Projects," *Onion*, June 11, 2003.

25. Leon Lazaroff, "Satirical Weekly 'The Onion' Takes Root in Minneapolis/St. Paul," *Chicago Tribune*, August 7, 2004.

26. "Bush 2004 Campaign Pledges to Restore Honor and Dignity to the White House," *Onion*, January 28, 2004.

27. "Democrats Somehow Lose Primaries," *Onion*, February 4, 2004.

28. "Bush to Cut Deficit from Federal Budget," *Onion*, February 25, 2004; "Bush Addresses 8.2 Million Unemployed: 'Get a Job,'" *Onion*, March 31, 2004.

29. "Kerry Names 1969 Version of Himself as Running Mate," *Onion*, June 9, 2004.

30. "Kerry Unveils One-Point Plan for Better America," *Onion*, August 11, 2004.

31. "Small Group of Dedicated Rich People Change the World," *Onion*, September 1, 2004.

32. "Hundreds of Republicans Injured in Rush to Discredit Kerry," *Onion*, September 8, 2004.

33. "Documents Reveal Gaps in Bush's Service as President," *Onion*, September 29, 2004.

34. "Cheney Vows to Attack U.S. If Kerry Is Elected," *Onion*, October 13, 2004.

35. "Countdown to Recount 2004," *Onion*, October 27, 2004.

36. "U.S. Inspires the World with Attempt at Democratic Election," *Onion*, November 3, 2004.

37. For a complete account of the Republicans' election tampering in Ohio and elsewhere, see Mark Crispin Miller, *Fooled Again: How the Right Stole the 2004 Election and Why They'll Steal the Next One Too (Unless We Stop Them)* (New York: Basic Books, 2005).

38. "Nation's Poor Win Election for Nation's Rich," *Onion*, November 10, 2004.

39. "Republicans Call for Privatization of Next Election," *Onion*, November 17, 2004.

40. "Swift Boat Veterans Still Hounding Kerry," *Onion*, November 24, 2004.

41. "Bush to Appoint Someone to Be in Charge of Country," *Onion*, October 12, 2005.

42. Katharine Q. Seelye, "Protecting the Presidential Seal. No Joke," *New York Times*, October 24, 2005.

43. "White House Had Prior Knowledge of Cheney Threat," *Onion*, February 20, 2006.

44. "Oil Executives March on D.C.," *Onion*, May 17, 2006.

45. "Bush Grants Self Permission to Grant More Power to Self," *Onion*, August 1, 2006; "Bush Urges Nation to Be Quiet for a Minute While He Tries to Think," *Onion*, August 30, 2006.

46. "Bush: Thousands of Registered Democrats Needed for 'Extremely Important Mission,'" *Onion*, November 1, 2006.

47. "Politicians Sweep Midterm Elections," *Onion*, November 7, 2006.

48. "Rumsfeld: Iraqis Now Capable of Conducting War Without U.S. Assistance," *Onion*, March 17, 2006.

49. "Bush Announces Iraq Exit Strategy: 'We'll Go Through Iran,'" *Onion*, March 9, 2005.

50. Paul Krugman, "Who Lost the U.S. Budget?" *New York Times*, March 21, 2003; Paul Krugman, "Un-Spin the Budget," *New York Times*, July 11, 2005.

51. Frank Rich, "Will We Need a New 'All the President's Men'?" *New York Times*, October 17, 2004.

2. A Liberal Franken-stein:
The Rise and Fall of Air America

1. Jeane Kirkpatrick, *New York Times Book Review*, January 7, 1996.

2. Al Franken, *Lies and the Lying Liars Who Tell Them: A Fair and Balanced Look at the Right* (New York: Dutton, 2003), 179–85.

3. For the Franken-Lowry exchange, see "Spinsanity Debate: Al Franken vs. Rich Lowry," March 15–18, 2004, www.spinsanity.org/debates/franken-lowry.html.

4. Ibid.

5. Franken, *Lies*, 5–16.

6. Ibid., 69–86.

7. Ibid., 91–111.

8. Russell Shorto, "Al Franken, Seriously," *New York Times Magazine*, March 21, 2004.

9. "Transcript: Interview with Howard Dean," *Larry King Live*, CNN, August 4, 2003.

10. Roger Simon, "The Doctor Is In—In Your Face!" *U.S. News and World Report*, August 3, 2003.

11. See Shorto, "Al Franken."

12. Vincent Morris, "Al Franken Knocks Down Dean Heckler," *New York Post*, January 27, 2004.

13. Kevin McKeough, "Left of the Dial," *Chicago Magazine*, December 2003.

14. See Shorto, "Al Franken."

15. Peter Johnson, "Talk Radio's Dial Will Get a Turn to the Left," *USA Today*, March 28, 2004.

16. See Shorto, "Al Franken."

17. Kurt Andersen, "Taking Back the Dial," *Mother Jones*, May/June 2004.
18. Ibid.
19. Transcript, *Today Show*, NBC, March 31, 2004.
20. Matthew Lasar, *Pacifica Radio: The Rise of an Alternative Network* (Philadelphia: Temple University Press, 1999), 3–26.
21. Clinton quoted in Lizzy Ratner, "Amy Goodman's 'Empire,'" *Nation*, May 23, 2005.
22. For a history of right-wing talk radio, see Steve Rendall, "Rough Road to Liberal Talk Success: A Short History of Radio Bias," *Extra!*, January/February 2007.
23. Center for American Progress, *The Right-Wing Domination of Talk Radio and How to End It*, June 2007.
24. See Andersen, "Taking Back the Dial."
25. Rachel Straus, "The Air America Factor: Are You Listening?" *Alternet*, May 7, 2004.
26. "Randi/Nader Air America Transcript," *Daily Kos*, April 1, 2004.
27. Quoted in John Hayes, "Hannity Takes Shots at Democratic Elite," *Pittsburgh Post-Gazette*, April 1, 2004.
28. Quoted in Scott Canon, "Radio Network Starts Small," *Kansas City Star*, April 1, 2004.
29. Andrew Gumbel, "Liberal Radio in Legal Fight After Just Two Weeks," *Independent* (London), April 16, 2004.
30. Quoted in ibid.
31. See the *Drudge Report*, April 14–20, 2004.
32. David Skinner, "Al Franken vs. Rush Limbaugh," *Daily Standard*, March 26, 2004.
33. Jonah Goldberg, "A Liberal Self-Esteem Factor," *National Review*, May 16, 2004.
34. Byron York, "Liberal Radio Talks, Nobody Listens," *National Review*, April 6, 2004.
35. Byron York, "Air America's Year of Decline," *National Review*, May 26, 2005.
36. Byron York, "Radiogate," *National Review*, August 19, 2005.
37. Michelle Malkin, "Why Are Hustlers Silent on Liberal Radio Scandal?" *Advocate* (Baton Rouge, LA), August 4, 2005.
38. *The O'Reilly Factor*, Fox News, September 27, 2005.
39. Danny Goldberg, "Right-Wing Media Gets Desperate," *Huffington Post*, September 28, 2005.

40. Danny Goldberg, *How the Left Lost Teen Spirit* (New York: RDV/Akashic Books, 2005), 321–24, 354, 280.

41. Ibid, 364–65.

42. Nicholas von Hoffman, "Calling Air America," *Nation*, May 23, 2005. Emphasis in original.

43. Danny Goldberg, reply to Nicholas von Hoffman, *Nation*, June 6, 2005.

44. Quoted in Paula Span, "Radio Waves," *Washington Post Magazine*, September 12, 2004.

45. Goldberg, *How the Left Lost Teen Spirit*, 328.

46. Rowley and Franken quoted in Theodore Hamm, "Have the Democrats Become the Party of Al Franken?" *Brooklyn Rail*, November 2005.

47. Franken and Packer quoted in ibid.

48. "Air America Future? Radio Watchers Split," *New York Daily News*, October 16, 2006.

49. Ibid.

50. "The Top Talk Radio Audiences," *Talkers Magazine*, October 2007.

51. See FAIR (Fairness & Accuracy in Reporting) media advisory, "Air America on Ad Blacklist?" www.fair.org, October 31, 2006.

52. Maria Aspan, "Some Advertisers Shun Air America, a Lonely Voice from Talk Radio's Left," *New York Times*, November 6, 2006.

53. Hamilton Nolan, "Liberals May Have to Look Beyond the Radio," *PRWeek*, October 18, 2006.

54. Steve Rendall, "The Trials of Air America," *Extra!*, January/February 2007.

3. The Passion of Michael Moore

1. Michael Moore, "Final Election Day Letter," MichaelMoore.com, November 7, 2000; *Real Time with Bill Maher*, July 30, 2004.

2. Michael Moore, "*Bowling for Columbine* Wins Cannes Prize," MichaelMoore.com, May 27, 2002.

3. Academy Awards, March 23, 2003, video available on YouTube.com.

4. Michael Moore, "Mike's Letter: I'll Be Voting for Wesley Clark," MichaelMoore.com, January 14, 2004.

5. Michael Moore, "Independent Voice Rings Out Among Dems," *Chicago Sun-Times*, September 21, 2003; David S. Broder, "Clark: Bush Guard Duty Not an Issue," *Washington Post*, January 18, 2004.

6. Larissa MacFarquhar, "The Populist," *New Yorker*, February 16, 2004.

7. Ibid.

8. Jim Rutenberg, "Disney Is Blocking Distribution of Film That Criticizes Bush," *New York Times*, May 5, 2004.

9. Ibid.

10. Michael Moore, "Disney Has Blocked the Distribution of My New Film," MichaelMoore.com, May 5, 2004.

11. "Disney's Craven Behavior," *New York Times*, May 6, 2004.

12. A.O. Scott, "Now Playing: Eisner and Me," *New York Times*, May 16, 2004.

13. Ibid.

14. A.O. Scott, "Moore's 'Fahrenheit 9/11' Wins Top Honors at Cannes," *New York Times*, May 23, 2004.

15. MPAA and Moore quoted in " 'Fahrenheit 9/11' Slapped with R Rating," Movie/TV News, IMDb.com, June 15, 2005.

16. Michael Moore, "Some People Still Don't Want You to See My Movie," MichaelMoore.com, June 18, 2004.

17. Valenti quoted in Gary Strauss, "Moore's 'Fahrenheit' to Keep Its R Rating," *USA Today*, June 22, 2004.

18. David Rooney, "Org Ignites '9/11' Fight," *Daily Variety*, June 15, 2005.

19. Richard Leiby, "A Website's Push for Less Moore," *Washington Post*, June 16, 2004.

20. Moore, "Some People Still Don't Want You to See My Movie."

21. George Rush and Joanna Molloy, " 'Fahrenheit' Has Elder Bush Boiling," *New York Daily News*, June 1, 2004.

22. MacFarquhar, "The Populist."

23. " 'Scarborough Country' for June 16," *Real Deal* transcript, MSNBC, June 17, 2004.

24. Phillip Shenon, "Michael Moore Is Ready for His Close-Up," *New York Times*, June 20, 2004.

25. Kaloogian quoted in Bill Werde, "Friends and Foes of *Fahrenheit* Lobby Everyone," *New York Times*, June 30, 2004.

26. Martin Kasindorf and Judy Keen, " 'Fahrenheit 9/11': Will It Change Any Voter's Mind?" *USA Today*, June 24, 2004.

27. A.O. Scott, " 'Fahrenheit 9/11': Unruly Scorn Leaves Room for Restraint, but Not a Lot," *New York Times*, June 23, 2004.

28. Robert Denerstein, "Moore's 'Fahrenheit 9/11' A Drive-By Attack on Bush," *Rocky Mountain News*, June 25, 2004.

29. Nicholas D. Kristof, "Calling Bush a Liar," *New York Times*, June 30, 2004.

30. Christopher Hitchens, "UnFairenheit 9/11: The Lies of Michael Moore," *Slate*, June 21, 2004.

31. Ibid.

32. *Scarborough Country*, MSNBC, June 30, 2004.

33. *Reliable Sources*, CNN, July 4, 2004.

34. Ibid.

35. Despite his constant harangue, it's not clear what actual "lies" Hitchens ever identified in Moore's work. Moore's assertion that the bin Laden family was given special permission to fly out of the United States when the airspace was still closed after 9/11 does remain debatable. But Hitchens most frequently cited Moore's attempt to connect a gas pipeline project initiated by Unocal to the U.S. effort to topple the Taliban regime in Afghanistan. Hitchens stated that the project had been scuttled in 1998, after bin Laden blew up two American embassies in Africa, causing the Taliban to be isolated. That was true, but so too was the fact that the Bush administration had resumed negotiations for the project after taking office; and in late 2002, the new Afghan president, former Unocal consultant Hamid Karzai, signed an agreement for the pipeline project. To argue, as Moore's film did, that the project had at least some bearing on the U.S. interest in Afghanistan was thus valid. Hitchens also slammed Moore's "astonishing falsification" in the film that "Iraq had never attacked or killed or even threatened (his words) any American." Here the writer pointed to the presence of international terrorist Abu Nidal, who had found a safe haven in Iraq, as well as the casualties of the Gulf War, Hussein's attempt to kill George Bush I, and the fact that "Iraqi forces fired, *every day, for 10 years*" on the aircraft that patrolled the no-fly zones created after the Kuwait conflict. Moore, however, had obviously meant that Saddam had not threatened to kill, via support for terrorism or direct warfare, American civilians, as opposed to the U.S. fighting forces or its heads of state. Once again, the charge of "lies" was itself a distortion.

36. *Reliable Sources*, CNN, July 4, 2004.

37. Byron York, "Michael Moore and the Myth of Fahrenheit 9/11," *National Review*, April 11, 2005.

38. "Moore: Bush 'Didn't Tell the Truth,'" *The O'Reilly Factor*, Fox News, July 27, 2004.

39. Ibid.

40. Alessandra Stanley, "What We Missed in Boston," *New York Times*, August 1, 2004.

41. *The O'Reilly Factor*, Fox News, July 28, 2004.

42. Moore quoted in Byron York, "The Passion of Michael Moore: Fun and Games with Fahrenheit 9/11," *National Review*, April 25, 2005.

43. Michael Moore, "My First Week with Fahrenheit 9/11," Michael Moore.com, April 4, 2004.

44. Ibid.

45. *Charlie Rose Show*, PBS, July 1, 2004.

46. *Scarborough Country*, MSNBC, July 13, 2004.

47. *Nightline*, ABC, July 27, 2004.

48. John McCain, "President Deserves Our Support, Admiration," *CNN.com*, August 31, 2004.

49. Michael Moore, "The Ebert and McCain Show," *USA Today*, September 1, 2004.

50. Mark Binelli, "Michael Moore's Patriot Act: How a Blue-Collar Screw-Up Became the White House's Worst Nightmare," *Rolling Stone*, September 16, 2004.

51. Michael Moore, "Why I Will Not Seek Best Documentary Oscar," MichaelMoore.com, September 6, 2004.

52. Ibid.

53. Robert Boynton, "How to Make a Guerrilla Documentary," *New York Times Magazine*, July 11, 2004.

54. Michael Moore, "Michael Moore on Tour; Slackers of the World, Unite!," MichaelMoore.com, September 25, 2004.

55. Michael Moore, " 'Fahrenheit 9/11' Out on Home Video/DVD Today! Pass It Around . . . ," MichaelMoore.com, October 5, 2004.

56. *The O'Reilly Factor*, Fox News, September 27, 2004.

57. Michael Moore, "Republicans Out of Ideas, Ask Prosecutors to Arrest Michael Moore," MichaelMoore.com, October 6, 2004.

58. Michael Moore, "One Day Left," MichaelMoore.com, November 1, 2004.

59. Michael Moore, "The Kids Are Alright," MichaelMoore.com, November 7, 2004.

60. Al From and Bruce Reed, "Get the Red Out," *Wall Street Journal*, December 8, 2004.

61. Michael Moore, "It's Time to Stop Being Hit," MichaelMoore.com, December 13, 2004.

62. York, "Michael Moore and the Myth of Fahrenheit 9/11."
63. *The O'Reilly Factor*, Fox News, November 8, 2004.
64. Ralph Nader, "Will the Real Michael Moore Ever Re-Emerge?" *Counterpunch*, December 8, 2004.
65. Ralph Nader, "Sicko and the Politics of Health Care," *Counterpunch*, June 26, 2007.
66. *The Situation Room*, CNN, July 9, 2007.
67. David Denby, "Do No Harm," *New Yorker*, July 2, 2007.
68. Atul Gawande, "Sick and Twisted," *New Yorker*, July 23, 2007.
69. *The O'Reilly Factor*, Fox News, July 11, 2007.

4. Netroots I: The Rise of MoveOn

1. Helen Kennedy, "Put a Plug in It, Net Petitioners Tell Lawmakers," *New York Daily News*, October 2, 1998.
2. Katie Hafner, "Screen Grab; Mobilizing on Line for Gun Control," *New York Times*, May 20, 1999.
3. Weiss quoted in Rona Marech, "Grass Roots from Berkeley Sprout On-Line," *San Francisco Chronicle*, December 29, 2000.
4. Charles Burress, "Making Their Move: Online Anti-War Movement in Full Flower," *San Francisco Chronicle*, February 9, 1993.
5. George Packer, "Smart-Mobbing the War," *New York Times*, March 9, 2003.
6. Ibid.
7. Randy Furst, "Thousands Take Stand for Peace," *Minneapolis Star Tribune*, March 17, 2003.
8. Eric Alterman, *What Liberal Media? The Truth About Bias and the News* (New York: Basic Books, 2004), 244.
9. David D. Kirkpatrick, "Putting a Face to a Cause," *New York Times*, May 29, 2003.
10. David von Drehle, "From Screen Savors to Progressive Savior?" *Washington Post*, June 5, 2003.
11. Ibid.
12. Brian Faler, "Democratic Hopefuls to Vie for Early Endorsement," *Washington Post*, June 14, 2003.
13. Harold Meyerson, "Net Worth; Why MoveOn.org's Backing Could Be Priceless to a Democratic Candidate," *Washington Post*, June 18, 2003.
14. Ryan Lizza, "Dean.com," *New Republic*, June 2, 2003.

15. "Happy Days Are Virtually Here Again," editorial, *New York Times*, June 27, 2003.

16. Meyerson, "Net Worth."

17. Anne E. Kornblut, "Democratic Primary Season Unofficially Opens with Web Poll," *Boston Globe*, June 28, 2003.

18. David von Drehle, "Dean Leads in Online 'Primary,' " *Washington Post*, June 28, 2003.

19. Ibid.

20. David von Drehle, "Among Democrats, the Energy Seems to Be on the Left," *Washington Post*, July 10, 2003.

21. Robert Schlesinger, "Antiwar Groups Turn Their Focus to Bush," *Boston Globe*, June 20, 2003.

22. Evelyn Nieves, "Antiwar Group Says Public Ire Over Iraq Claims Is Increasing," *Washington Post*, July 22, 2003.

23. Andrew Boyd, "The Web Rewires the Movement," *Nation*, August 4, 2003.

24. Peter S. Canellos, "Gore Speech Fuels Campaign Talk," *Boston Globe*, August 7, 2003.

25. Laura Mecoy, Alexa H. Bluth, and Gary Delsohn, "Schwarzenegger on the Defensive; Davis Says He's Unfit to Be Governor," *Sacramento Bee*, October 4, 2003.

26. Stephen Koff, "Lewis Pledges $12 Million to Oust Bush," *Cleveland Plain Dealer*, November 12, 2003.

27. Michael Janofsky and Jennifer 8. Lee, "Net Group Tries to Click Democrats to Power," *New York Times*, November 18, 2003.

28. "Mr. Soros's Millions," editorial, *Washington Post*, November 22, 2003.

29. George Soros, "The Bubble of American Supremacy," *Atlantic Monthly*, December 2003.

30. MoveOn ad quoted in Michelle Goldberg, "Dazed and Confused About Iraq," *Salon*, October 27, 2003.

31. In his recent memoir, the veteran Democratic Party insider Bob Shrum, a senior consultant to the Kerry campaign, maintains (based on the campaign's polling) that it was not Kerry's first two flip-flops—voting against the Gulf War, then voting for the Iraq War, and voting for the current war, then voting against the $87 billion appropriation for it—that made the charge stick. Instead, it was the candidate's Kerryesque explanation of his spending vote: "I voted for the $87 billion . . . before I voted against it." See Robert

Shrum, *No Excuses: Confessions of a Serial Campaigner* (New York: Simon & Schuster, 2006), 451–52.

32. Robert Novak, "Soros Shrinking from Dean," *Chicago Sun-Times*, December 21, 2003.

33. Julia Malone, "Campaign 2004: Soros Pins His Hopes on Defeat for Bush," *Atlanta Journal-Constitution*, January 13, 2004.

34. Brian Faler, "MoveOn Decides Not to Decide," *Washington Post*, January 13, 2004.

35. Howard Kurtz, "Anti–Bush Ad Contest Includes Hitler Images," *Washington Post*, January 6, 2004.

36. "Raw Rage at Bush During MoveOn.org Awards," *Drudge Report*, January 13, 2004.

37. Lloyd Grove, "Cho-Time for Moby vs. Drudge," *New York Daily News*, January 23, 2004.

38. Deanna Zandt, "Taking It to the People," *Alternet*, January 14, 2004.

39. Jim Rutenberg, "Ad Rejections by CBS Raise Policy Questions," *New York Times*, January 19, 2004.

40. David Kaplan, "Super Bowl XXXVIII; Ad's Rejection Giving Group Free Publicity," *Houston Chronicle*, January 24, 2004.

41. Jim Rutenberg, "Activist Group Plans New Ads Attacking Bush in Swing States," *New York Times*, February 12, 2004.

42. Eli Pariser, "Dear MoveOn Reader," MoveOn.org, April 8, 2004.

43. Clarke quoted in "Election Ad," *USA Today*, April 1, 2004.

44. Byron York, "Going Viral," *National Review*, April 7, 2005.

45. Jim Rutenberg, "The 2004 Campaign: Advertising; Kerry Denounces New Ad on Bush's Service in Guard," *New York Times*, August 18, 2004.

46. George Raine, "Ad That Won Web Award Criticizes Bush for War," *San Francisco Chronicle*, August 14, 2004.

47. Robert Scheer, "Kerry Made a Bush League Error on Iraq," *Nation*, August 17, 2004.

48. "As Iraq Veers out of Control, New Ad Calls for Change in Leadership," *CommonDreams.org*, September 16, 2004.

49. Glen Justice, "Political Group's Antiwar Ad Draws Ire of the Bush Campaign," *New York Times*, September 17, 2004.

50. *Wall Street Journal* ad, September 29, 2004, cited in Oliver Burkeman, "Soros Goes on Tour to Do His Bit to Defeat Bush," *Guardian*, September 30, 2004.

51. "Transcript: First Presidential Debate," *WashingtonPost.com*, September 30, 2004.

52. "Transcript Part I: Candidates Tackle Iraq," *CNN.com*, October 8, 2004.

53. "Transcript: Bush, Kerry Debate Domestic Policies," *CNN.com*, August 14, 2004.

5. Netroots II: The Rise of the Blogosphere

1. Tanya Schevitz, "MoveOn Groups Asking, Where To? Progressives Talk It Over at 1,680 Parties," *San Francisco Chronicle*, November 22, 2004.

2. Dan Balz, "DNC Chief Advises Learning from GOP," *Washington Post*, December 11, 2004.

3. Ibid.

4. James Harding, "Soros in New Pledge to Leftwing Causes," *Financial Times*, January 12, 2005.

5. For the early history of the Democracy Alliance (which originated in 2003, as the Phoenix Group), see Matt Bai, *The Argument: Billionaires, Bloggers, and the Battle to Remake Democratic Politics* (New York: Penguin, 2007), 34–48.

6. Michael Tomasky, "How Democrats Should Talk," *New York Review of Books*, May 31, 2007.

7. Ari Berman, "Big $$ for Progressive Politics," *Nation*, October 16, 2006.

8. See Bai, *The Argument*. Bai, a Clintonite, portrays Moulitsas as more of an entrepreneur than a political thinker, insisting that he does not "give a second's thought to the perils of economic transformation or the new threat posed by nonstate actors with advanced weaponry—identifying the progressive argument [is] someone else's job" (150–51). But unlike the Clintons or the leadership of the Democratic Party, Moulitsas was smart enough to see that the invasion of Iraq would be a disaster.

9. Jerome Armstrong and Markos Moulitsas, *Crashing the Gate: Netroots, Grassroots, and the Rise of People-Powered Politics* (White River Junction, VT: Chelsea Green Publishing Company, 2006), 148–51.

10. *ABC's This Week with George Stephanopoulos*, January 9, 2005, excerpt of transcript posted by Chris Bowers, "More on Roemer," *MyDD.com*, January 9, 2005.

11. Jerome Armstrong, "Netroots for Howard Dean," *MyDD.com*, December 2002.

12. For Kos's bio and claim of 20 million, see www.dailykos.com/special/about (accessed October 19, 2007); the number from site meter.com, his preferred tracking site, averaged out to between 14 to 15 million monthly visitors (accessed October 19, 2007). For 100,000 figure, see Spec20, "The Real Traffic Numbers for dKos," *Daily Kos*, August 25, 2007.

13. Noam Scheiber, "Wooden Frame," *New Republic*, May 23, 2005.

14. Matt Bai, "The Framing Wars," *New York Times Magazine*, July 17, 2005.

15. Markos Moulitsas, "Day 1," *Daily Kos*, May 26, 2002.

16. Markos Moulitsas, "Iraq Invasion Loosing Steam," *Daily Kos*, May 26, 2002.

17. Markos Moulitsas, "Chickenhawks Push War," *Daily Kos*, August 21, 2002.

18. Ibid.

19. Markos Moulitsas, "War Vote as Campaign Issue?" *Daily Kos*, September 6, 2002.

20. Markos Moulitsas, "A Disappointing Failure," *Daily Kos*, September 19, 2002.

21. Markos Moulitsas, "What's Up with Gephardt?" *Daily Kos*, October 3, 2002.

22. Markos Moulitsas, "Moving On," *Daily Kos*, October 26, 2002.

23. Markos Moulitsas, "Democrats Are Masters of GOTV," *Daily Kos*, October 31, 2002.

24. Markos Moulitsas, "Democrats Will Not Have a Big Night," *Daily Kos*, November 4, 2002.

25. Markos Moulitsas, "Congrats to Republicans," *Daily Kos*, November 5, 2002.

26. Markos Moulitsas, "The Bush Administration Is Out of Control," *Daily Kos*, February 2, 2002.

27. John Podhoretz, "The Internet's First Scalp," *New York Post*, December 13, 2002.

28. Markos Moulitsas, "Dean Tops MyDD/dKos Poll," *Daily Kos*, December 30, 2002.

29. Markos Moulitsas, "Cattle Call 2004: 1/27," *Daily Kos*, January 27, 2003.

30. Markos Moulitsas, "Dean Brings Down the House," *Daily Kos*, February 21, 2003.

31. Markos Moulitsas, "Time for Kucinich to Drop Out," *Daily Kos*, February 26, 2003.

32. Markos Moulitsas, "Cattle Call 2004: 4/17," *Daily Kos*, April 17, 2003.

33. Markos Moulitsas, "Clark 2004? I'm Leaning That Way," *Daily Kos*, March 30, 2003.

34. Armstrong and Moulitsas, *Crashing the Gate*, 140.

35. Markos Moulitsas, "CDP Convention, Day Two; Dean Cleans Up," *Daily Kos*, March 13, 2003.

36. Markos Moulitsas, "Full Disclosure," *Daily Kos*, June 9, 2003.

37. Markos Moulitsas, "Cattle Call 2004: Comment Period 6/4" *Daily Kos*, June 4, 2003.

38. Markos Moulitsas, "What I Will Tell McAuliffe," *Daily Kos*, June 17, 2003.

39. Markos Moulitsas, "A Different Noise," *Guardian*, September 28, 2004.

40. Markos Moulitsas, "Divide and Rule . . . for Now," *Guardian*, November 3, 2004.

41. Armstrong and Moulitsas, *Crashing the Gate*, 148–51.

42. Ryan Lizza, "The Democratic Divide. The Outsiders," *New Republic*, February 14, 2005.

43. Ibid.

44. Dean quoted in Adam Nagourney and Edward Wyatt, "Rivals Condemn Dean for Flag Remark," *New York Times*, November 5, 2003.

45. "Dems Battle Over Confederate Flag," *CNN.com*, November 2, 2003.

46. See Armstrong and Moulitsas, *Crashing the Gate*, 40–42.

47. John Nichols, "Blog: Kate Michelman for Senate?" *Nation*, March 4, 2006; John Nichols, "Democratic Alarms in PA," *Nation*, February 27, 2006.

48. Gwen Shaffer, "Dem's the Breaks," *Philadelphia Weekly*, July 6, 2005.

49. "A Pair of Fighters," editorial, *Cincinnati Enquirer*, July 24, 2005.

50. David Goodman, "The Ohio Insurgency," *Mother Jones*, November/December 2005.

51. Jerome Armstrong, "More Hackett Jobs," *TomPaine.com*, August 3, 2005.

52. Benjamin Wallace-Wells, "Kos Call," *Washington Monthly*, January/ February 2006.

53. For Kos's 2006 keynote address, see www.chelseagreen.com/about/ politicsandpractice/news/2006/june9.

54. Boxer quoted in Matthew Continetti, "Betting on the Bloggers," *Weekly Standard*, February 26, 2006.

55. Adam Nagourney, "Gathering Highlights Power of the Blog," *New York Times*, June 10, 2006.

56. Maureen Dowd, "Bloggers Double Down," *New York Times*, June 10, 2006.

57. Eli Sanders, "Kos: Maureen Dowd Is an Insecure, Catty Bitch," *Slog (Stranger* blog), June 10, 2006, http://slog.thestranger.com/2006/ 06/04–10.

58. Ryan Lizza, "Liberal Activists on the Strip. Wag the Blog," *New Republic*, June 26, 2006.

59. *Meet the Press*, NBC, June 11, 2006.

60. Markos Moulitsas, "The Fighting Dem Phenomenon Spreads," *Daily Kos*, December 28, 2005.

61. Garance Franke-Ruta, "Why the 'Fighting Dems' Didn't Win. Tug of War," *New Republic*, November 20, 2006.

62. Nicholas Jahr, "General Kos' Army," *Brooklyn Rail*, April 2006.

63. Markos Moulitsas, "IL-06: Tuesday Fighting Dem: Tammy Duckworth," *Daily Kos*, January 17, 2006.

64. See "George Allen Introduces 'Macaca,'" YouTube.com, August 11, 2006.

65. Tim Craig and Michael D. Shear, "Allen Quip Provokes Outrage, Apology," *Washington Post*, August 15, 2006.

66. Richard Lowry, "The Macaca Campaign—How George Allen Fell," *National Review*, December 4, 2006.

67. Markos Moulitsas, "Memo to the Media, Pundits," *Daily Kos*, November 9, 2006.

68. Markos Moulitsas, "VA-Sen: Webb's Son Off to Iraq," *Daily Kos*, August 31, 2006.

69. Markos Moulitsas, "CT-Sen: Looks Like Ned Lamont to Take on Lieberman," *Daily Kos*, January 7, 2006.

70. Matt Stoller, "The Risks for the Blogosphere of Taking on Lieberman," *MyDD.com*, January 19, 2006.

71. Matt Stoller, "Ned Lamont, Political Entrepreneur," *MyDD.com*, February 17, 2006.

72. Markos Moulitsas, "Lieberman Freaking Out About Lamont," *Daily Kos*, January 17, 2006.

73. Democracy for America press release, May 23, 2006.

74. Eli Pariser, "Lamont Wins MoveOn's Endorsement in Online Primary," *CommonDreams.org*, May 26, 2006.

75. Ronald Brownstein, "Support for a Challenger to Longtime Sen. Joe Lieberman Indicated Tensions over Iraq War," *Los Angeles Times*, May 26, 2006.

76. William Yardley, "Lieberman's Support for War Leaves Him Embattled on Left," *New York Times*, May 19, 2006.

77. Brownstein, "Support for a Challenger."

78. David Brooks, "Respect Must Be Paid," *New York Times*, June 25, 2006.

79. David Brooks, "The Liberal Inquisition," *New York Times*, July 9, 2006.

80. Cokie Roberts, *This Week*, ABC, August 6, 2006.

81. David S. Broder, " 'A Terrible Tug' for Democrats," *Washington Post*, July 30, 2006.

82. Jonathan Alter, "Putting First Things First," *Newsweek*, August 7, 2006.

83. "A Senate Race in Connecticut," editorial, *New York Times*, July 30, 2006. As the *Times* noted, "The race has taken on a national character. Mr. Lieberman's friends see it as an attempt by hysterical antiwar bloggers to oust a giant of the Senate for the crime of bipartisanship."

84. Mike McIntire and Jennifer Medina, "In Race, Bloggers Throw Curves and Spitballs," *New York Times*, August 4, 2006.

85. Ari Melber, "Ned Lamont's Digital Constituency," *Nation* (online only), August 9, 2006.

86. Harry Reid, "You Got Us Here," *Daily Kos*, November 7, 2006.

87. Ibid.

6. The Success of *The Daily Show-Colbert Report*

1. Joe Bargmann, "Broadcast Bruise," *Esquire*, January 1, 1998.

2. Tad Friend, "Is It Funny Yet?" *New Yorker*, February 11, 2002.

3. Bargmann, "Broadcast Bruise."

4. John Colapinto, "The Most Trusted Name in News," *Rolling Stone*, October 28, 2004.

5. "Nice Guy Finishes First," *Newsweek*, September 28, 1998.

6. Friend, "Is It Funny Yet?"

7. Howard Kurtz, "The Campaign of a Comedian," *Washington Post*, October 23, 2004.

8. "Bill Moyers Interviews Jon Stewart," *Now*, PBS, July 11, 2003.

9. Remnick quoted in Stephen Kiehl, "Digging for the Meaning of Fake News' Acceptance," *Baltimore Sun*, October 12, 2006.

10. "Bill Moyers Interviews Jon Stewart,"

11. Kurtz, "The Campaign of a Comedian."

12. Maureen Dowd, "America's Anchors," *Rolling Stone*, October 31, 2006.

13. On *That Was the Week That Was*, see Stephen E. Kercher, *Revel with a Cause: Liberal Satire in Postwar America* (Chicago: University of Chicago Press, 2006), 379–88.

14. Peabody Awards Web site, www.peabody.uga.edu.

15. Steve Hedgepeth, "Comedy Central's 'Daily Show' Will Put Its Spin on Conventions," *San Diego Union-Tribune*, July 28, 2000.

16. Jim Rutenberg, "TV Notes; News Is the Comedy," *New York Times*, November 22, 2000.

17. Friend, "Is It Funny Yet?"

18. *The Daily Show*, Comedy Central, September 26, 2002.

19. Laura Miller, "TV's Boldest News Show," *Salon*, April 8, 2003.

20. Frank Rich, "Jon Stewart's Perfect Pitch," *New York Times*, April 20, 2003.

21. Friend, "Is It Funny Yet?"

22. "Bill Moyers Interviews Jon Stewart."

23. *The Daily Show*, Comedy Central, September 15, 2003.

24. *The Daily Show*, Comedy Central, November 14, 2006.

25. Pew Research Center, "Cable and Internet Loom Large in Fragmented Political News Universe," report, January 11, 2004, http://people-press.org/reports/display.php3?ReportID=200.

26. Annenberg Public Policy Center, "Daily Show Viewers Knowledgeable About Presidential Campaign, National Annenberg Election Survey Shows," news release, September 21, 2004.

27. *The Daily Show with Jon Stewart—Indecision 2004* (Comedy Central, 2005), disc 1.

28. Lisa de Moraes, "Seriously: Kerry on Comedy Central," *Washington Post*, August 24, 2004.

29. *The Daily Show*, Comedy Central, August 24, 2004.

30. *The Daily Show with Jon Stewart—Indecision 2004*, disc 2.

31. Ibid.

32. *Nightline*, ABC, July 28, 2004.

33. *The O'Reilly Factor*, Fox News, September 20, 2004.

34. "Bill Moyers Interviews Jon Stewart."

35. *Crossfire*, CNN, October 15, 2004.

36. Ibid.

37. Lauren Baker, "Jon Stewart's Humiliation of Tucker Carlson the Most Popular Blog Story of 2004," *Search Engine Journal*, December 15, 2004.

38. Michael Moulitsas, "Carlson Doesn't Get It—Stewart Won," *Daily Kos*, October 18, 2004.

39. Alessandra Stanley, "No Jokes or Spin. It's Time (Gasp) to Talk," *New York Times*, October 20, 2004.

40. "CNN Host Rips Cranky Comic," Page Six, *New York Post*, October 20, 2004.

41. *Crossfire*, CNN, August 18, 2004.

42. *Daily Show*, Comedy Central, August 18, 2004.

43. Phil Rosenthal, "CNN Ready to Call Cease-Fire on Cross-Fire," *Chicago Sun-Times*, January 6, 2005.

44. Edward Wyatt, "Arts, Briefly; Banned in Wal-Mart," *New York Times*, October 22, 2004.

45. Jon Stewart, Ben Karlin, David Javerbaum, et al., *America (The Book): A Citizen's Guide to Democracy Inaction* (New York: Warner Books, 2004), election guide.

46. *The Daily Show*, Comedy Central, October 11, 2004.

47. *The Daily Show with Jon Stewart—Indecision 2004*, disc 3.

48. George Rush and Joanna Molloy, "No Kidding, Stewart Down Over Vote," *New York Daily News*, November 4, 2004.

49. Jacques Steinberg, "'Daily Show' Personality Gets His Own Platform," *New York Times*, May 4, 2005.

50. David Remnick, "Reporter Guy," *New Yorker*, July 25, 2005.

51. *The Daily Show*, Comedy Central, July 6, 2004.

52. Steinberg, "'Daily Show' Personality.'"

53. Alessandra Stanley, "Bringing Out the Absurdity of the News," *New York Times*, October 25, 2005.

54. Nathan Rabin, "Interview: Stephen Colbert," *Onion*, January 25, 2006.

55. *The Colbert Report*, Comedy Central, October 18, 2005.

56. *The Colbert Report*, Comedy Central, August 24, 2006.

57. *The Colbert Report*, Comedy Central, January 24, 2007.

58. "Transcript: Stephen Colbert's Take at the White House Correspondents Dinner," *Daily Kos*, May 1, 2006.

59. Lisa de Moraes, "Colbert, Still Digesting His Correspondents' Dinner Reception," *Washington Post*, May 2, 2006.

60. Amy Argetsinger and Roxanne Roberts, "The New Bush Twins: Double Dubya," *Washington Post*, May 2, 2006.

61. Richard Cohen, "Not So Funny," *Washington Post*, May 4, 2006.

62. Richard Cohen, "Digital Lynch Mob," *Washington Post*, May 9, 2006.

63. *The Colbert Report*, Comedy Central, April 6, 2006.

64. *The Colbert Report*, Comedy Central, July 31, 2006.

65. *The Colbert Report*, Comedy Central, August 10, 2006.

66. *The O'Reilly Factor*, Fox News, January 19, 2007.

67. *The Colbert Report*, Fox News, January 19, 2007.

Conclusion: 2008 and Beyond

1. *New York Times*, September 10, 2007; ad available at http://pol.moveon.org/petraeus.html. Led by Rudy Giuliani, the Republican candidates and the right-wing media called attention to the special advertising rate the *Times* gave to MoveOn for the ad. See Sam Youngman, "Giuliani Demands MoveOn's Times Ad Rate," *The Hill*, September 13, 2007.

2. See Paul Krugman, "All the President's Enablers," *New York Times*, July 20, 2007; "Snow Job in the Desert," *New York Times*, September 3, 2007; and "Time to Take a Stand," *New York Times*, July 10, 2007. In all three columns, Krugman cited an op-ed in the *Washington Post* that Petraeus wrote in late September 2004, in which the general saw "tangible progress" being made in Iraq. In Krugman's estimation, such cheerleading by Petraeus amounted to a de facto endorsement of Bush's bid for reelection.

3. "Lieberman Blasts MoveOn; Petraeus Goes on Fox," blogs.abcnews.com, September 10, 2007.

4. Glenn Greenwald, "Brit Hume and the Administration Take Propaganda to a New Level," *Salon*, September 11, 2007.

5. "GOP Calls on Top Senate Dem to Condemn Anti-Petraeus Ad," *CNN.com*, September 10, 2007.

6. "Bush: MoveOn.org Ad on Petraeus 'Disgusting,' " *CNN.com*, September 18, 2007.

7. The Cornyn Amendment passed 72–25, with Senators Leahy and Webb voting yes, Senators Boxer, Clinton, Kerry, and Schumer voting no, and Obama not voting. The vote on the Boxer Amendment, which needed 60 to pass, was 50–47 in favor, with all of the above—including Obama—voting yes. By voting for the Boxer measure, the Democrats were repudiating both the Kerry/Cleland attacks *and* the MoveOn ad. Only Russ Feingold voted against both measures. See U.S. Senate Roll Call, 110th Congress—1st session, September 20, 2007.

8. "Limbaugh: Service Members Who Support Withdrawal Are 'Phony Soldiers,' " *MediaMatters.org*, September 27, 2007.

9. *The O'Reilly Factor*, Fox News, October 3, 2007.

10. See "House Resolution Commending Rush Limbaugh for His Support of Our Troops," RushLimbaugh.com, October 1, 2007.

11. John Nichols, "Al Franken Seeks the Wellstone Seat," *Nation*, November 5, 2007.

12. Mark Green, "Why 2008 Will Be a Perfect Storm for Republicans," *Huffington Post*, October 15, 2007; and "GOP, Batten Down the Hatches, a Huge Storm Is Coming," *New York Daily News*, October 15, 2007.

13. "The Top Talk Radio Audiences," *Talkers Magazine*, October 2007.

14. See Maureen Dowd, "A Mock Columnist, Amok," *New York Times*, October 14, 2007.

15. *The Daily Show*, Comedy Central, October 16, 2007.

16. *The Colbert Report*, Comedy Central, October 16, 2007.

17. Jacques Steinberg, "Colbert Consulted Parties Before Announcing Run," *New York Times*, October 18, 2007.

18. Chris Bowers, "Republicans Fall to Third-Party Status Among Young Voters," *Open Left*, October 24, 2007.

19. Chris Cillizza, "The Fix: Poll Tries to Measure Colbert Effect," *Washington Post*, October 22, 2007.

20. Markos Moulitsas, "Dem Cattle Call 2008: 6/1/07," *Daily Kos*, June 1, 2007.

21. Markos Moulitsas, "What I Think About the Prez Candidates," *Daily Kos*, January 19, 2007.

22. Moulitsas, "Dem Cattle Call 2008: 6/1/07."

23. Of the spending vote, Edwards said that Clinton and Obama "went

quietly to the floor of the Senate, [and] cast the right vote. But there is a difference between leadership and legislating." See "New Hampshire Democratic Presidential Debate," transcript, *CNN.com*, June 3, 2007.

24. "John Edwards Vows to End All Bad Things by 2011," *Onion*, July 21, 2007.

25. "Study: Iraqis May Experience Sadness When Friends, Relatives Die," *Onion*, July 28, 2007.

26. "Giuliani to Run for President of 9/11," *Onion*, February 21, 2007.

27. Thomas Friedman, "9/11 Is Over," *New York Times*, September 30, 2007.

28. "Reaganomics Finally Trickles Down to Area Man," *Onion*, October 13, 2007.

29. Marvin Kitman, "Olbermann Rules!" *Nation*, October 8, 2007.

30. Chris Bowers, "Hillary Clinton and the Netroots Survey," *MyDD .com*, June 12, 2006.

31. For a transcript of the MoveOn event (held on April 10, 2007), see http://pol.moveon.org/townhall/iraq/transcripts_p.html.

32. Helene Cooper, "Hillary's Iran Vote: The Fallout," *New York Times*, October 14, 2007.

33. For the MoveOn results, see http://pol.moveon.org/prezsurvey/ ?id=11853-7525852-eF9o8P&t=1.

INDEX